Towards Better Peacebuilding Practice

Towards Better Peacebuilding Practice

On Lessons Learned, Evaluation Practices and Aid & Conflict

Edited by

Anneke Galama and Paul van Tongeren

European Centre for Conflict Prevention

P.O. Box 14069
3508 SC Utrecht, the Netherlands
info@conflict-prevention.net
www.conflict-prevention.net

ISBN 90-5727-043-9

EUR 7,50

Editing and production Bureau M&O, Amsterdam
Typesetting and design MMS Grafisch Werk, Amsterdam
Cover pictures Liberia *Ron Giling/Lineair*; Sri Lanka, Flag for Peace campaign *AFP*
Conference photos Bas Jongerius
Printing Macula bv, Boskoop, the Netherlands

Contents

The international project Lessons Learned in Peacebuilding is financially supported by:
Alan B. Slifka Foundation, United States of America
Central Mission Board, (CMC), the Netherlands
Catholic Organisation for Relief and Development, (Cordaid), the Netherlands
Charles Stewart Mott Foundation, United Sates of America
Ministry of Foreign Affairs, the Netherlands
Ministry of Foreign Affairs, Switzerland
Societas Verbi Divini, Catholic Missionary Congregation, (SVD), the
     Netherlands
Triodos Bank, the Netherlands
Van Berch en Heemstede Foundation, the Netherlands
WNM, Funding Organisation for Dutch Missionaries, the Netherlands

Acknowledgements

The international project, Lessons Learned in Peacebuilding, was initiated by the European Centre for Conflict Prevention in order to facilitate and stimulate the field of conflict prevention and peacebuilding in the relatively new task of evaluating and learning practices. Field and office staff dealing with peacebuilding and conflict resolution projects, feel the need to improve their knowledge of the impact of the work they do. So too, external pressure from donors to increase the accountability of projects has stimulated reflection within organizations. As these activities are increasingly included in organizations' agendas, it was felt that addressing the issue would be a relevant task for the ECCP in its position of secretariat of the European Platform for Conflict Prevention and Transformation. However, the field of conflict prevention and peacebuilding is known for the diversity of its actors, activities and approaches and consequently, establishing a coherent framework to include, summarize and also disseminate the lessons learned has been no easy task. In this book we have tried to bring together the work of organizations and their staff who have reflected upon their work, who have developed tools and instruments to conduct these evaluation activities and who have formulated implications of the lessons they have learned. In the course of the project we have received sometimes difficult but nevertheless crucial criticism on how to collect lessons and what to do with these collections afterwards. These comments sprung from co-operative and constructive contributions from many people whom we would therefore like to thank.

First of all we would like to thank all participants at the expert meeting we held in Londonderry, February 2001. At this meeting, the first attempts to structure the project on lessons learned was made. We would especially like to thank the staff of INCORE who hosted this conference. Also thanks to Mark Salter of the International Institute for Democracy and Electoral Assistance (International IDEA) Sweden, for editing the conference's report which helped us further in the project. Thanks too to all the people who participated in the regional workshops we held in Sarajevo, New Delhi, Colombo, Accra and Almaty. They shared with us their experiences, issues and problems which gave us much more perspective on regional lessons. Thanks are also due to the reference group, Mari Fitzduff, Ada van der Linde, Michael Lund, Ronald Lucardie, Carolyn Kerr, Thania Paffenholz, Luc Reychler and Oliver Wolleh who spent two days with us in July and helped us further in programming the large international conference Towards Better Peace Building Practice, which took place in October 2001. The conference was hosted by the Soesterberg conference centre, Kontakt der Kontinenten, who with this conference celebrated their 40th anniversary and showed generous hospitality for the more than 300 participants. The summary, as included in this book, indicates the quality of people who were gathered at this conference. Special thanks are also due to the following organizations and persons who were mainly responsible for organizing one of the seventeen working groups: the Berghof Research Center for Constructive Conflict Management (Germany), the Centre for Peace Building (Switzerland), Field Diplomacy Initiative (Belgium), Collaborative for Development Action (United States of America), Cordaid (the Netherlands), European Centre for Common Ground (Belgium), Initiative on Conflict Resolution and Ethnicity, INCORE, (Northern Ireland), International Alert (United Kingdom), International IDEA (Sweden), Institute for Multi Track Diplomacy (United States of America), Justitia et Pax (the Netherlands), Kontakt der Kontinenten (the Netherlands), Nairobi Peace Initiative-Africa, (Kenya), National Council of Churches (Kenya), Netherlands Institute of International Relations 'Clingendael' (the Netherlands), Norwegian Church Aid (Norway), Pax Christi (the Netherlands), Responding to Conflict (United Kingdom), Saferworld (United Kingdom), Search for Common Ground (United States of America), Swiss Peace Foundation (Switzerland), Voluntary Organisations in Co-operation in Emergencies (VOICE) (Belgium), Emmanuel Bombande, West African Network for Peace Building (WANEP) Ghana, Jonathan Goodhand, (United Kingdom), Manuela Leonhardt (Germany), and Nick Lewer, Bradford University, (United Kingdom).

We would also like to thank the journalists of Bureau M&O, Amsterdam, Jos Havermans, Hans van de Veen and Jim Wake who successfully grasped the complex gathering of issues on lessons learned, evaluation and learning practices and the difficult but crucial debate on aid and conflict. Also thanks to all the other people who permitted us to include their papers in this book.

The project and the conference gave us an interesting, but also a heavy burden of work. Therefore the staff of the European Centre for Conflict Prevention deserves much gratitude for their support and assistance during this project.

This publication has been financially supported by the Dutch Ministry of Foreign Affairs, the Swiss Ministry of Foreign Affairs and the Van Berch Heemstede Foundation (the Netherlands). We thank them for their generous support.

Reflection leads to learning. Therefore, the things we learn and the experience we gain in the field of peacebuilding, conflict prevention and humanitarian aid and development, should be widespread. This will enable our field to move forwards. Putting these lessons on paper as we have tried in this book therefore will hopefully serve this purpose.

Paul van Tongeren, executive director
Anneke Galama, project officer

European Centre for Conflict Prevention

Preface

By PAUL VAN TONGEREN AND ANNEKE GALAMA

Since the events of September 11 and the violent as well as non-violent reactions that followed, the challenge for all people concerned with conflict reduction and building peaceful environments, or assisting civilians suffering the consequences of war, has increased enormously. This challenge lies in a straightforward but nonetheless difficult and unavoidable question. Do the incomprehensible attacks on the US and their unforeseeable consequences throw doubt on the value of their work? Or, conversely, do they demonstrate even further the importance of working for peace and reflection on the world in which we live?

This is a question which also faces the still relatively youthful field of conflict prevention and peacebuilding. A rigorously proven answer is impossible as we do not know how the world would look without this area of research and activity. In other words, we cannot 'delete' the influence of actors trying to address the causes and consequences of violent conflict and then see whether or not the attacks in the United States would have taken place. But, in trying to answer this question, it is possible, and indeed necessary, to reflect upon the *impact* of peacebuilding and conflict prevention. It is important to know what you are doing and why. So rather then attempting to answer questions about the value of continuing to work for peace, it may be more useful to examine the state of the art as it is right now. What are the successes and failures in peacebuilding and moreover, how can they be interpreted or used to bring safety and prosperity back to those parts of the world currently caught up in violence?

Recently we have seen the publication of much valuable work on lessons learned in peacebuilding which draws on years of field experience and academic research. This body of work shows that the field is moving from a pioneer stage into a reflective stage characterized by increased professionalism. Consequently, the time is ripe for defining what has been learned so far. The field has been challenged to become more reflective and conclusive not only by its own organizations but also by donor agencies and governments. More precise answers are needed on a range of questions including, what kinds of preventive action actually work in specific contexts, what can be learned from this in other situations, and according to what criteria do we call certain initiatives a success or a failure?

The European Platform for Conflict Prevention and Transformation has taken up the challenge of addressing the need for more and better methodologies of reflection in order to enhance the learning capacity of practitioners and policymakers in the area of conflict prevention and peacebuilding. As a direct result of this challenge, the international project "Lessons Learned in Conflict Interventions and Peace Building" was initiated in 2000. The project's aim is not only to collect lessons but also to disseminate them in such a way that the lessons will be accessible to other organizations and actors involved in violent and non-violent situations. This publication tries to summarize the activities initiated in this project so far and to give an overview of the lessons learned, collected, shared and disseminated so far by different actors and organizations in this field.

One of the first initiatives within this Lessons Learned project was an expert meeting in Londonderry (Northern Ireland), which was co-organized with INCORE (Institute for Conflict Resolution and Ethnicity) and in cooperation with the Coexistence Initiative and took place in February 2001. It brought together the main experts and practitioners dealing with evaluation methodologies and institutional learning processes. One of its conclusions was that the initiatives and projects dealing with lessons learned in peacebuilding are there, but they lack a coherent framework. The process of collecting lessons continued at regional seminars in Bosnia-Herzegovina, Sri Lanka, India, Ghana and Kazakhstan. At these meetings regional experts were invited to share their perspectives and ideas on the specific issues of their region and the type of conflict with which they were dealing. The relations between Western - often more academic - analysis and local views and perspectives were discussed. Also, the question was raised whether or not regional lessons should be linked to more international debate on peacebuilding practice. It became clear during these seminars that there is a great amount of knowledge and experience amongst practitioners but again, a format in which all these lessons can be collected within the organization often does not exist.

The next step in the Lessons Learned project was the international conference, "Towards Better Peace Building Practice", which took place October 24-26, 2001. More than 300 practitioners from over 50 countries came together in Soesterberg, the Netherlands. Key NGOs organized a total of seventeen working groups and assessed the work and projects of different areas in peacebuilding such as gender, religion, early warning and security. Learning methodologies and evaluation practices were also discussed. Bringing together so many people, not only from non-governmental organizations but also from other sectors including international organizations and governments, was another step towards a more coherent process of learning and reflecting on the work in peacebuilding and conflict prevention.

This publication opens with the conference summary that brings together the discussions, debates and presentations made during the proceedings at Soesterberg. The following chapters are based on the main issues as described in this summary.

The chapter *Evaluation and Best Practices: Picking Appropriate Strategies, Gauging their Impact, and Remembering What Works,* deals with the process and practice of learning. Learning is a process that takes place in people's minds and is mostly directly shared within an organization or project. However, to disseminate what has been learned and to link up with actors and projects in other areas and sectors, it is important to develop methodologies and frameworks to collect these lessons.

Secondly, the chapter *Lessons Learned from Ten Years Experience in Peacebuilding* summarizes the large amount of lessons, best practises, failures and successes, as been collected and experienced by practitioners and policymakers so far. It is rightly argued that there are no overall recipes for ending or preventing conflicts; every conflict is unique and so are its consequences. However, the main lists of lessons composed so far are brought together, but are also challenged by some interesting views and opinions of practitioners in the field.

One of the most important lessons that fieldworkers, academics and policymakers have learned is that aid and conflict are not two separate issues. Moreover, the context in which humanitarian agencies provide food, shelter and other necessary material to people affected by war, cannot be separated from the conflict or post-conflict situation. Therefore, the linkage or debate on aid and conflict was one of the main issues at the Soesterberg conference and will also be discussed in the chapter *Aid and Conflict: Feeding Armies and Militias or Supporting a Path to Peace?* The issue is being addressed extensively by a number of development NGOs, including the American network of voluntary organizations involved in humanitarian assistance and development aid, InterAction. As they say in one of their recent reports, "recognizing the importance of an effective civil society to move communities from conflict to peace and development, NGOs also work to strengthen civil society associations and institutions that promote the interests of the community as whole." However, it also acknowledges that these activities are not yet well enough understood for best practices to be identified.[1]

Each of these three chapters is followed by appendices which include short descriptions of projects and overviews of the lessons learned. Further, the book contains papers on the Soesterberg conference written and compiled by the NGOs who organized the separate working groups. Areas such as gender, religion and security generated such interesting reflection and learning initiatives that it was felt they should be included in this publication. An annotated bibliography of important reports and books on these topics is also included.

Collecting lessons as such is not difficult. It is the conclusions and recommendations that have to be extracted from the lessons that complicate the task. And this is further complicated by the challenge of integrating the lessons learned into the various levels of activity — regional, national and international. A linkage also has to be made between policy makers in headquarters and employees in field offices. One problem, however, which frequently hampers the practice of reflection and evaluation is a lack of funding. Learning requires time and staff capacity. These two factors are often limited in this field and therefore priorities are likely are to be set which favor existing projects. However, donors and other funding agencies should be made aware of the importance of evaluation and impact assessments as these processes will in the end benefit the projects and their outcomes.

Although the field of conflict prevention and peacebuilding is growing from its infancy to a more adolescent phase, and despite the fact that the events of September 11 sometimes makes us wonder what political and moral space remains for alternatives to violence, the potential of the work should not be underestimated. Just as peacekeeping is in a process of redefining itself through reports and assessments such as the Brahimi Report, so too the field of peacebuilding and conflict prevention should also tackle its weaknesses and emphasize its strengths. In Bruce Jentleson's words: "There is no non-position for international actors."[2] Whether negative or positive, international political actors involved in conflict always play some sort of role. Consequently, influencing this role or challenging it with other perspectives is as necessary today as it has ever been.

Notes

1 *Development Relief: NGO Efforts to promote Sustainable Peace and Development in Complex Humanitarian Emergencies,* prepared for InterAction's Transition Working Group, Kimberley Mancino, Anita Malkley, and Santiago Cornejo, June 2001.
2 *Opportunities Missed, Opportunities Seized: Preventive Diplomacy in the Post-Cold War,* Bruce W. Jentleson, (ed.), Carnegie Commssion on Preventing Deadly Conflict,, Rowman & Littlefield Publishers, Inc., 2000

Summary of International Conference
Towards Better Peace Building Practice
October 24-26, 2001
Soesterberg, the Netherlands

Contents

I. Introduction

During the conference "Towards Better Peace Building Practice", some 250 people from many different parts of the world discussed issues, problems and best practices related to conflict prevention and peacebuilding. This document presents the output from the working groups and the plenary sessions and debates that were held during the conference. In addition, some input from already existing literature was used to clarify and complement some of the points.

In order to enhance the clarity of the document, the output of the conference is organized in four separate sections. In the first section, some general lessons in the field of conflict prevention and peacebuilding are outlined. These, from our perspective, apply to all practitioners working on development, peacebuilding and conflict prevention. Then the next three sections cluster some issues of particular relevance for Evaluation Practices and Reflections, the debate on Aid & Conflict, and some of the specific areas that were discussed in the working groups, such as Gender, Media and Peacebuilding, and many more. Finally, paragraph 7 includes some of the remarks and suggestions that were made during the conference, related to the September 11th events and their consequences for the field of peacebuilding and conflict resolution.

Lively atmosphere at the Soesterberg conference

In each of these different sections, the output is presented as 'Lessons Learned' and 'Problems'. This way, a division is made between those issues that have to some degree already been clarified, and those issues that need to be debated and developed further. This division was made for clarification purposes only. It is not intended to fragment the field. Peacebuilding and conflict prevention practices are by their very nature holistic, comprehensive activities and therefore many of the issues mentioned in this document interlink and overlap.

II. General Lessons for the Field

a. General Lessons

Conflict prevention is no longer in its infancy
"As each successive bloody crisis has hit the headlines, there is less heard about how they are inevitable tragedies resulting from age-old animosities (and thus something the international community cannot do anything about). Instead, more doubts seem to be publicly voiced that perhaps the calamity could have been avoided...In sum, conflict prevention, while clearly not yet mature, is no longer in its infancy." (Michael Lund)

Because the nature of conflicts has changed since the end of the Cold War, it is necessary to change the process, the goals and the actors that can lead to peace
Such alternative peace processes require changes in processes, in goals and in actors. In all three domains, the basic changes relate to a broadening of the processes, goals and actors included in the peace process. Political, structural and social processes should be included and they should work towards agreement, joint activity, concrete improvement on the ground and changed attitudes. Each of these processes reinforces the others. Finally, peace processes should make 'more room at the table' and involve people at international, national and sub-national regions. (Robert Ricigliano)

The role of 'ordinary people' in peacebuilding
"If efforts to prevent, resolve and transform violent conflicts are to be effective in the long-term, they must be based on the active participation of local civil groups committed to building peace." (*People Building Peace*)

Peacebuilding must be seen as a process, rather than a goal
"Peace is not an abstract goal but a process. It must be built up over a long period of time Building peace must be an organic process, growing at all levels of society." (*People Building Peace*) "A slow and steady process of trust-building is often necessary before negotiations can start, if they are to succeed." (*War Prevention Works*)

Sources
- *16 Lessons Learned* in: People Building Peace, 35 Inspiring Stories from Around the World, European Centre for Conflict Prevention, 1999
- Michael Lund, *Learning Lessons from Experience; Preventing Violent Intra-State Conflicts*, in: Working Document for International Conference Towards Better Peace Building Practice, 2001
- Robert Ricigliano, keynote speech at International Conference Towards Better Peace Building Practice, the Netherlands.
- *War Prevention Works; 50 stories of people resolving conflict*, by Dylan Mathews, Oxford Research Group, 2001

b. Guiding Principles

Lessons Learned

Build upon local experiences/peace initiatives
Many organizations have in recent years emphasized this basic principle for peacebuilding. Local culture, including traditions, methods and structures related to peacebuilding and conflict transformation, should not just be understood or taken into account; they should be a foundation for peacebuilding and conflict transformation efforts that are undertaken by

outside interveners. The process of peacebuilding should begin with the people who are affected by conflict, with their experiences, questions and their own experiences towards peacebuilding.

Include all relevant actors in decision-making

The inclusion of all relevant actors in the decision-making processes and planning concerning all kinds of interventions in conflict-affected societies is very important. If certain actors are excluded from these processes, be it at the grass roots or at higher political levels, this can become a source of further conflict. Therefore, the careful consideration and inclusion of all relevant actors can contribute to sustainable peacebuilding efforts.

Partnerships with local organizations

Partnerships with local organizations have become an important part of the mandates of many organizations working in peacebuilding and conflict transformation. There is widespread belief that, in order for conflict transformation to be sustainable, effective co-operation with individuals and organizations within conflict-affected societies is necessary.

Cooperation with other organizations in the field, at the NGO, intergovernmental as well as governmental level

Many have emphasized the importance of co-operation between organizations in the field of conflict prevention and transformation. Peacebuilding will be most effective only when it takes place at different levels of society simultaneously, e.g. local, governmental and international levels. Therefore, co-operation with different organizations on these levels is vital. Consideration should be given to who can do what best.

Long-term engagement

It has been mentioned by many practitioners and scholars that peacebuilding is never a short-term effort. Peace is not an end goal, but a process in itself, related to transformations of society.

Use comprehensive approaches

Peacebuilding and conflict transformation efforts should be comprehensive in many different ways. Important actors at different levels in society should be included in the process. A thorough understanding of the conflict and its history is important, so that root causes can also be addressed, next to its effects. Peacebuilding should also be comprehensive in the use of different techniques and instruments as each situation requires.

Impartiality

NGOs need to be impartial in instances where this is required by the type of involvement, for example in mediation and dialogue where high-level political leadership is involved. However, NGOs always come from a certain setting and have certain perspectives on peace and justice. Therefore, in some instances their power is to use these perspectives and insights as these can support other parties in their talks and peacebuilding activities.

Gender perspective
Many have pointed out the importance and the great potential of the role of women in peacebuilding. In most conflict-affected societies, women have no interest in escalating or continuing violent conflict. Therefore, they can play a powerful role in conflict transformation and peacebuilding efforts.

Importance of interpersonality/trust building
A great part of peacebuilding work is based on person-to-person contact. Therefore, stable and trusting relationships are vital.

Empowerment
Peacebuilding and conflict transformation are essentially about changing society and people's attitude towards conflict. Therefore, the empowerment of people as individuals, or in organizations or governments, lies at the core of peacebuilding work. Peacebuilding assists people in taking responsibility for their own destinies.

The need for qualified staff
Because peacebuilding activities can be precarious, difficult and long-term, it is extremely important to find the right kind of people for the job. Important qualifications include commitment, openness, flexibility, self-confidence and the ability to adapt.

Forgiveness is internal and begins with the self, reconciliation is external and deals with the outside world
Fear, pain, suffering, anger, revenge, and compassion must all be dealt with if one is to forgive. Spirituality is an important element of forgiveness.
Forgiveness always comes before reconciliation but you can also have public reconciliation without forgiveness, especially at the political level. *(Conclusion of working group sessions on Reconciliation, facilitated by Institute of Multi-Track Diplomacy, United States)*

Sources
Main source:
•   International Alert, *Guiding Principles for Conflict Transformation Work*
Other sources:
•   Institute for Multi-Track Diplomacy, *Twelve Principles of Multi-Track Diplomacy* (www.imtd.org)
•   Search for Common Ground, *Best Practices and Lessons Learned Pilot*, summary of principles
•   Berghof Research Center for Constructive Conflict Management, European

Centre for Conflict Prevention, International Alert and Life & Peace Institute, *Code of Conduct/Guidelines for Conflict Transformation*, Seminar Report, April 27-29, 1999.
- Responding to Conflict, *Short Courses draft guidelines.*
- Catholic Relief Services and the Joan B. Kroc Institute for International Peace at the University of Notre Dame, *Summer Institute on Peacebuilding*, Final Report August 2001
- Report from working group: Guiding Principles for Conflict Prevention and Peace Building, *Institute for Multi-Track Diplomacy, USA.*

III. On Reflection, Learning and Evaluation Practices

Sources
- Report from working group: Reflecting on Peace Practice Project, *Collaborative for Development Action, USA.*
- Report from working group: Institutional Learning, Better Practices and Lessons Learned in Conflict Resolution, *Search for Common Ground, USA* and *International Alert, UK.*
- Report from working group: Framework for the Evaluation of Peacebuilding Initiatives - Approaches to Self-Evaluation, *Berghof Research Centre for Constructive Conflict Management, Germany* and *Nairobi Peace Initiative-Africa, Kenya.*
- Report of working group: Peace and Conflict Impact Assessments, *Jonathan Goodhand, United Kingdom, Jos De la Haye, Field Diplomacy Initiative, Belgium, Manuela Leonhardt, Germany, Nick Lewer, Centre for Conflict Resolution, United Kingdom*

Introduction
Within the field of conflict resolution there is a growing realization that in order to become more reflective and more effective in our work, we need to examine the lessons we are learning and how we are learning them. We must aim to be reflective practitioners, cognizant of our role, our mandate, our contribution and the state of the process at each state. Two processes of learning lessons will be discussed in this chapter. Firstly the various approaches and methodologies developed by and/or available to peacebuilding and development aid organizations. They are known under such names as *Peace and Conflict Impact Assessment* (PCIA) and *Conflict Impact Assessment Systems* (CIAS). However, as a relatively new field, conflict resolution faces many new challenges and dilemmas. For the sake of convenience, hereafter, all evaluation tools are referred to as PCIAs. Secondly, a more process-oriented approach towards learning is described mainly by the working group on institutional learning. Their starting point was that learning is relatively 'subjective' and difficult to 'pin down'. Learning as a process is less prescriptive and therefore different from evaluation methodologies.

Although not an evaluation effort in itself, the Collaborative for Development Action's Reflecting on Peace Project (RPP) has also contributed to the evaluation field by creating a forum for reflection among practitioners in the field. As RPP is one of the most elaborated projects on reflecting and learning processes, it is shortly introduced in this chapter.

Aid agencies have become increasingly aware of the fact that aid and conflict are intimately connected to each other, and that this has serious implications for their work. Both of these developments have had enormous impact on approaches to evaluation and on the evaluation field as a whole. However, as they did not see peacebuilding as their main field of activities, many aid organizations searched for a tool that could guide them in deciding what work to do or support. Questions were asked about how their policies interacted with the dynamics of conflict and peace. With the help of experienced peacebuilding organizations, work started to develop with the idea of "providing non-specialist donors, aid agencies and local organizations with accurate, yet user-friendly methodologies to plan, assess and monitor development and humanitarian assistance in the context of armed conflict" (Manuela Leonhardt).

a. Impact, Evaluation and Learning

Lessons Learned

A sustained peace process has a value of its own. The focus thus should be on the actual process towards peace rather than just on the result, however peaceful.
Peacebuilding is a long-term process full of small successes and many setbacks. Conventional planning and evaluation methods may not always be appropriate for assessing whether an initiative is successful or not.

Focus should be on long-term monitoring and learning instead of one-off evaluations
Initiatives may have an unintended impact on the conflict setting i.e. consequences as a result of an initiative's organization and delivery rather than its actual activities. Thus, it is important to monitor the unintended in a long-term perspective and 'learn as-we-go-along'. Indicators may unfold as the initiative progresses.
"[...] evaluation should be seen less as a validation or invalidation exercise pegged only to credibility, and more as a process where learning is extracted from practice and incorporated in new planning and thinking. This is the 'evaluation as learning' paradigm." (George Wachira)

A wide range of stakeholders should be involved in the planning and monitoring process of any initiative in order to integrate different peace visions

Definitions of peace and conflict may vary among stakeholders thus creating (additional)conflict. Shared values and a clear understanding of what is about to be achieved are essential among all stakeholders in order to evaluate whether an initiative has been successful or not. Not only may definitions of peace and conflict vary, stakeholders may also have different perspectives on what constitutes goals, progress or success in relation to a project. Evaluation activities should be thought of already at the planning stage of a project.

To achieve sustainable development, the evaluation/learning process must be owned by the partners/recipients

Thus, the relationship between donors and recipients needs to be clarified, particularly in determining the objectives, goals, and methodologies of the evaluation itself. In addition, shared understanding before and during a project starts will increase the possibility of success and of implementation of whatever is learned. This also means that the evaluation process must be understood and accepted by beneficiaries as well. In this respect, evaluation is like any other peacebuilding activity: It requires participatory, inclusive approaches that are respectful of local realities.

The linking of the micro-level of the intervention to the macro-level of the conflict is essential when evaluating an initiative

As an external intervention can only play modest role in influencing the course of a conflict, it is important to find creative ways to pose the question whether an initiative has a positive impact or not on the conflict, and in what way. Furthermore, evaluations have to be put into perspective in relation to other political, economical and social trends in a region. In other words, they must be based in a regional context, not only in the context of the particular conflict setting where the project is carried out.

The creation of a self-regulating and self-accountable practitioner community is needed

Practitioners need to evolve a culture of accountability, a code of ethics, among themselves that can help define rules and ethics of good practice. A common understanding of what peacebuilding means is also essential. Peacebuilders should be cognizant of the skills they have, as well as the skills they need in this sector.

In evaluation activities, as in any other development activity, the safety of informants, partners and beneficiaries must be addressed

Peacebuilders are frequently at risk and it is sometimes difficult to balance between the loyalty to partners and the need for transparency. The use of informal and oral means of reporting should not be underestimated.

Institutional learning needs to be prioritized
'Learning' is a costly exercise, both in terms of time and money. It is very important that lessons that have been learned not only stay with those that were involved in the exercise but also be communicated within the organization and to the outside world. As staff turnover is often high in peace agencies, it is very important that organizational structures are developed that ensure that the acquired knowledge can stay in the organization and be passed on to future staff members.

Good peacebuilding is about being good human beings and embodying and reflecting personal and organizational integrity
The focus should be kept on one's own and others' humanity and the partnerships, relationships and trust that are central to this work.

PCIA could be used as a connector by organizations in the field to similar organizations in other conflict settings around the world
Many partners/organizations in the field feel isolated from other organizations working with the same issues in other conflict settings. PCIA tools could create a common ground where different organizations could come together to share experiences.

Problems

For whom and by whom is the PCIA done? Who is driving the process?
It is not always clear whether a PCIA is done in order for a donor to control a project, a project leader to control its partner or for partners to become more efficient in their work. In other words, the issue of capacity building is not always explicit in PCIA work. As a PCIA can be used both as an instrument of control and also as an instrument of feedback, creativity and empowerment, the question of how to balance these factors becomes crucial.
Different actors have different needs when it comes to evaluation. This is especially true for the donor and the practitioner. The needs of the donor (accountability, planning, predictability, impact) must be balanced with the needs of the practitioner (learning, flexibility, unpredictability, serendipity, adaptations)
The needs of the donor are likely to prevail over the needs of the practitioner. The former is mostly interested in short-term and measurable results and this has implications for how the work is carried out in the field, not necessarily addressing root causes that require a structural change and a long-term involvement.

Indicators are an important part of PCIA, but how do you select them, when and by who are they selected?
Depending on for whom the PCIA is intended, indicators are chosen. For a PCIA to be user-friendly, users should choose their own indicators. This

Paul van Tongeren, European Centre for Conflict Prevention, Opening statement

implies that some indicators may be chosen as the project goes along i.e. not all indicators should be pre-set. Furthermore, peacebuilding has more to do with qualitative developments than quantitative which makes the whole issue even more difficult.

What is the theoretical base for PCIA and how do you translate theory into practice?

The academic community does not always feel at ease with the fact that much of PCIA seems to involve a certain amount of "gut feeling" i.e. to 'learn as you-go along' does not always seem sound from a theoretical point of view. Vice versa may also be true. Not all theories or methodologies are easily applicable to the field of operations.

Is mainstreaming of the field desirable or even possible?

There is no generic method available that is applicable to all purposes and types of users. Also, it may be that specific ideas or techniques may not be transportable from one situation to another.

Do PCIA tools take all issues into consideration in the appropriate way?

There is a danger of de-positioning a conflict when using PCIA tools i.e. everything gets boxed in neat tables and the real issues and dynamics run the risk of "disappearing". However, PCIA has a critical and empowering potential that needs to be examined further to be fully understood.

Are there resources enough within organizations involved to carry out a PCIA?

Nowadays, many other assessments such as environmental and gender screening are obligatory before a project starts. The PCIA-tool runs the risk of being seen more as a burden than an aid for field staff. How do you balance this so that a PCIA does not become "just another tool"?

Are there sufficient resources within organizations to work on institutional learning?

It is not only donors who need to be convinced of the importance of institutional learning. Organizations themselves also need to allocate money, time and staff capacity for reflection and evaluation practices. In addition there is a need to balance 'reacting', which is an organization's main activity, with 'reflecting', an activity to which organizations devote too little time.

Is there donor openness to lessons learned and a willingness to allow mistakes?

There is a need to 'desensitize' and 'de-stigmatize' learning from the mistakes NGO feel they make. They need to consider the relationship with donors as a mutual learning process. This is, however, a difficult task to carry out in practice, as NGOs also have to meet donor criteria for indicators and outputs in order to secure funding. How to find ways then of stimulating 'proving' and 'improving' what NGOs are doing?

Lessons can be subjective, relative or contextual

Lessons are mostly individually experienced so the question is how do we know what to share and why? Moreover, how should staff turnover be balanced with institutional memory, project (funding and organization) security and time frames?

b. *The Reflecting on Peace Practice Project:* Reflections on the Effectiveness of Peace Work

The RPP project is working to understand what are the most effective contributions 'outsider' agencies can make to peace processes. It is not an evaluation effort but rather an inclusive forum for reflection on what works, what doesn't and how we understand this from a practitioners' perspective. Through 26 case studies of different peace projects, practitioners around the world participating in the project have identified the following issues for further examination in feedback workshops to being held around the world in 2001 and 2002.

Intersecting themes
1. The role of linkages between levels/sectors/peace initiatives
2. The roles and relationship of insider/outside agencies
3. Balance and tradeoffs between working for peace and working for social justice
4. How peace NGOs deal with parties whose interests are in war, not peace
5. What kinds of context analysis lead to more effective strategies

Understanding impact
1. Effectiveness criteria for peace work
2. Indicators of impact
3. Inadvertent negative impacts

Specific approaches and tools
1. Role and impact of dialogue projects
2. Role and impact of training
3. Unique dilemmas for humanitarian / development aid organizations that take up explicit issues of conflict

Better understanding of the above, practitioners feel, would improve the effectiveness of international efforts to support peace processes. Issue Papers detailing initial findings and dilemmas regarding these issues are available, and will be "tested" and expanded on in the feedback workshops series, with findings to be issued in late 2002.

The two workshop sessions at the conference were among the first of these workshops. As such, their findings are not conclusive, but tentative and suggestive. In these sessions, two of the above issues were discussed through a case study based on real NGO interventions in Burundi and additional concrete experiences of the participants.

The linkage between context analysis and designing peace strategies
Agencies say that analysis of the context which they hope to affect is critical to
designing effective strategies for their peacebuilding efforts. There are several
common approaches to context analysis that are currently used by
peacebuilding agencies. *Root causes analysis* (historic, economic, political and
social issues people say they are fighting over); *dividers and connectors analysis*
(systems, events, groups, values and institutions that divide ordinary people in
the society and those that, despite the conflict, still connect them across
conflict lines); *issues and interests analysis* (the concrete contemporary issues
people claim they are fighting over and the interests of key groups with respect
to those issues).

The workshop showed that each of these types of analysis highlights some
similar, and also some different, aspects of the conflict. It also showed that
many peace programs being undertaken by NGOs are often only indirectly
related to the key issues driving the conflict that such analytical lenses
highlight. In practice, peace efforts undertaken seem equally the result of
agencies' implicit theories of "how peace happens", and their particular skills
and resources. This may lead to some peacebuilding projects that, though well
intentioned, miss the mark and have little potential to affect the issues driving
the conflict. The process that shapes agencies strategies and what role analysis
really plays in them needs to be better understood. Part of the analytical
process clearly requires that agencies 'theories of peace' be made more
explicit, so they can be analyzed and their validity in the particular context
examined.

Effectiveness criteria for peacework
RPP is testing six broad and generic 'criteria for effectiveness' that can apply to
the wide range of peace programs and across a range of settings. These are
derived from the process to date, and point to ways that one could understand
whether a specific program is having a beneficial impact. Through gathering
further experience about what kinds of larger level processes are linked to
furthering peace, it is hoped that more refined criteria will emerge from the
process.

Additional sources
- A Practitioners Reflections on the Evaluation of Peacebuilding by George
  Wachira, Nairobi Peace Initiative-Africa, key-note speech at International
  Conference Towards Better Peace Building Practice, the Netherlands.
- Strategic and Responsive Evaluation of Peacebuilding: A Framework for
  Learning and Assessment, NPI-Africa/NCCK, 1999, Conference Report
- A Sectorial Conflict Impact Assessment: Guidelines for Peace Education by
  Jos De La Haye, Field Diplomacy Initiative, Belgium
- Reflections on Peace Practice, phase II - background paper from
  Collaborative for Development Action

- The Coming of Age of PCIA: What Have We Learned? Where Are We Going? - Manuela Leonhardt
- Conflict Sensitive Approaches to Development, A Review of Practice by Cynthia Gaigals with Manuela Leonhardt, Saferworld, International Alert, International Development Research Centre 2001
- Presentation held by Cheyanne Church (INCORE, Northern Ireland) on Questions and Challenges on Evaluation and Lessons Learned in Conflict Interventions and Peacebuilding, Expert Meeting on Lessons Learned, February 2001, Londonderry.

IV. Lessons on Aid and Conflict

Sources
- Report from working group: Options for Aid in Conflict: Lesson from the Local Capacities for Peace Project, *Collaborative for Development Action, USA*
- Report from working group: Development NGOs in Conflict Areas: extending the humanitarian mandate, *Norwegian Church Aid, Norway*
- Report from working group: Peace Building and Development, *Cordaid* and *Pax Christi, the Netherlands*
- Report from working group: Links between Development and Peace with focus on Sri Lanka, *Simon Harris and Nick Lewer.*
- Report from working group: Humanitarian Aid and Peace Building, *Voluntary Organizations in Co-operation in Emergencies, Belgium*

Lessons Learned

General lessons on the linkage between aid and conflict
Aid agencies can work *around*, *in* **or** *on* **conflict**
Aid agencies have the possibility to stop work in areas where violent conflict arises, work *around* conflict, and go back in when peace occurs. Also, organizations can continue work *in* conflict areas, taking the safety risks and changed working context into account. And NGOs can even work *on* conflict as well, addressing directly the consequences of the conflict and the need for peacebuilding activities.

Working in conflict can be harmful
When agencies ignore or fail to address the realities of a conflict, aid and development have the potential not only to have a positive impact on the peacebuilding process and peacebuilding initiatives.

Aid agencies have to decide to what extent they wish to work 'in ' and 'on' conflict

Working in conflict means addressing the realities of the conflict situation without doing harm to the dynamics of the conflict. Working on conflict implies a step further in the sense that the agency takes up an explicit peacebuilding and conflict prevention role as well.

A paradigm shift is needed in donor policies and in the policymaking of NGOs

Development projects and humanitarian assistance have to be become 'conflict sensitive'. This means that financial and human resources have to made available to address this new approach. However, peace or conflict on the one hand and development on the other are part of an indivisible reality, and should be interpreted with the same process approach and paradigm.

Conflicts are characterized by dividers and connectors

Conflicts imply intergroup divisions and tensions but also embody connectors or 'local capacities for peace'. People used to live together and they continue to do so in wartime. This means there are still connecting features, which could be used for peacebuilding initiatives. Aid can become a vehicle for both divisions and connections in a given social context.

Aid delivers 'messages' as well as resources

The ways and manner in which aid is supplied; staff interacts with the aid-receivers; and how the protection and safety of staff and goods is arranged all imply messages that can either reinforce the modes of conflict or reduce them.

The objective standards of 'peace' have to be identified if you want to include peacebuilding activities in policymaking

Justice might be an overarching principle but it is culturally defined as well. However, further mechanisms for pursuing justice and truth during protracted conflict should further be explored. Also, it is crucial to start identifying codes of conduct for aid agencies in specific areas and operations.

Donors and NGOs

Donor education is a key element in ensuring that aid is 'responsible'

NGOs need to take up more initiatives to inform their donor agencies sufficiently on the linkage between aid and conflict.

NGOs themselves need to become more articulate in their explanations to donors as to why peacebuilding should be included in the programs and the training of staff

For this purpose, NGOs need to re-define their mandates and explicitly include the link between their aid policy and the particular conflict area they are working in.

Recognizing that donors are steered by (international) politics, integrated lobbying and advocacy work by NGOs is crucial
Donor-agencies are intrinsically linked with the decision-making levels within politics. Therefore, linking humanitarian and development aid to conflict could endanger funding possibilities for NGOs.

Problems

There is an organizational competition amongst NGOs in the South for funding
Local organizations tend to have a more nuanced understanding of the conflict. A lesson from practice is that donors also need to engage in deep analysis of conflicts in which they plan to work or which they plan to fund. Local agencies engaged in competion for funding may be drawn into attempting actions which seem unlikely to succeed based on their own understanding of the situation, both because they want the funding and because they hope the donor may know something they don't know. For these reasons, shared analysis is an important part of partnership.

A complicating factor in peacebuilding and development is the dominance of political, and international actors working in the background of this field
International political actors often focus solely on military and geo-political conflict dynamics and not on the broader interactions and consequences of conflict in general.

There is a lack of in-depth analysis of cultural, social understandings of peace and conflict
Practitioners and policy makers often fail to address the linkages between the local and international levels of peacebuilding and conflict prevention initiatives. Also, too little cross-cultural interpretation and analysis is being undertaken.

Although it is likely for 'development' to have a broader impact, outright politicization of aid is probably not desirable
Advocacy and lobby activities by aid agencies can endanger ongoing work and also place the field staff in dangerous situations.

The risk of mainstreaming
Mainstreaming conflict prevention and peacebuilding strategies in development policies demand such different skills from policymakers and field workers that NGOs should avoid 'punching above their weight'.

V. Areas Assessing Lessons Learned

A. Early Warning

Source
- Report from working group: Early Warning and Conflict Prevention. *Swiss Peace Foundation, Switzerland*
- Heinz Krummenacher, Susanne Schmeidl, "Practical Challenges in Predicting Violent Conflict - FAST: an Example of a Comprehensive Early-Warning Methodology", in: Swiss Peace Foundation, Working Paper No. 34, Berne, 2001.

Lessons Learned
No blueprint for early warning
It is difficult to draw up a general blueprint for early warning activities. Much depends on the specific situation and not all methods work everywhere. It is important to adapt to the needs of the end user and to take into account the region on which you are providing information.

Uniformity in reporting is important
It is important to provide early warning reports in uniform structures and formats. This way, it becomes easier for the end user to locate information.

Early warning reports should be concise
Early warning reports should be brief and to the point in order to make sure the most important information reaches the end user. Lengthy descriptions take too much time to read and can lack clear structure.

Early warning must be practiced as on-going monitoring
Early warning cannot be practiced in an ad-hoc way by bringing out some reports on certain developments. Early warning should always be an on-going monitoring process.

The role of theoretical frameworks
In early warning practice, there is a definite need for the use of a good theoretical framework. However, it is equally important that such a framework is flexible. It should not block new knowledge that can be gained from new experiences.

Problems
Too little attention to capacities for peace
The practice of early warning concentrates only on the early warning of conflicts. There is not enough attention as yet on the windows of opportunity and local capacities for peace.

The timeframe of early warning is often too short
Often the timeframe that is used in early warning is skewed toward operational, often military action aimed at preventing the immediate outbreak of violence. However, early warning should also focus on long-term prevention and pay attention to issues such as democratization, development, etc.

Unclear institutional landscape
There are a number of organizations involved in early warning, but it is not clear exactly who does what, how information exchange takes place, etc. Networking could help to clarify some of these issues.

Too little focus on cost analyses
Another additional role for early warning could be to clarify the relatively low costs of prevention when compared to humanitarian assistance after the fact. This possible role needs more attention and should be developed further.

B. Media and Peacebuilding

Source
• Report from working group: Media and Peacebuilding, *European Centre for Common Ground, Belgium.*

Lessons Learned
Media can provide linkages within society
In conflict-prone societies, Track I political negotiations often have too little impact on what happens on the grass-roots level, and vice versa. The media can be a useful tool in linking the top level and bottom level of society by providing information that can go from top to bottom and vice versa.

'Practice what you preach'
NGOs that broadcast or print peacebuilding media programs should try to get people from different groups in society to work together on the production of these programs. This is also important in convincing the audience of the impartiality of the reporting.

Media is an element in a holistic approach to peacebuilding
Peacebuilding through media programs should be seen as part of a larger set of factors that can contribute to peacebuilding. Media do not have a decisive influence in this respect; they should be part of a holistic approach to peacebuilding. Therefore, it is also important for media peacebuilders to create networks and link with other peacebuilding actors in society.

The role of research
Elaborate research about context, society etc. is needed before the production of media programs.

The need to link foreign media with local media

NGOs can try to get international media to use local reporters, instead of sending in many foreign reporters. This way, Africans can report on Africa, etc.

Three categories of peacebuilding media objectives

The objectives that different media programs pursue can be divided into three different categories:

- Unitarian reporting - speedy reporting on local/national levels to target groups who seek this specific information.
- Conflict prevention - working with local civil society institutions to try and devise strategies for how to best reach people; speed is less important.
- Institutional development - building media as a component of a long-term democratization strategy.

Such a classification can be useful in educating donors about media and peacebuilding projects.

Local partnerships

NGOs should work together with local media and try and integrate with them. Local partners, their needs and perspectives are important.

Problems
Media can work both positively and negatively for NGOs

How can NGOs work with the media to bring peacebuilding activities in the spotlight? How can an NGO use the media as a constructive element? This can be problematic when negotiations or others projects are confidential. Also, many NGOs have little experience in working with the media. Western media reporting can create problems as they can have their own agendas.

Problems of impartial journalism

The people who want to provide impartial information can be seen as traitors. In many situations, there is no law to protect journalists. Therefore, news often comes only from the conflicting parties, and impartial journalists can be subject to security threats.

The problem of getting access to mainstream media

It can be difficult to reach the main media arteries in societies. It is becoming more and more difficult to get your stories into the mainstream media.

C. Networking

Source

- Report from working group: Lessons Learned on networking on national and international levels and interactions of NGOs with governments, *Centre for Peacebuilding, Switzerland* and *European Centre for Conflict Prevention, the Netherlands*.

Lessons Learned

Networking has a large role to play in pulling together an expanding, but dispersed field

The field of conflict prevention and peace building is expanding rapidly. More and more organizations, non-governmental as well as governmental, have become involved in peace building and conflict prevention activities. However, the field is dispersed over a great number of mostly small organizations. In order to pull all these efforts together and identify gaps in the field, the sharing of information and co-operation is becoming more and more important. Different organizations working in conflict resolution and peacebuilding often pursue very different activities. Networking can help to avoid a duplication of activities. Also, a broad network is the best guarantee against one-sided approaches to the complex issues involved in peacebuilding and conflict resolution.

Complementary partnerships are necessary to deal with little resources

Because the field of conflict prevention and peacebuilding has few resources, in financial as well as in personnel terms, it is important to try and achieve a certain complementarity in the activities of different organizations. Networks of different organizations can help to set up such complementary partnerships.

The joining of forces is important to strengthen impact of the field

Joining forces can strengthen the outreach capacities of the field of conflict prevention and resolution and increase the impact of the lobbying and advocacy activities of different organizations. A coalition of NGOs speaks louder than one alone.

How to build an effective network

Some of the following recommendations may help to establish effective networks:
- Begin with a small group
- Find a common interest
- Establish clear rules of membership
- Network around clear issues
- Clarify the distinction between this network and others
- Clarify the benefits of joining the network
- Network participants define the role of the network, not the other way around

Problems

Too little complementarity between Northern and Southern networks

A persisting problem is the growing intervention of Northern NGOs in issues of peacebuilding and conflict prevention in the South, whereby they take on roles and functions that should be/had been left to local NGOs. The respective roles of Northern and Southern NGOs should be complementary, not competitive.

There are problems in the functioning and financing of a secretariat
An important determinant of the strength of a network is the existence of an active secretariat. However, financing a secretariat can be difficult, because donors are often unwilling to provide core funding. It is also difficult for such a secretariat to find a balance between the interests of the different network members as they often fear losing their profile in a network structure.

It is difficult to establish networks between governments and NGOs
The institutionalization of co-operation between governmental and non-governmental organizations is necessary in order to develop coherent peacebuilding policies. In some countries, this institutionalization has already taken place, in others it is very difficult because NGOs are seen as opposition to the government or NGOs see their governments as part of the conflict. It is difficult to bring together these two levels; both sides often have different procedures and cultures and use different terminology. Therefore, it is important to look for common objectives, agree on the terminology used and exchange best practices and success stories.

D. Gender and Peacebuilding

Source
• Report from working group: Gender and Peace Building, *International Alert, United Kingdom* and *Cordaid, the Netherlands.*

Lessons Learned
Increase women's voices in peacebuilding processes
Opportunities should be created and supported for women to take up more leadership roles. This way, they could have more influence on peacebuilding processes. The possibilities for women to gain more decision-making power in peacebuilding processes can be present within existing structures.

Engendering peace processes means not only including women, but also men
The word gender is still frequently perceived as referring to women only. However, engendering is about creating an equal relationship between men and women. To this end, men need to be approached and included in this process as well. In particular, men should not be stigmatized as the 'violent gender'.

Understanding the gender aspects of conflict in order to engender peacebuilding
In order to engender peace processes, it is important to understand the male and female ideologies of peace. In which positive ways can male and female

identities contribute to peacebuilding? There is a need to rethink both the roles of women and men in terms of violence, victimization and sexuality.

Problems
Violent conflict can change the position of women in a positive way, but how should these changes be sustained?
In war situations, women often take on different roles. This can in effect change their position in a positive way. However, the question is how to sustain these positive effects after violent conflict has ended?

More research on different aspects of the role of women in conflict is needed
There is a need to look more closely at the causes of conflict and the role that women play in these. Also, more research should be done on the impact of violence on women. Finally, more work can be done in research on women's roles in peacebuilding.

E. Religion and Conflict

Source
- Report from working group: Lessons Learned on 'Religion: source of both peace and conflict?', *Justitia et Pax* and *Cordaid, the Netherlands*

Lessons Learned
Focus on various levels within faith based communities
The role of religion with respect to peacebuilding is ambiguous. Religious communities are frequently to be found at the forefront of conflict prevention and peacebuilding activities, but can sometimes also fail to promote peace and can even fan the flames of conflict. Research has shown that influential peace initiatives can derive either from religious institutions (as in the case of Mozambique), from specific religious leaders (South Africa) or from the laity (Rwanda). It is important not to get frustrated if either one is not able to get involved actively, but to support those who are ready to work for change.

Non-discrimination on the basis of religion or belief is the key, instead of a specific State - Church relation
Around the globe a great variety of legal arrangements exist, governing relations between states and specific religions or belief. The existence of systems recognizing a religion as an official religion or of systems of established churches is not in itself a violation of international law, provided that the state does not discriminate against other religions or beliefs. To guarantee this national and international lobby, legal proceedings as well as education on religious tolerance are necessary.

Careful analysis of the causes of conflict is necessary to prevent their meaning too easily labeled as 'religious conflicts'

Today's conflicts have complex social, political, economic and cultural causes. The disturbing fact is that they often tend to be simplified as a confrontation between religious groups, values and virtues. By analyzing, one will notice that religious tensions may arise from the politicization and manipulation of religion, existing antagonism between religions and a mixture of religion and politics. Each factor asks for specific redress. Religious groups have a specific task to be reflective towards their own faith community (recognize possible faults and weaknesses) and, also, to make local people and leaders alert through exchange of information and joint research to unmask the motives and agents of 'religious violence' and expose the victims.

Interreligious dialogue and co-operation are fundamental to curbing religious intolerance

The dangers of growing intolerance between people and movements of different religious backgrounds have become urgently visible in the wake of the events of September 11, 2001. In order to overcome suspicion and animosity renewed efforts are required to stimulate interreligious dialogue and cooperation: both on a theological and on a practical level. An open attitude is needed, a readiness to critize each other and be criticized. Also, this requires agreement on common goals and the essence of religious freedom and pluralism. In some societies theological encounters are already quite a challenge, in others even more should be possible: from the understanding of each other's differences towards a joint effort to face common problems. Non-violence and true acceptance involves a personal process: try to move from fear, to healing, to trust.

Problems
Conflict potential within religion itself

The positive, resourceful side of religion or belief is inextricably linked to its more restrictive, negative side. If religion enhances a creative side in human beings this is, basically, because it is able to provide an ultimate meaning of life, a founding truth. It is for this reason that it becomes difficult for believers to tolerate other faiths that offer contrasting claims to truth. Even more, the mere existence of competing faiths opens up, at least potentially, the possibility of doubting religious claims to truth. This jeopardizes the resourceful character of religion. Thus, to an extent, religious *freedom* conspires against *belief* and its positive psychological consequences. Therefore, it is essential that religious conflict is kept within the boundaries of symbolic confrontation. It could be argued that verbal and ritual condemnation should be allowed for but no institutional or physical attacks, as these would objectively limit the liberty and rights of others.

F. Security and Peacebuilding

Source
- Report from working group: Security and Peacebuilding, *International Alert* and *Saferworld, United Kingdom*.

Lessons learned

Lack of governance of the security sector (armed forces, police, intelligence services, etc.) is often a source of conflict and a key obstacle to peacebuilding
Of the 44 countries in conflict in the world many have security forces that are symbolic of societal cleavages (either ethnic or political) that are at the heart of violence, and are frequently associated with repressive acts against civilians and violations of human rights. The transformation of the security sector is critical to the success of peace agreements and the fostering of structural stability so that societies can live in a safe and secure environment.

Security institutions could play an effective, legitimate and democratically accountable role in society
The overall aim of security sector reform is the transformation of security institutions so that they play an effective, legitimate and democratically accountable role in providing external and internal security for their citizens. It includes on the one hand the professionalization of security forces, but equally so on the other the strengthening of civil institutions to provide proper public management and oversight of the security sector.

If law-breakers face prosecution and social disapproval, people will be discouraged from engaging in armed violence
The role of civil society is to lead efforts to change minds and attitudes towards guns and violence. At the same time, the authorities should obtain legitimacy if they are effective, transparent and accountable, and respect and protect citizens rights and liberties.

Problems

Security is essential to development - people must be safe and feel safe
This means that the threat of armed violence must be reduced; when people see better ways of achieving security, justice and progress they are less inclined to engage in armed violence.

Involvement of local communities
Local communities should be consulted and involved in police reform processes. Local partners are able to build trust and confidence between the police on the one hand and the communities they work in on the other hand.

The police should gain from reform
There has to be something in the reform for the police (for example
recognition of past work or financial compensation to officers who leave).
Although very difficult and sensitive, some form of continuity should be
maintained and all identity groups also should feel represented in the newly
established security structures.

Broad engagement of donors is crucial
Donors should work both with governments, helping them to reform their
security forces, and civil society, encouraging them to play a critical and
supportive role in the prevention of violence. Therefore we need both capacity
building of governments and civil society

VI. September 11 and its Aftermath

On the evening of the first day of the conference, interested participants came
together to listen to some reflections on the September 11 events from
practitioners from different parts of the world. In addition, the events were
discussed in some of the working groups and came up in some of the plenary
sessions. Also, many different NGOs and practitioners have made statements
and written articles on the consequences of the attacks for the peacebuilding
and conflict prevention field. In this paragraph, some of these reflections and
concerns are presented.

Concern about the abuse of the term 'terrorism'
After the attacks on the World Trade Centre and the Pentagon, terrorism has
become a focal point in the international arena. With the current black and
white view of the world, the label of terrorism could be extremely damaging to
what might be in essence legitimate causes. In other words, the term
'terrorism' can now easily be abused by people to discredit opposition
movements at any kind. In this respect, the abuse of the term terrorism can
further deepen divisions and heighten existing tensions.

Concern about the shifting of priorities to the 'war on terrorism'
The world has become very focused on fighting terrorism. This has been felt
immediately in some of the countries in the South. Priorities are being shifted
towards the 'war against terrorism'. This could have serious consequences for
attention to the problems in the South, as is becomes more difficult for
Western governments to justify spending on development support.

Concern about possible polarization between 'the West' and 'the Islam'
The war on the United States and the West declared by Islam fundamentalists
like Osama bin Laden has created a lot of questions regarding Islam as a
religion in general. Already, incidences of violence have taken place against

Ragnar Ångeby, Ministry of Foreign Affairs, Sweden, key-note speaker

Muslim people in different parts of the world. At the same time, the attacks of the United States and its allies on Afghanistan have further deepened some of already existing antagonisms towards the West in some Islamic societies. The field of conflict prevention and peacebuilding could have an important role to play in trying to prevent further polarization and establish co-operation across these lines.

Concern about possible spillover of the conflict in Afghanistan
From South and Central Asia come many voices of concern about the possible influence of the war in Afghanistan on the surrounding region. As events unfold in Afghanistan they could have destabilizing consequences for the Kashmir conflict and the regime in Pakistan. The presence of nuclear armaments in the region makes this an even more pressing issue.

The link between the fight against terrorism and the resolution of the conflict in the Middle East
This link has already been explored by many. Although it can be debated whether resolving the conflict in the Middle East would actually prevent further terrorist attacks, it is definitely an important part of a strategy to try and take away some of the arguments that are being used by anti-Western Islamic fundamentalists. Hopefully, this link will therefore serve to bring back

some of the attention that is necessary to push the parties in the Middle East towards a solution.

The added need of early warning from the conflict prevention field
The early warning activities undertaken by some NGOs in the field of conflict prevention field could serve as a valuable counterpart to the more military/security focused reports coming from the intelligence sources. In addition, the early warning that is already being done, in particular in the Central and South Asian region, has now become even more valuable and should be taken more seriously by policy makers.

The added need for institutional co-operation
More than ever, it is important for the field of conflict prevention and peacebuilding to demonstrate the necessity and the potential of preventing and transforming conflict into non-violent interaction. Therefore, as the coalition for terrorism has been initiated, perhaps a coalition for peacebuilding should be put into place as well.

VII. Concluding Remarks

This summary represents the reflections, findings and conclusions of the conference's participants. Collecting people's experiences as such is not so difficult, the challenge of this document lies in its practical implications. What do these lessons and dilemmas mean for the people formulating policies and what implications do the same lessons have for the people doing the actual work in the field? In other words; how further to implement and disseminate the knowledge we have already gained, while at the same time facing the new dilemmas and problems formulated? These are the challenges for the future. However, the lessons learned as put together in this document demonstrate that we are indeed moving forward; towards better knowledge that will hopefully lead to more and better lessons and an improvement of our work.

Conference summary written and compiled by Anneke Galama, Mats Lundstrom, Paul van Tongeren, and Iris Wielders, European Centre for Conflict Prevention, the Netherlands. Thanks to Mark Salter, IDEA, Sweden, for his advice and comments.

Part I
Evaluation and Best Practices

Picking Appropriate Strategies, Gauging their Impact, and Remembering What Works

Too often, conflict prevention interventions are simply based on the "best guesses" of generally well-intended but under-informed parties about what may work. To identify the best practices appropriate to the great variety and unfathomable complexity of conflicts, it is clearly desirable to engage in methodical assessments of the whole range of interventions. Evaluating such activities is, however, just a starting point for a more generalized evaluation component. A significant body of knowledge on best practices in the field of conflict prevention can only be assembled if practitioners understand that they have a responsibility to pass on the knowledge they gain to others who will face similar challenges in the future. Which is to say, the evaluation of conflict prevention activities is by no means a mere academic exercise.

By JIM WAKE

Introduction - A medical metaphor

While life may at times seem to be just one continual headache, in point of fact, for most of us, the headaches are actually rather sporadic. And nonetheless, when the pain is severe, many of us will reach for a bottle of our preferred analgesic - and sure enough, within hours, the pain is gone.

Just what effect has the pill had on the headache? How long would we have suffered without taking the pill? Did the medication actually have a palliative effect before the headache finally faded away? And what about the side effects? To what should we attribute that overwhelming feeling of drowsiness at the end of the workday? Not to mention the recent realization that the fine print in the newspaper is harder and harder to read.

Come to think of it, why should anyone believe that a little pill ingested with a glass of water is going to chase away a headache? Why not just rub your head, and swathe it in hot (or cold) towels?

These may seem like silly questions, but they suggest a bit of the problem with the inexact science of conflict prevention. We're looking for effective treatments for the painful afflictions of our species, and sometimes we think that we've just got to do something. We've got some remedies available - some of them recently developed, a few of them studied by experts and academics, some accepted on faith, some rooted in ancient traditions, some counter-intuitive. There are even, as in the world of physical disease, treatments that cure the disease by killing the patient, and remedies peddled by quacks or promoted by corporate and political entities with an eye towards profit and self-aggrandizement and little regard for their suitability or effectiveness. Not only that, but sometimes, just as with human disease, soothing words and the appearance of treatment is enough to provide significant relief.

In the health care world, an extensive body of practice has been built up over the years. It relies on a combination of anecdotal evidence, intuition, and of course, carefully conducted scientific research in the form of objective analysis of double blind trials, cold statistical calculations of the probable relationship between treatment and the course of the disease, and peer review of published findings. In the conflict prevention arena, nothing would ever get done if the treatment required such rigid standards to be applied, but that doesn't mean that the sort of evaluation which has served the medical world can't also serve as a metaphorical model for peace practitioners. As it is, all too often, interventions are simply based on the "best guesses" of generally well-intended but under-informed parties about what may work.

To identify the best practices appropriate to the great variety and unfathomable complexity of conflicts, therefore it is clearly desirable to engage in methodical assessments of the whole range of interventions aimed at conflict prevention (and conflict management and conflict resolution - the semantics here are not relevant to the general thrust of this argument), as well as other activities, including development assistance, political and social development, and cultural contexts. Evaluating such activities is, however, just a starting point for a more generalized evaluation component. For evaluation should not be viewed as simply a retrospective activity, but as a continuum (or, perhaps more accurately, a spiral) that starts prior to an intervention, and remains an essential activity throughout the intervention and after its conclusion, with the information gleaned from the ongoing process channeled into subsequent peacebuilding efforts. Furthermore, evaluation needs to take place on a global level - that is, the effectiveness of peacebuilding activities needs to be compared, with consideration to the similarities and differences between not only the types of interventions, but also the types of conflicts. We shouldn't delude ourselves into imagining that we can produce a 'Peacemaker's Desk Reference' as exacting as the *Physicians Desk Reference* which describes the indications, contraindications, and side effects of every pill on the market, but it is, nonetheless possible to assemble a significant body of knowledge on best practices in the field of conflict prevention - but only if practitioners themselves (along with outside evaluators) understand that however hard-pressed they may be to work effectively under difficult circumstances, they have a responsibility to pass on the knowledge they gain (both of positive and negative outcomes) to others who will face similar challenges in the future. Which is to say, the evaluation of conflict prevention activities is by no means a mere academic exercise.

Executive Summary

Evaluation is an essential and integral part of effective peacebuilding activities. With the knowledge that comes from evaluation, those involved in peacebuilding can draw on the pool of knowledge concerning best practices, to assure themselves of the best possible chances of success. This chapter provides an overview of evaluation practices. It starts with a discussion of a number of the most important issues that peacebuilders need to consider. These include structural impediments to evaluation, the problems of identifying appropriate indicators to measure effectiveness and impact, the question of who should be involved in carrying out evaluation (including a discussion of self-evaluation), and the difficulty of determining causality - that is, whether, in fact, an effect can be attributed to a particular intervention or activity. Following this discussion is a section on a "user-friendly" evaluation methodology, variously known as PCIA (Peace and Conflict Impact Assessment) or CIAS (Conflict Impact Assessment System), which has played an increasingly important role in evaluation activities in the past few years. This is then followed by a closer examination of the different functions that evaluation activities serve, depending on what stage in an intervention they take place - prior to an intervention to help determine appropriate intervention activities; during a project, to make certain the intervention is carried out effectively, and to make adjustments based on changes in the situation that may develop; and following an intervention to discover if it has succeeded and what lessons (both positive and negative) can be learned. This section also includes a short discussion on the role evaluation can play in making more general appraisals of activities on the global level. The chapter concludes with a discussion on best practices, which includes numerous practical tips for better peace-building activities based on the knowledge that has been gained from thoughtful evaluations of past experience.

1. Issues for Consideration

Evaluation may be necessary, but it certainly isn't easy. There are a number of problems that are facts of life for almost anyone involved in peacebuilding when they set out to undertake proper evaluation activities. This section addresses those problems, and offers some suggestions that may be helpful in addressing those problems.

On impediments and indicators

It may be helpful to understand that intervention in conflict situations, be it pre-emptive or reactive, can generally be described with the same sorts of models that managers in the business world and the world of public administration use, which means, obviously, that despite the fact that evaluation is a relatively recent topic of discussion in conflict prevention circles, there's a considerable body of knowledge available to peace practitioners. As John Welton, of the Quaker Council for European affairs notes, "There's nothing that we can come up with that hasn't already been tried in the business world." Business builds various evaluation mechanisms into its project implementation schemas. Those same schemas are applicable in conflict prevention/management activities: a project management cycle that begins with problem analysis, and then proceeds with the establishment of goals and objectives, design and selection of a response, implementation, accompanied by monitoring and evaluation on an ongoing basis, modifications and adjustments in response to these ongoing evaluation activities, and then, upon completion, or in the case of a long-term project, after a sufficient amount of time has elapsed, a more comprehensive review with the findings of that review compiled in a report that serves as a reference for future activities and/or continuation of the project.

Thus, in any intervention, as in any business venture, "evaluation"[1] will generally be built into the process. But that does not necessarily mean that it gets done (or gets done thoroughly and systematically) for a variety of reasons.

In particular, four "impediments to evaluation" are particularly noteworthy: inadequate resources, time pressure, apprehensions regarding the consequences of reporting on unsuccessful or less successful interventions, and confidentiality issues.

Not surprisingly, one of the chief impediments to satisfactory evaluation of conflict prevention activities is insufficient funding. Funds for peacebuilding are all too scarce and the needs are great. So it is almost to be expected that, given a choice between funding peacebuilding activities and paying for evaluations, funders are likely to choose peacebuilding. Nor is it surprising that implementing agencies will submit budgets in which scant attention is paid to the evaluation process. Retired diplomat John McDonald, now

Bineta Diop, Africa Women Solidarity, Switzerland, key-note speaker

affiliated with the Institute for Multi-Track Diplomacy, tells of the frustrations he experienced in attempting to carry out an evaluation of a project in the Balkans. He found two skilled evaluators, but their initial budget was far above what McDonald considered feasible. After further discussion, they agreed to a budget of $100,000 and presented the proposal to the primary funder. "But," recalls McDonald, "the funder said 'Oh, I was thinking $10,000.' That wouldn't get you to Bosnia and back. So it never happened. And that happens again and again."

And then - inextricably linked to the issue of resources - there are the competing demands on staff - whether they be staff of the implementing organization or the donor. Obviously, if there is sufficient funding, additional personnel can be hired, but when that is not the case, the same sorts of hard choices that funders need to make between conflict prevention activities and evaluations confront staff. In the sense that "the squeaky wheel gets the grease", it stands to reason that staff will respond to today's crisis, even if a well-considered project implementation plan allocates x amount of hours to evaluation activities. On the other hand, in many cases where a formal evaluation process is not carried out, or not fully carried out, the process does take place informally at any rate. Peter Woodrow, of CDR Associates, a U.S. based non-profit organization involved in conflict resolution services, asks rhetorically "how do we do organizational learning when there's no time, even for staff meetings?" and then answers his own question: "We do it by telling stories to each other." And Joseph Ayindo, of the Amani People's Theater in Nairobi, Kenya, remarks that informal evaluation of the performances is a routine occurrence - after a show, the performers naturally reflect on what worked and what didn't, and how the audience has responded, and the shared information gets processed, even if there is no record of that sort of evaluation.

A third impediment to the evaluation process is the apprehension that many people, especially local people working on conflict prevention activities, feel regarding the possible negative consequences of reporting on unsuccessful or less successful interventions. Where it is difficult or impossible to point to progress, or indeed, when an initiative does not lead to the hoped for outcomes, would-be evaluators may be inclined to avoid asking the pertinent questions about the reasons expectations went unfulfilled, and to leave the report unwritten. Again, with fierce competition for scarce resources, an honest discussion of a disappointing outcome can have serious negative consequences. But of course, as the Senegalese director of Femmes Africa Solidarité Bineta Diop remarks, "Learning from our failures is just as important as learning from our successes."

"Learning from our failures is just as important as learning from our successes."

John McDonald also stresses that protecting the confidentiality of individuals involved in peacebuilding activities in conflict zones can impede the evaluation process. "Scientific evaluation," says McDonald, "is not possible in the depth that some scholars want because we work with confidentiality, which means that whenever you do a training ... you can talk about process but not who said what to whom."

The Nairobi Peace Institute-Africa (NPI-A), in its 1999 paper entitled *Strategic and Responsive Evaluation of Peacebuilding*,[2] notes the inherent conflict between a need for transparency, comprehensiveness, and regularity in reporting, on one hand, and the need to "respond appropriately to sensitive and confidential issues" on the other hand. The report adds that "in a field that is quickly becoming competitive rather than co-operative, pressure for progress reporting can lead to audacious claims to success and achievement while in fact, the reality on the ground is different. For this reason, there is a potential conflict between accountability and transparency on the one hand, and confidentiality, modesty and sensitivity, on the other. Therefore, in order to report without creating any problems for the people and the process, ways and means of balancing accountability and the demands for confidentiality need to be devised." NPI-A goes on to explain that it engages in annual, in-depth discussions with its funding partners while producing considerably less in writing, adding that it is "important that peace workers do not use claims of confidentiality to cover for lack of accountability."

Beyond these impediments to evaluation, there are a number of related issues which emerge over and over again. These are related to the differing needs of donors, practitioners, and (to a somewhat lesser extent) the local population which can include not only parties to the conflict, but others who may be impacted by peacebuilding activities:

Who carries out the evaluation?

Who is viewed to be the beneficiary of the information gleaned during the evaluation?

What are the criteria and indicators that guide the appraisal of the processes and the outcomes, and who establishes them?

As George Wachira of NPI-Africa points out, "the needs of the donors and those of the practitioner regarding evaluation are not necessarily the same."[3] Donors, he points out, need to account for the way funds have been spent, to demonstrate that the activities they support have made a difference. They will be inclined to zero in on the "success" or "failure" of an activity, and more than likely will want to measure success against stated goals and schedules, and concrete, observable indicators of achievement. But practitioners want to effect change, and the measures of whether or not their activities have enabled change, empowerment, and shifts in attitudes and relationships are highly subjective and rarely quantifiable.

Wachira further points out that similarly, the root causes of violent conflict are seldom neatly and easily quantified. "Working with some of the pastoralist communities in Kenya," he writes, "it is quite clear that there are fundamental security, subsistence, relational and developmental concerns that drive the conflicts and an accumulation of a deadly arsenal of firearms. Yet it appears easier to get funding for numerous research projects and conferences on small arms and light weapons than it is to get funding to organize longer term processes that could address the wider question and root causes of the problem. So what drives us to focus on the small arms ... while ignoring what the actors in the conflict themselves view as the central concerns? Of course, one realizes the difficulty of assessing the impact of structural change in the long-term and we therefore seem to prefer short-term, measurable interventions. After all, it is easier to see the number of firearms recovered from communities than it is to see the evolution of the capacity of the people involved to articulate the root causes of their conflicts." In other words, in some cases, the evaluation is not only carried out for the benefit of the donor, but "evaluability" - the perception that results can be measured and described for the benefit of the donor - actually drives the programming, rather than needs on the ground.

Wachira argues passionately - as a practitioner - that without due consideration for the dynamics of both the conflict and the intervention process, any assessment of peacework is likely to provide an incomplete picture:

"Peaceworkers initiate processes aimed at introducing change into an environment that is itself changing or has recently changed. Relationships, dynamism, process, flexibility, hope, adaptation, discovery, unpredictability, etc., are the words and phrases that the peaceworker lives by. The predictability implied or assumed at the level of planning seems to evaporate as the day-to-day experience takes over and drives the process. Critical discernment of the moment becomes important. Flexibility becomes a commandment. ... we discover that peacebuilding is not merely finding solutions for specific issues of conflict; it also requires that people be empowered to fully engage with and understand better all aspects of social, economic and political structures that give rise to violence and how they could be changed. Measuring achievement at this level is a major challenge. Above all, it cannot be done within the short time, funding and project framework that often drives our interventions. The peaceworker therefore needs the kind of evaluation language and methodology that is sensitive and responsive to the fluid progression of process."

By means of a concrete example, Wachira describes a series of training programs which took place in Liberia, Uganda, and Kenya. Measured against the stated goals of the programs, an evaluator would likely conclude that the programs had not achieved those goals; Wachira states that little training had been achieved. But what was achieved was mediation and confidence building between participants which served to facilitate further contact among those who participated. In other words, as Wachira puts it, "in practice the indicators unfold as you go along." Sometimes, he observes, the practitioner will judge progress by "indicators" that seem almost inconsequential, and that might not even get recorded and/or reported, such as people drinking together who wouldn't have done so previously.

The Kenyan peaceworker Jebiwot Sumbeiywo, of the National Council of Churches of Kenya, puts it rather succinctly: "Human relations cannot be quantified. It is not the number of meetings that is important but what is said in the meeting."

Still, says conflict prevention scholar and current International Alert Secretary General Kevin Clements, some agreement on desirable outcomes is clearly wanted. "You can say 'it doesn't really matter whether there's an outcome - that it's the process that's important in itself. That may be true, but unless you can identify some steps in the process - some outcomes - how do you know if the process is positive or negative?" And Michael Lund, who has also written extensively on conflict prevention, adds that the analysis needs to be sufficiently methodical so as to have some credibility - but at the same time, flexible enough so that the more abstract (and therefore less quantifiable) issues related to peace and conflict get due consideration. It is important, says Lund, "to broaden the set of criteria by which interventions are judged to include poverty, social injustice, and participation.[4]"

"Who determines the indicators is very important," says Clements. "In the past there has been a notion that the indicators are determined in the log frames, by donors, and by implementers. They determine your indicators, and the people you are working with are your partners. They are the recipients of your indicators and they'll determine what you do and what happens and likely outputs. I think there's a new movement to find indicators of progress and collaboration with the parties you are working with, and that makes a lot more sense to me. In fact in terms of doing good baseline analysis, you need to sit down with your key partners and say, 'what is the situation you are confronting, and what do you want to see come out of this process?'"

"I think there's another way to understand indicators," says Mary B. Anderson, whose *Do No Harm* approach has profoundly influenced the thinking of peaceworkers around the world. Anderson, who is president of the Collaborative for Development Action, Inc., launched the Local Capacities for Peace Project (LCPP) in 1994, and in 1999, initiated the Reflecting on Peace Practice Project, which has, to date, undertaken 26 case studies to understand and improve the effectiveness of efforts by international agencies to support peace efforts in areas of violent conflict.[5]

"If you look at the six criteria of effectiveness that we have identified in the 26 case studies we're carried out," says Anderson, "they seem at least to capture a 'generalizable' way of assessing progress - whether your activity adds up to something or doesn't. The indicators are always context specific, but within the context, everyone can agree on the indicators. It's not as though your indicators and my indicators would be different. If we say, for example, that more people, as a result of the work that you have done, are speaking out or acting on efforts to promote peace than had previously been the case, or that fewer people are actively speaking out or are engaged in war than was previously the case - that's generalized. Whether you've gotten more people on board - that's pretty straightforward."

Six Criteria of Effectiveness

1. The project increases the number of people actively working, or speaking out, for peace (or reduces the numbers of people actively engaged in or promoting conflict).
2. It engages people in positions to make or influence formal peace agreements in the process of doing so.
3. It promotes a peace-related activity that, when violence worsens or threats are made, is able to sustain its efforts and maintain its membership.
4. It establishes a link between leadership and the general public by which either the leadership or the general public communicate to the other in ways that encourage their support and involvement to move toward settlement.
5. Specific acts of violence are stopped (when these acts are themselves unjust and breeders of further violence).
6. A specific cause of conflict is solved. This could be either through:
   - addressing injustice (note: this criterion explicitly relates to the building of a just society on which sustainable peace can be based; the other criteria could promote justice though not necessarily).
   - addressing the lack of institutions to deal with conflict in non-violent ways

Source: Mary B. Anderson "Effectiveness Criteria" Reflecting on Peace Practice: Issue Papers, April 2001

Anderson goes on to make the point that *the context* provides the baseline from which to measure progress. A few thousand more people supporting a peace initiative when popular sentiment is already strongly biased towards an end to conflict may sound good on paper, but its value may be questioned. However, as Anderson puts it, "If you've been in a country for twenty years and nobody dared to stick his or her head up at all, and now you've got groups of twenty people who have really taken a stand, then from your baseline to that point it's probably more significant in terms of effectiveness."

Mary B. Anderson, Collaborative for Development Action, USA, key-note speaker

Anderson observes that the anecdotal evidence of effectiveness - people on the street who make reference to a turning point that is associated with an intervention, for example - does indeed need to be taken seriously, but she also cautions that "you have to watch how you collect" such evidence. It is easy to gather anecdotal evidence of progress from the participants in one or another activity, but it is also possible that such evidence will only "affirm what you want to hear as opposed to the reality." In other words, anecdotal evidence has its value, but that value very much depends on what the sources are and how it is gathered.

Who does the evaluation?

The question of who actually carries out an evaluation is intimately linked to the determination of indicators and the ultimate beneficiaries of the evaluation and has been a matter of considerable debate among peace practitioners at all levels - local activists and peace workers in conflict areas, outside experts engaged in project implementation in conflict regions, and funders and scholars. Traditionally, most evaluations were undertaken by outsiders on behalf of the funding agencies. They, of course, wanted to know if their money was well spent, if their local partners were motivated and competent, and if their interventions led to the intended and hoped for impacts.

But such top-down evaluations will inevitably lead not only to flawed conclusions, but they can also skew the entire project in undesirable ways, impede creativity and innovation (because local implementation staff will feel bound to "play it safe"), and -perhaps most significantly - fail in the essential task of sharing useful knowledge for improved effectiveness.

At the other end of the spectrum, there is growing interest in "self-evaluation", in part as a reaction to (or resentment of) outside evaluations, and in part because more and more peacebuilding activities are the direct result of local initiatives. Discussions during the "Towards Better Peace Building Practice" conference held in the Netherlands in October, 2001[6] indicated - as would be expected - considerable support for the self-evaluation approach, but also understanding for the limitations of the approach.

With self-evaluation, it is certainly easier to overcome the problems of confidentiality that can impede effective evaluation from outside, and local participants can also factor in the intangible and the unquantifiable impacts that they sense in their personal contacts and observations - selecting, in effect, indicators of which outside evaluators cannot possibly be aware. "If communities are able to come to an agreement over a resource," says Jebiwot Sumbeiywo, "that is an indicator, [as is] a road that is open, or the use of a bridge that wasn't used before." She expresses frustration that it has been difficult to persuade donors to "embrace a different log frame" that would give due consideration to such indicators.

Using, once again, the business world as a model, it can be argued that self-evaluation is actually the logical and normal approach; except for financial reporting purposes (auditing, that is) most businesses only call in an outside evaluator when they are in trouble. And several participants at a "self-evaluation workshop" held during the "Towards Better Peace Building Practice" conference indicated that they view self-evaluation as an important "management tool" or "management process".

George Wachira notes that the demands of evaluating the effectiveness of one's work implies the need to "create a self-regulating and self-accountable practitioner community" and that practitioners need to "critically examine their work and what is learned from it." In fact, he is arguing that practitioners should take the initiative to be self-critical, so as to enhance their credibility with outside organizations and donors.

Still, there is a consensus among both local practitioners and outside parties that ideally, evaluation should be "participatory". It should include outsiders, who can bring perspective and objectivity lacking at the local level, as well as insiders, who have insights and knowledge not available to the outside evaluators, and stakeholders, who, after all, have the most to gain or lose from

George Wachira, Nairobi Peace Initiative-Africa, Kenya, key-note speaker

any peacebuilding intervention. "You need a range of perspectives," say Mary B. Anderson. "You need people close to the context who can explain why things happened, and people from outside, who can ask the kinds of overarching questions that people inside often can't ask, because they're so enmeshed in the details that they forget the questions."

On causality and attribution

Of course, whether the changes in a situation are measured empirically or reported anecdotally, an important question still remains: what does any particular activity have to do with the overall situation?

Conflict prevention researcher Manuela Leonhardt identifies the difficulty of showing causality in interventions as one of several challenges that must be addressed in the PCIA methodology which she has examined in her academic work, and offers some guidance on how to approach the issue:

"External interventions can play only a modest role in influencing the course of conflicts. This poses the question of causality and attributing (positive) changes, [which] means linking the micro-level of the intervention to the macro-level of the conflict. One possibility to deal with this challenge consists in recording the development of the conflict at the macro-level, yet without appropriating any positive changes for the particular program. At the same time, one evaluates the outcomes of individual initiatives with more traditional methods at the micro-level. This approach has the advantage of offering some insight into the general development of the situation, while remaining realistically modest about the project's impact."

Teresa Barnes, of the International Institute for Democracy and Electoral Assistance (International IDEA) offers some further strategies for determining if "results" can indeed be attributed to the actions that purport to cause them[7]:

"How do we know that a particular result can be attributed to a particular preventive action? The most common approach is sequential analysis or 'process tracing'. But the mere existence of temporal sequence (when this happened, that occurred) does not in itself prove a causal relation. Further tests could include the following: is there a causal logic that connects the intervention to the result?; do the conflict protagonists believe there was an impact?; is the causal link plausible in view of other knowledge?; were no such impacts seen where the intervention was not applied?; and are the same results found in many cases?"

Acknowledging the difficulty of attributing progress to interventions, as well as the danger of dismissing benefits when "positive steps become overwhelmed by destructive violence", particularly in view of the complexity of most conflict situations, Mary B. Anderson argues that it is frequently possible to discern patterns and that often they are valid indicators of impact (positive or negative)."[8]

"... LCPP was able to identify clear, repeated and prevalent patterns in the interaction between aid and conflict. The cumulative evidence, for example, of the manipulation of food aid to support armies or force population movements, drawn from specific, grounded experiences in multiple settings, became as compelling as any direct measure of the impact of food aid on nutritional status. The specificity and precision of this cumulative experience provided empirical data that was seen by aid workers to be accurate and valid."

Causality and attribution (continued): People know
Anderson is convinced that a lot of peacebuilding, and a lot of the analysis of effectiveness in the field, has more to do with common sense than it does with complex, elaborate schemes. "People seem to think there's a mysterious process to learn how to understand [these things] - but it's not that hard." Her point is not so much that evaluation methodologies are not helpful, but rather that, just as anecdotal evidence of progress has value, so do the visceral feelings of people on the ground.

"In LCPP's work," she writes "it became clear that often people in conflict situations do attribute outcomes to specific actions. They 'know' whether an aid agency's programs fuel the fires of suspicion and competition, or are rather seen as fair, even-handed and inclusive. And they can provide clear indications of why they know what they know. They cite evidence of cause and effect. They have opinions on impacts. These opinions provide the best source of attribution available to aid agencies. Knowing what people are saying about a program's impacts is an exceedingly important measure of its real effect. This is true even if the impact is only visible through the opinions of local people because, if opinions shape observable behaviors, they will then become reality. That is to say that they will reinforce further engagement in, or increasing disengagement from, conflict."

She does add one cautionary note; acknowledging that opinions may vary and "attribution through public opinion is, therefore, only partially reliable."

2. User-friendly Methodology: PCIA

The non-specialist does not need to "re-invent the wheel" to carry out an evaluation; over the past several years, a number of experts in the field have been developing "user-friendly" methodologies for this purpose. This section looks at the PCIA approach to evaluation.

As has been noted previously, one significant trend in evaluation methodologies applied to conflict situations which has emerged since the second half of the 1990s involves an approach known variously as PCIA (for Peace and Conflict Impact Assessment) or CIAS (Conflict Impact Assessment Systems), as well as a variety of other similar names for related methodologies. Manuela Leonhardt credits Jean-Paul Lederach and Jay Rothman with laying the groundwork for the approach, (which, for the sake of simplicity, is subsequently referred to here as PCIA), and Kenneth Bush and Luc Reychler for developing the methodologies [9]. What makes PCIA attractive, says Leonhardt, is that it provides "non-specialist donors, aid agencies and local organizations with accurate, yet user-friendly methodologies to plan, assess and monitor development and humanitarian assistance in the context of armed conflict.

The PCIA approach is applicable all along the evaluation continuum - that is, as a planning tool, for monitoring activities, and for ex-post evaluation. Leonhardt also notes that, while it has mostly been seized upon by larger NGOs, a number of advocacy-oriented NGOs have encouraged civil society organizations in developing nations and/or conflict regions to use the methodologies of PCIA "to enhance their capacity to critically monitor and report on conflict-related government and donor policies." PCIA can also be applied at various levels - at the country, sectorial or programmatic, project, or community level. Additionally, Leonhardt distinguishes between "primary" purposes, related more or less directly to assessment, and "secondary" purposes, which relate more generally to the environment in which the intervention takes place. This is most clearly illustrated by the following table, where secondary purposes are italicized and indented:

	Planning	**Monitoring/Evaluation**
Country	Strategic Conflict Assessment Country Strategy *Political Dialogue* *Multi-Stakeholder* *Consultation*	Policy/Portfolio Analysis Impact Assessment *Steering* *Learning*
Sector/ Program	Sectorial Conflict Assessment Sectorial Strategy *Consensus-building*	Sectorial Portfolio Analysis *Steering*
Project	Local Conflict Analysis Project Planning and Assessment *Team building* *Trust building*	Project Monitoring/Evaluation Impact Assessment *Control* *Management/Steering* *Learning* *Accountability*
Initiative/ Community	Participatory Situation Assessment Joint Planning *Local dialogue/mediation*	Participatory Monitoring Civil Society Monitoring *Feed-back/Advocacy* *Stakeholder Perceptions &* *Priorities*

Because PCIA is still a developing methodology, there is still considerable discussion about its applications, and there are a variety of conceptual and practical challenges that, in Leonhardt's view, must be addressed. These challenges include, for example, considerations for the time frame of peace building activities; the very thorny issues of reaching consensus on values and definitions (such as the meaning of "peace", and what constitutes "progress") and allowing for the inevitability that perspectives of various parties will differ, perhaps radically; the need to be aware of unintended impacts, including negative impacts; and the difficulties of determining causality and attribution, and protecting confidentiality.

Just how does a Peace and Conflict Impact Assessment work? In a paper prepared for the "Towards Better Peace Building Practice" conference, Jos De la Haye of the Field Diplomacy Initiative provides a handy, six step "road-map" that describes the PCIA process concisely[10]:

1. **Conflict mapping.** Conflict mapping or conflict analysis is designed to offer an analysis of the conflict and the conflict dynamics, which may include such considerations as conflict history, conflict context, conflict parties, conflict issues, conflict dynamics, dividers and connectors, an assessment of conflict trends and peace opportunities, etc.
2. **Sector mapping.** Here, attention is focused on the range of activities taking place in the particular sector (such as education, or journalism), with a discussion of how a project will impact the sector, discussion of objectives, assessment of resources, personnel, needs, etc.
3. **Impact analysis.** Here, the focus is on how and to what extent the aims of the projects are realized. This implies a) a description of the baseline (or startline), b) a description of the target line, and c) the specification of the chain of impacts and indicators of progress.
4. **Conflict impact analysis.** The conflict impact assessment, which complements the above mentioned impact analysis, assesses the positive or negative impact of the projects on the peacebuilding efforts in other sectors or other levels, and the overall impact on the conflict transformation and peace building in the area in which the project is being planned or implemented.
5. **Conflict impact interpretation.** In this "interpretation", the significance and implications of the activity and its outcomes are considered, and attention is also directed to the "blind spots" and the "missed opportunities". The conflict impact interpretation should be very accurate and look at the multiple layers of the society and take account of longer-range processes that may take time to unfold. Distinctions should be made between indirect conflict impact (when there is no impact on the conflict dynamics at all), intermediate conflict impact (when there is an expected impact on the conflict dynamics), and direct conflict impact (when there is an impact on the conflict dynamics).
6. **Design or re-design of policy.** The final step is design and architecture. Based on the perceived conflict impact of the intervention and an accurate needs assessment concrete suggestions are formulated so as to increase the conflict impact in the following implementation phase or in future projects. Here De la Haye makes reference to a remark from Jonathan Goodhand that "the challenge is to find the right balance between 'off the peg' tools that are too general and 'customized' tools that are too specific and make comparisons difficult."

PCIA may provide a "user-friendly" methodology for evaluators, but it does not eliminate the inherent problems of evaluation, including, first and foremost, that nagging issue of finding a measuring stick that provides the kind of information that will be helpful for stakeholders, practitioners, and donors. Here, Mark Hoffman and Ken Bush differ fairly sharply on a way forward. Bush, whose *A Measure of Peace* was largely responsible for initiating the discussion around PCIA in 1998, is insistent that different indicators are relevant for different actors in peace interventions. The debate between the two is worth citing at length, beginning below, with Bush[11]:

"In essence, *A Measure of Peace* calls for a 'kaleidoscope' set of indicators that can accommodate the different needs, interests and worldviews of the different project stakeholders (in the broadest sense), as well as of the participants in an assessment process. This is essential if PCIA is to even stand a chance of having an empowering impact on communities affected by outside interventions. ... Any willingness to accept such methodological messiness [of different indicators] can only serve to highlight the paradigmatic difference between standard evaluation tools that create and then *capture a single reality* on the one hand, and the notion of PCIA as an approach that *interprets multiple realities* on the other." [Bush's emphasis]

"The embracing of *competing indicators* is founded upon the understanding that there is no single socio-political reality or impact, but rather a multiplicity of realities and impacts that coexist and often clash with one another. The different stakeholders' choice of these different indicators allows for a clearer examination and understanding of these multiple, overlapping realties."

This, says Bush, is not only a problem *for* traditional evaluation approaches, but also "a major difficulty *with* traditional evaluation" because it "imposes the worldview and implicit interests of the evaluator's system over those on the ground."

Hoffman sees it rather differently, even if he is sympathetic to the Bush's concerns:

"While the reluctance to produce a set of indicators cast in stone is understandable and correct, the limited success so far in detailing any sort of even illustrative, suggestive indicators for use in PCIAs is regrettable. If the desire is to move away from inappropriate evaluation methodologies and criteria, and transcend the constraints of log frame methodology and similar approaches, then part of what will make a convincing case for alternative approaches is the articulation of usable criteria and indicators."

These can be articulated on the theories that lie behind particular types of interventions as well as drawn from practical experience and case studies. This is not to argue in favor of 'magic bullets', but rather to suggest that broad, contingency related patterns and categories need to be identified. It is simply not good enough to invoke the contexts and the particularities of certain situations, important as those are, as a defense against the failure to name such indicators.[12]

3. A closer look: Evaluation approaches at various stages in the project cycle

As noted earlier, evaluation is important at all stages in a peacebuilding intervention, from before a project begins to after it has been implemented. This section looks at some of the considerations which are relevant to each stage in the project cycle, and concludes with a discussion of evaluation at the more "global" level.

Ex-ante assessment: looking before you leap

Good intentions are clearly not enough to ease tensions and keep conflicting parties from murdering each other. Effective intervention begins with a well-grounded analysis of the situation - "ex-ante conflict impact assessment". Jos De la Haye provides a concise description of the essential elements of such an analysis. "The ex-ante PCIA or CIAS a) analyses the conflict situation describing problems in a particular area, b) sets out the objectives of the aimed intervention and c) looks at the appropriateness of proposed measures and ways of translating them into action." Citing Ken Bush, De la Haye observes that this ex-ante analysis functions "as a 'screening' exercise that examines the dynamics of the conflict and its likely impact on the proposed project. However, the analysis goes further. The ex-ante PCIA or CIAS is also to be considered as a 'screening' exercise that examines the likely impact of the proposed project on the dynamics of the conflict."[13]

Michael Lund discusses this preliminary process in some detail in his paper, *Learning Lessons from Experience: Preventing Violent Intra-State Conflicts.*[14] Lund identifies five steps during "conflict analysis" and "prevention analysis" to undertake prior to beginning the active portion of any conflict prevention intervention. The following is an abridged version of Lund's discussion of these first five steps:

Conflict Analysis: the initial steps structure the problem and identify specific objectives

Step 1: Identify the sources of potential conflict ("What is the Problem?")
This includes identifying the nature of the conflict situation by pinpointing as clearly and explicitly as possible the main risk factors and conflict dynamics that could produce violent conflict and conflict escalation.

Step 2: Identify entry points and objectives
This involves first identifying possible *entry points, leverage points,* or *angles of attack* that can be taken with regard to each of the identified sources of conflict.

Prevention Analysis: these steps match specific preferred preventive measures to the identified conflict causes and existing peace capacities, generate an array of possible options, try to forecast the likely outcomes of each choice, and finalize the most promising options.

Step 3: Identify an array of possible preventive measures to achieve the objectives ("What is appropriate to do?")
Consider various plausible programmatic means or activities ("preventive measures", "policy tools", "instruments") for achieving the various objectives.

Step 4: Do prior appraisal of the likely effectiveness and implementability of preventive measures (prospective evaluation — "Will these work in this context?)
This task asks the question "Will they be effective in this context?" Using clearly identified peace and conflict impact criteria, they should each be screened for their likely effectiveness in contributing to limiting violence, building peace capacities, or alternatively, worsening aspects of the conflict.

Step 5: Identify a preferred total mix or combination of preventive measures
This involves identifying the overall set of measures that will be required to address all the major sources of the conflict, and thus are ultimately needed for effective conflict prevention - the various blocks that are needed to construct stable "peacebuilding."

Hoffman cites the four pre-assessment "areas of concern" that Ken Bush identified: **location, timing, political context**, and **other salient factors**.[15] Without adequate consideration of these areas of concern, it is unlikely, if not impossible, to design an appropriate intervention, or to reliably anticipate the outcomes of an intervention.

Hoffman goes on to elaborate on the subsequent evaluation activities suggested by Bush, which can be broadly divided into three sorts of considerations:

- Environmental / contextual considerations - these include assessment of the political and security structures, risk, infrastructure, as well as the feasibility or "window of opportunity" for a peace-building activity;

- Project specific considerations - here, issues such as resources, competencies of implementing agencies, and availability of suitable personnel are examined;

- Project - environment correspondence - consideration here is given to support at local, regional and national levels, as well as within the implementing and funding organizations, issues such as trust and participation of local authorities, and sustainability of a project.

Taken together, Lund's five steps and the Hoffman/Bush considerations discussed above suggest a clear approach that should be applicable for most ex-ante evaluation activities. Manuela Leonhardt adds that the analysis of conflict dynamics requires "an intimate knowledge of the local context", and that effective programs need to be based on "a thorough needs assessment".[16] Leonhardt also argues forcefully that the full range of impacts, both negative

Thematic area	Risks	Opportunities
Governance	aid reinforces illegitimate political structures aid weakens local government by creating unsustainable parallel structures aid replicates authoritarian structures aid undermines local capacities and creates dependency	aid strengthens local formal and informal structures aid encourages participation and local ownership aid recognizes local ownership of peace process aid agencies assume engaged, but neutral position in conflict
Economics	aid distorts local economies aid cements existing socio-economic divisions aid encourages unsustainable use of natural resources aid supports contentious claims to natural resources	aid strengthens local economy aid promotes more equal opportunities aid delivery encourages collaboration and cohesion aid encourages sustainable resource management aid strengthens equal access to resources
Socio-Cultural Factors	aid agencies duplicate and reinforce war images aid grafts western conflict resolution methods on to local peace processes	aid agencies support trust building and reconciliation aid empowers people to resolve violent conflict in their own ways
Arms and War Economy	aid subsidizes the war economy	aid avoids instrumentalization by warlords aid develops alternative livelihoods to violence

and positive, must be taken into consideration whenever any activity - including not only conflict prevention activities but also development or humanitarian assistance, is undertaken in a conflict prone area. Thus, writes Leonhardt, "ex ante project appraisals and conflict impact assessments are crucial for identifying both the conflict risks and peace opportunities of particular initiatives, as well as unintended negative effects in worsening conflicts.

As an example, Leonhardt summarizes the risks and opportunities associated specifically with aid in conflict-affected regions in the table (page 65).

Process Monitoring: keeping things on track
Any ongoing process needs to be monitored to ascertain that the actual implementation is proceeding according to plan, that the premises upon which an implementation plan have been based correspond to reality, that the strategies adopted lead to the intended and desired results, to consider how changes in the environment may effect the ongoing implementation, and to consider whether the originally stated objectives are still relevant or need to be adjusted in the light of new realities, additional information, and better understanding of the facts.

Conflict prevention activities are no different in this respect than other processes, be they business or industrial processes. Of course, in conflict prevention activities and interventions, the situation is likely to be more fluid than in the business world, and the stakes can oftentimes be considerably higher. Indeed, the very sensitivity of the situation in conflict prevention activities is an argument for rigorous monitoring, as well as flexibility in responding to new findings and modifying strategies if need be.

"Given the nature of the peacebuilding endeavor," says George Wachira, "... as a practitioner I need the kind of feedback that helps me to know how to adapt to the dynamics of process, how to manage change, and if I am managing it well. The evaluation of peacebuilding should not just aim at measuring the results, but should, more importantly, capture the unfolding process, particularly the adaptations and new initiatives and relationships that are brought into play."[17] Wachira adds that in stressing the importance of a focus on *process* rather than *outcomes* during intermediate or ongoing evaluation, a process-focused approach is likely to reveal the development, for example, of an expanding peace infrastructure or other underlying developments that can be important for long-term progress towards greater stability and less violence.

"Process monitoring" should include assessment of the actual implementation - are the tasks properly and professionally carried out; is there sufficient staff to successfully implement the plan; are funds sufficient and properly allocated, etc. - as well as assessment of the strategies and objectives.

This sort of process monitoring is an iterative process. It is ongoing, and as objectives and implementation strategies change to accommodate new conditions and new perceptions, the monitoring activities need to take these new facts into consideration as well. How well have the changes in planning been implemented? Have the perceived changes on the ground proved to be correct? And so on. It is interesting to note here that in the particular peacebuilding activities to which George Wachira was referring - the growth of a peace infrastructure - the primary feature has been the formation of over eighthundred peace committees in rural Kenya - a key feature which *"was not foreseen at the initial stages but was itself the product of adaptation"*[emphasis added]. Wachira concludes here that "evaluation should be seen less as a validation or invalidation exercise pegged only to credibility, and more as a process where learning is extracted from practice and incorporated into new planning and thinking. This is the 'evaluation is learning' paradigm. It recognizes what we have come to call 'serendipitous arrivals or discoveries', how we learn from what 'we have come to', and how this helps to clarify our goals, objectives and activities, and the theories behind them."

A suggested strategy for carrying out this "intermediate" evaluation process is "action evaluation", proposed by conflict resolution scholar Jay Rothman of Antioch University in a paper for the journal *International Negotiation* in 1997,[18] further elaborated by various scholars, including Prof. Marc Howard Ross of Bryn Mawr College.[19] "Action evaluation," writes Ross, "encourages an active and continual focus on goal definition and achievement throughout an intervention." Ross further observes that "action evaluation explicitly rejects that it is either possible or desirable for initiatives to fully articulate goals at the outset and to fail to modify them over time," and further, that "an implicit objective of the method is to make participants seriously reflect on and discuss their goals, so they will be less likely to accept vague, general goals such as bringing peace to a long-troubled region."

Action evaluation is a particularly useful strategy for evaluation of the ongoing process because it sees the evaluation process as inextricably linked to the dynamic implementation process. "Action evaluation incorporates goal setting, monitoring and evaluation into a conflict resolution initiative rather than seeing these as distinct activities to be conducted independently and at different points in time. It seeks to make explicit the goals and motivations of all stakeholders, to analyze how these evolve over time, and to encourage the stakeholders to use the goals which have been identified as a step towards identifying explicit, contextually defined criteria of success by which a project might be judged."

An important feature of action evaluation is that it envisions a leading role for a member of the project implementation team, the "action evaluator". In articulating his ideas about action evaluation, Rothman relied on "the participation hypothesis", which presumes that active involvement in a process builds commitment to the process and to the pursuit of the project's goals. The lead evaluator canvasses, consults and engages stakeholders, project participants, and "organizers" (funders, officials of implementing agencies, etc.), with a particular focus on project goals, in terms both of an assessment of the perceptions of the goals by various participants, and progress towards these goals. Ross notes that this monitoring of goals serves as a way of developing context-specific standards or criteria of success which can be employed both for internal evaluation and external evaluation. Because action evaluation is an ongoing process, it provides a mechanism that facilitates "self-correction" in response to contextual changes, as well as standards, reflecting the realities at any given moment, which "outside evaluators and others can use to determine the extent to which a project has established and met meaningful goals in terms of the large conflict in which it is embedded."

After the fact(s) - ex-post evaluation

When most people think of an evaluation, what they have in mind is a review of some activity following its conclusion, or if it is ongoing, after it has been established and has been functioning for long enough that its effectiveness can be appraised. In the conflict prevention world, such "ex-post" evaluations are also the sort most commonly requested and/or undertaken by outside agencies and funders.

There is, to be sure, something slightly threatening about the ex-post review - particularly when local implementers feel that an outside party is standing in judgement of their work. And indeed, one German peace worker involved in grass roots peacebuilding activities in the Balkans acknowledged that she and her colleagues were involved in evaluation activities, but that they tended to carry them out for their own benefit, because they were lacking in self-confidence about their own effectiveness and capacities, and therefore somewhat apprehensive about sharing their findings with the donor.

To allay such fears, and to help assure the sustainability of peacebuilding activities, as was pointed out time and again during the "Towards Better Peace Building Practice" conference, it is of vital importance that the partners and stakeholders feel they have "ownership" of the evaluation process. It is also essential that a high priority be placed on the "institutional learning" aspects of evaluation.

Ken Bush, in summing up his PCIA approach, provides an extensive list of questions, divided along the lines of five "potential peace and conflict impact areas",[20] which he suggests can serve as a framework for evaluation activities. For Bush, this framework need not be restricted to ex-post evaluation activities (nor, he stresses, is the list of questions comprehensive), but his suggested areas of inquiry are indeed useful for guiding any review of an intervention.

These "impact areas", with a brief explanation of what each encompasses, are as follows:

Institutional Capacity to Manage/Resolve Violent Conflict and to Promote Tolerance and Build Peace - the impact on capacity to identify and respond to peace and conflict challenges and opportunities; organizational responsiveness; bureaucratic flexibility; efficiency and effectiveness; the ability to modify institutional roles and expectations to suit changing environment and needs; financial management.

Military and Human Security - the direct and indirect impact on the level, intensity, and dynamics of violence; violent behavior; insecurity and/or security (broadly defined), in particular as experienced in the daily lives of the general population; defense/security policy; repatriation, demobilization and reintegration; reform and retraining of police and security forces/structures; disarmament; banditry; organized crime.

Political Structures and Processes - the impact on formal and informal political structures and processes, such as government capabilities from the level of the state government down to the municipality; policy content and efficacy; the decentralization or concentration of power; political ethnicization; representation; transparency; accountability; democratic culture; dialogue; conflict mediation and reconciliation; the strengthening or weakening of civil society actors; political mobilization; the impact on rule of law; independence or politicization of the legal system; human rights conditions; labor standards.

Economic Structures and Processes - the impact on strengthening or weakening equitable socio-economic structures and processes; distortion or conversion of war economies; the impact on economic infrastructure; supply of basic goods; availability of investment capital; banking system; employment impact; productivity; training; income generation; production of commercial products or service; food security; impacts on the exploitation, generation, or distribution of resources, especially non-renewable resources and the material basis of economic sustenance or food security.

Social Reconstruction and Empowerment - the impact on quality of life; constructive social communication (promotion of tolerance, inclusiveness and participatory principles); displaced people; adequacy of health care and social services; compatibility of interests; levels of trust; inter-group hostility/dialogue; communications; transport; resettlement/displacement; housing; education; nurturing a culture of peace.

Michael Lund, in his keynote address at the "Towards Better Peace Building Practice" conference, proposed a somewhat different set of criteria, drawing on the work of George Wachira and Mary B. Anderson, that also provides useful guidance for evaluators:

Is the initiative contributing to increasing the assets of the community?

Is it fostering relationships?

Did it introduce promising peacemaking methods and spread them?

Is it advancing debate among leaders?

Is it encouraging conciliatory statements and/or reducing violence?"

Another way of gauging progress (or negative impacts) in a conflict situation, suggested by Mary B. Anderson, is based on her notion that within a society there are "dividers" and "connectors" - processes, organizations, even individuals, that function to drive the disparate elements of society apart or to bring them together. By identifying the particular dividers and connectors within a conflicted society, it is then possible to use them as indicators of change and impact. "Once aid agency staff have identified and analyzed connectors," writes Anderson, "they can observe whether their use is increasing or decreasing. For example, if trade has traditionally been a connector, are people still (again) meeting in markets or do they instead avoid them? Do they send their children to schools together, do they build new and separate schools, do they just keep their children at home?"[21]

Among the many important points that Mary B. Anderson has made, none have been so well received - probably because she managed to articulate what many others sensed - than her point that development work and even peacebuilding activities can have unintended negative impacts. In 1996, drawing on what she had learned during the Local Capacities for Peace Project (LCPP) she published *Do No Harm: How Local Aid Can Support Peace or War* (revised and expanded in 1999). The "Do No Harm" approach, which some observers view as a kind of PCIA colored by a set of specific values and concerns, has subsequently been applied and studied in at least twelve projects around the world.

To the extent that the approach focuses attention on the "ancillary effects" of aid on conflict, rather than the direct impacts of aid, writes Anderson, it requires "aid agencies to effect a significant shift in their understanding of accountability: accepting responsibility for the unplanned and often unintended political and social impacts of their work." This, she notes, raises the concern among aid agencies "that this might involve them in areas where they [have] no expertise and also require that they measure what are essentially immeasurable outcomes."

Anderson offers five very straightforward conclusions or "lessons", gleaned from the LCPP project, as general guidance in assessing the impacts of interventions to reduce conflict and support peace. While these conclusions are drawn from experience involving aid programs in conflict areas, Anderson suggests that they probably have more general relevance. Her lessons:

1 Impacts are not abstract: they are observable. On site it is often not difficult to determine, without ambiguity, local impact of a program activity.
2 Numbers matter (if a particular outcome is observable again and again ... the sheer numbers of examples and breadth of agreement will support the credibility of the findings)
3 Disaggregation of goals helps - assessment of how a program eliminates a harmful consequence is easier than knowing with certainty just how a program promotes a positive effect on conflict. It is less difficult to assess one's effectiveness in 'doing no harm' than in bringing about the ultimate goal of reconciliation. Disaggregation of large goals (such as peace) into smaller, clear "steps" along the way, provides a useful way of assessing progress.
4 People "know" - as noted above, people closely involved with a situation in which programs are carried out have opinions - often valid ones - and they often attribute outcomes to particular events.
5 Impacts are as dynamic and changing as the surrounding events — it is important to follow impacts over time to determine whether and how they are changing. Impact assessment cannot be carried out on a one-shot basis.[22]

The Big Picture: evaluating the effectiveness of international peacebuilding activities

Nearly all peace work is local, and most of what passes for "evaluation" is concerned with assessing local situations and local interventions, where "local" may mean a village dispute, or at the opposite end of the spectrum, war between two neighboring nations. And so, most often, reflections on the adage "think globally, act locally" conjure up images of local activists inspired by some "global" perspective.

But Kevin Clements and Michael Lund are both keen to make the point that how the world fits together, in a political sense, is an appropriate topic for the consideration of peacebuilders, and that those concerned with preventing and managing conflict really do need to engage in an analysis of social and political structures that feed conflict (and implicitly, to change them if possible). The events of September 11, both agree, have- quite properly - already begun to focus attention on more global issues.

Those concerned with conflict management, says Clements, need to consider the issues of global governance, the global welfare contract, and organizations at the regional and global level that have the capacity to deliver (or withhold) security. "To some extent," he notes, "we have to evaluate our work in the context of whether we're strengthening civil society, whether we're developing a kind of participatory state system, and whether we've got an international framework which moves in that direction." He wonders aloud if it is conceivable for a global political movement to develop that can address such issues, noting that the "anti-globalization movement" may be, in some nascent form, such a movement.

"Evaluation has been focused on programs, particular interventions, particular organizations, and specific situations," says Lund. "But the field is starting to recognize that it's not just a matter of everybody evaluating their own activity, but to also ask, 'what does it add up to within a country?', and now, in terms of all these activities by international organizations, 'what does this lead to in terms of a broader notion of a more secure globe?'"

How can one apply the evaluation tools of conflict prevention and conflict management to global issues? Both Lund and Clements acknowledge that it is a difficult challenge and largely uncharted territory. Clements suggest that discussion around "social contract" and "human security" issues may be of some value. "There are sets of indicators which can help us in terms of determining whether or not we've got good governance or bad governance, effective economies or ineffective economies, more security or more insecurity, and more justice or less justice."

Better Practices

It is, of course, essential to take best advantage of the lessons learned from past experience. These lessons need to become part of a body of knowledge of best practices, so that with every intervention, the chances of a positive impact will increase. This section reflects on the challenges of compiling that body of knowledge, and offers practical suggestions based on some of the most thoughtful efforts to compile such a body of knowledge.

"Evaluation is one piece of a much, much bigger puzzle," says Susan Collin Marks, of Search for Common Ground. "What to me is much more interesting is [to understand] how we learn the lessons we learn, how institutions learn, how we create the space to be reflective enough to do it, and how we then gather those best practices and lessons learned and make them available not only within our organizations or within our project, but also out to the field and to the educational institutions."

In fact, Collin Marks insists on drawing a clear distinction between "evaluation" - a process which she equates with an appraisal or judgement on the effectiveness of an action or activity (and which, she fears, has a stifling effect on cooperation between peace activists in conflict areas and conflict prevention organizations and donors based outside the conflict zones), and "learning" - striving for constant improvement, better practices, and the sharing of information and transfer of knowledge. "People are doing great work around conflict," she says, "but the question that everybody has is how do they translate that into something usable. So that process that we're talking about is to gather the best practices. There has to be a framework of evaluation, but if we just talk about evaluation we're missing, in my view, 70 percent of the picture."

By focusing on "best practices", Collin Marks observes, cooperation in pursuit of the institutionalization of effective strategies is far more likely, as opposed to apprehension with respect to an outsider's judgement.

Jonathan Goodhand, an Associate of INTRAC (International NGO Training and Research Centre) and an experienced field worker and writer on conflict resolution, makes the point that "there's a lot of knowledge but it's not organized." Ideally, "systematization" of knowledge should be an integral part of conflict prevention and development activities, but frequently that has not been the case.

Frequently, but fortunately not always and not everywhere. An excellent example of "systematized" knowledge is Search for Common Ground's "tool box" of twenty-four conflict resolution techniques. These tools are derived from the core methodology which is reflected in the organization's name, and best expressed by the suggestion, offered by African National Congress Leader Andrew Masondo to "Understand the differences; act on the commonalities." Some of these tools are traditional methods such as mediation, while others are less traditional, such as the use of radio and television. Search for Common Ground notes that the impacts are increased when several tools are simultaneously applied in a conflict situation.

It is all well and good that some organizations are producing such valuable tools, but Goodhand still bemoans the fact that "lessons are usually spurned rather than learned," noting, for example, that a comprehensive assessment of Afghanistan was undertaken in 1993, and yet, while that report collects dust, the international community is preparing to repeat the same exercise. Obviously, he observes, "there was no learning and things got forgotten. The question then is 'why' and how to avoid it." Goodhand believes that the

The Search for Common Ground Toolbox[23]

1. Mediation and Facilitation
2. Dialogue Workshops
3. Conflict-Resolution Institution Building and Training
4. Policy Forum
5. Joint Action Projects
6. Cross-Ethnic Cooperation within Professions
7. Back-channel Negotiations
8. Domestic Shuttle Diplomacy
9. Community Organizing
10. Court-Based Mediation
11. Education in Schools
12. Interethnic Kindergartens
13. Images of the Other: Reduction of Stereotypes
14. Radio
15. Television
16. Children's TV
17. Video-Based Dialogues
18. Journalist Training
19. Cross-Ethnic Team Reporting
20. Publications
21. Arts and Culture
22. Music
23. Sports
24. Awards

continual rotation of field staff is one problem, and that more fundamental institutional structures impede knowledge transfer and learning. "The more that I'm involved in this, the less I think information is the problem," says Goodhand. "There are institutional political blockages which prevent people from acting upon information. That implies that it's not about lesson learning - it's about looking at the blockages and acting upon them. Another reason that there's an essential poverty of knowledge is because there's so much institutional competition. People don't want to relinquish sovereignty. They don't want to collaborate too much if it means they're going to lose some kind of power."

Michael Lund expresses a different concern with respect to the evaluation process, namely, that "a common frame of reference is lacking in which to classify findings so they can be communicated to relevant users of this advice, and can be further tested and cumulated by researchers." This makes it difficult for practitioners to know what experiences of previous interventions may be useful for their activities. "Without such a framework," he continues, "the business of deriving and offering lessons from preventive activity is like reading tea leaves or seeing shapes in the clouds on the sky - almost anything can be stated to anyone about any facet of the subject."[24]

Lund concludes that when it comes to more effective conflict management practices, "where there's a way, there can be a will", and suggests that serious reflection on what has and has not worked in the past is essential if that "way" is to be found:

"Putting more emphasis on examining recent prevention experience to understand what is effective prevention, and then incorporating these lessons in existing country level programming procedures conducted on some roughly joint basis will not by themselves dramatically change the existing political priorities at the top levels of decision making. But these steps might embolden various actors focused on particular countries so that they can take a preventive initiative when they have the opportunity. They can also build up a basis for sounder policymaking at the level of high policy, as conflict prevention advocacy increasingly garners more serious and detailed attention."

In this light, the value of the Local Capacities for Peace Project and the Reflecting On Peace Practice Project is clear. All those involved in peacebuilding activities owe Mary B. Anderson and the Collaborative for Development Action (CDA) a debt of gratitude not only for taking the initiative to gather a considerable body of knowledge, but also for beginning to make sense of it with keen observations and valuable recommendations regarding effective strategies not only for evaluation, but - more importantly - effective action.

LCPP began in 1994 with the first of fifteen field-based case studies of the interaction between aid and conflict, followed in 1996 and 1997 by some forty "feedback workshops" where participants were invited to reflect on and "test" the "lessons" learned during the case studies against their own experience. Following the workshops, from 1997 through the end of 2000, fourteen agencies involved in projects in conflict areas tested the "Do No Harm" framework developed as a result of the findings during the initial phase, in terms of design, implementation, monitoring, evaluation and re-design. Currently, the focus has shifted to "mainstreaming" the framework and the methodologies which emerged from LCPP. In addition CDA has produced a wide range of publications related to the project and the findings.

The Reflecting on Peace Practice Project began in 1999, and is more specifically focused on peace-building efforts. According to CDA, "the project systematically compares and analyses past conflict-focused actions through case studies and consultations with practitioners in order to identify what works, what does not work, and under what circumstances." Here again, CDA has carried out case studies (26 in all), published on its findings to date, and is now conducting workshops for a wide variety of participants, including actors in the conflict areas as well as representatives of local and international peace agencies, with the aim of further critiquing the methodologies and implementations, and distilling additional lessons from the information gathered.

In the initial phase of the RPP Project, a number of "critical issues" emerged which, says CDA, must be taken into consideration in virtually any intervention. CDA identifies the following as "critical issues":[25]

Linkages and levels: Inadequate linkages among peace efforts (at different levels or sectors) are widely reported as a reason for the inability of small-scale peace efforts to achieve larger scale impacts.

Insider-outsider roles and relationships: Outsider peace agencies/ practitioners play a wide variety of roles in their partnerships with insider peace agencies/practitioners. A distinct issue is the relationships that develop between insiders and outsiders, and whose agenda, models, approaches, and analysis dominate such partnerships and the programming decisions made.

Strategies and their relation to analysis of context: Thorough and ongoing analysis of the context in which they work is widely seen by agencies to be key to program effectiveness.

Tradeoffs between working for reduction of violence and social justice: Some interventions are meant to stop violence, while others are intended to promote or build peace through working for social justice. RPP Phase I showed that most agencies see dilemmas and tradeoffs between the two approaches in their work, though most agree both are critical for lasting peace. At a practical level, it remains unclear what balance between these leads to the most effective work.

How agencies deal with actions intended to disrupt peace processes: RPP experience shows that peace agencies seem unprepared for the actions of people who are NOT interested in peace.

Indicators of impact: RPP cases showed that indicators of the impacts of work on conflict are highly context specific. An indicator of a positive outcome in one setting is often an indicator of a negative outcome in another. As well, agencies face many dilemmas in attributing outcomes to agency work, assessing credibility of indicators, and choosing which indicators to monitor.

Robert Ricigliano, Peace Studies Programme, University of Wisconsin, Milwaukee, USA, key-note speaker

Effectiveness criteria for peace work: How do agencies that work on conflict establish interim benchmarks of success that apply to the broad range of types of peace work being done? The experience of peace and conflict agencies in the RPP cases studies and consultations suggested six tentative criteria for effectiveness [identified earlier in this chapter].

Inadvertent Negative Impacts: Phase I of RPP showed that most practitioners readily acknowledge that work on conflict can have inadvertent negative impacts that need to be examined more closely to improve programming.

The Role of Dialogues and Trainings: "Dialogues" and "trainings" are two of the most prominent intervention methods by international peace agencies. RPP Phase I showed that often these methods have positive impacts on (some) participants, but only rarely did they show visible and tangible impacts on peace processes writ large.

Development and humanitarian agencies in peace initiatives: Phase I showed that humanitarian and development agencies are increasingly undertaking programs to address conflict directly. Their long term presence in conflict areas, and their ability to deliver funds and projects to address people's survival and reconstruction needs are two factors which distinguish these agencies from other NGOs that undertake peace projects.

Search for Common Ground's toolbox, and CDA's critical issues, along with the many other recommendations that have been cited in this chapter, may all lead to better practices, and ideally, to positive change in conflict situations. But there are few hints offered with respect to the actual *process* of institutional learning. Here - once again - models from business will undoubtedly be instructive. But International Alert's Kevin Clements, and Rob Ricigliano of the University of Wisconsin have both reflected on these processes. Ricigliano speaks of "networks of effective action" and what he terms a "holistic" approach. The underlying notion is that a "network" consists of people and organizations at multiple levels, without a hierarchy, and that the values of inclusivity and diversity should enable greater exchange of information and more learning about strategies for peace building.
Clements focuses on what he calls "Shared Analysis", by which he means a collaborative relationship where "insiders" and "outsiders" work together to define strategy and determine objectives. "One of the most important contributions an outsider can make," says Clements, "is to act as an 'analytic mirror'."

It may be obvious, but it is also worth emphasizing as (or re-stating: these points were made in another context earlier in this chapter), that institutional learning is inextricably linked to the sort of iterative reflection on activities that takes place during "process monitoring" and so it is essential that such activities be built into an peace-building activity. The goal is to create an environment in which "lessons are learned" as a matter of course, and as part of the process.

At the "Towards Better Peace Building Practice" conference in the Netherlands, Kevin Clements delivered a final address during which he reflected on both the difficulties and the opportunities for peace building, particularly in the wake of the terrorist attacks on the United States which had taken place just six weeks earlier. He likened peacebuilding to untying a knot - "you have to find the ends and where to tug a pull," he said, or you may end up pulling from the middle and making the situation worse - and then offered twelve insights, borne of experience and reflection, that may point the way to finding the ends.

As peacebuilders, said Clements:

We need to acknowledge and understand the specificity and uniqueness of each conflict that we're dealing with;

We need to apply whatever academic perspectives are available to us;

We've got to increasingly consider the nature of the relationships between various conflicts, and to think in terms of conflict systems;

We need to understand about the political economy of war;

We need to start paying much more attention to conflict dynamics;

We need a division of labor and peer responsibility in the field, and much improved communication and coordination;

We've got to make sure that we fundamentally address these issues around the relationship between peace building and conflict resolution and development, and insure that we address peace building, development, justice, and democratization simultaneously;

We need to understand that *we* don't solve anyone's problems, and that as external actors, all we can really do is identify and work together with those who are working for peace;

We need to have a sense of proportionality about what external parties are actually contributing, and to recognize how meager the resources are that are invested in peace building;

We should be striving to establish mutually empowering and emancipatory partnerships and to keep in mind that the more peace builders and conflict resolvers are concerned about their own status and the status of their organizations, the less likely they are to be effective;

We need to aim for sustainability and to insure that when we leave, resources are still available for the people who've been working, and that not only will there be networks of effective action when we're there, but networks of effective action when we're not there;

And finally, we need to imbed our work in a theory of social and political change, and to have some sense of the mechanism we want to utilize to help others solve their problems.

Peacemakers, said Clements, must not lose sight of their visions of peace. "Without visions of peace, people can't realize peace. Without visions of a just world, people can't realize justice." The challenge, he concluded, is "to create the space to allow others to share their visions with you and for you to respond to their visions."

The point, in the end, is that best practices come about not only as at result of right thinking about how to achieve a more peaceful and more just world, but also right thinking about just what we want to achieve.

Jim Wake is a free lance journalist based in The Netherlands

The European Centre for Conflict Prevention would like to continue collecting and disseminating tools for evaluation and learning practices. It would also like to further facilitate the debate on the impact of these tools. Therefore, if you have, or know of any projects related to these issues, please contact us at info@conflict-prevention.net

Bibliography

Publications

Barnes, Teresa. "Lessons Learned in Conflict Prevention: State of the Art", in *Towards Better Peace Building Practice, Working Document*, Anneke Galama and Paul van Tongeren, eds. European Centre for Conflict Prevention, 2001

De la Haye, Jos. *A Sectorial Conflict Impact Assessment: Guidelines for Peace Education* (unpublished, 2001). Paper presented during the Peace and Conflict Impact Assessments workshop at the Towards Better Peace Building Practice Conference, The Netherlands, Oct 2001

Leonhardt, Manuela. "Improving Capacities and Procedures for Formulating and Implementing Effective Conflict Prevention Strategies - An Overview of Recent Donor Initiatives" in *The Impact of Conflict Prevention Policy*, Michael Lund and Guenola Rasamoelina, eds., Baden-Baden, Nomos Verlagsgesellschaft, 2000

Leonhardt, Manuela. *The Coming of Age of PCIA: What have we learned? Where are we going?* (unpublished). Paper presented during the Peace and Conflict Impact Assessments workshop at the Towards Better Peace Building Conference, The Netherlands, Oct. 2001

Lund, Michael. "Learning Lessons from Experience: Preventing Violent Intra-State Conflicts" in *Towards Better Peace Building Practice, Working Document*, Anneke Galama and Paul van Tongeren, eds. European Centre for Conflict Prevention, 2001. The paper appears in altered form in *Searching for Peace in Europe & Eurasia: An Overview of Conflict Prevention and Peacebuilding Activities*, a joint publication of Lynne Rienner Publishers and the European Centre for Conflict Prevention, due to be published in February 2002

Nairobi Peace Institute-Africa, *Strategic and Responsive Evaluation of Peacebuilding*, 1999

Ross, Marc Howard. "Action Evaluation in the Theory and Practice of Conflict Resolution", *Peace and Conflict Studies*, George Mason University, May 2001

Rothman, Jay. "Action Evaluation and Conflict Resolution Training: Theory, Method and Case Study". *International Negotiation.* 2:451-70, 1997

Wachira, George, "A Practitioner's Reflections on the Evaluation of Peacebuilding", keynote address at Towards Better Peace Building Practice Conference, The Netherlands in October, 2001

Websites and links for additional sources:

Berghof Research Center for Constructive Conflict Management
home page: www.berghof-center.org

Berghof Handbook for Conflict Transformation (available in HTML and PDF
format): www.berghof-center.org/handbook/cf.htm
Site includes:

> Anderson, Mary. "Reflecting on the Practice of Outside Assistance: Can we
> know what good we do?"

> Bush, Ken. Peace and Conflict Impact Assessment (PCIA) Five Years On:
> The Commodification of an Idea (response paper), in Berghoff Handbook
> for Conflict Transformation, Berghof Research Center for Constructive
> Conflict Management, 2001. Another in the series mentioned above.

> Hoffman, Mark. "Peace and Conflict Impact Assessment Methodology:
> Evolving Art Form or Practical Dead End?"

Bush, Kenneth. "A Measure of Peace: Peace and Conflict Impact Assessment
(PCIA) of Development Projects in Conflict Zones" (extracts), International
Development Research Centre, Working Paper No. 1, available at:
www.idrc.ca/peace/en/reports/paper01

Collaborative for Development Action
home page: www.cdainc (home page)

Local Capacities for Peace Project: www.cdainc.com/lcpp-index.htm

Reflecting on Peace Practice Project: www.cdainc.com/rpp-index.htm

Reflecting on Peace Practice Project, critical issues: www.cdainc.com/rpp-
description2.htm.

Search for Common Ground website
home page: www.sfcg.org

toolbox: www.sfcg.org/act2.cfm?locus=Toolbox

USAID
www.ussaid.gov

Appendix

Asking the Right Questions and Looking in the Right Places (Ken Bush)[26]

Institutional Capacity to Manage/Resolve Violent Conflict and to Promote Tolerance and Build Peace

- Did/will the project affect organizational capacity of individuals, or collectivities (institutions, social groups, private sector) - positively or negatively- to identify and respond to peace and conflict challenges and opportunities? If so, Which groups? To what degree? How and why? Did/will the project increase or decrease the capacity to imagine, articulate and operationalize realities that nurture rather than inhibit peace?
- "Organization capacity" might include: 1) the ability to conceptualize and identify peace-building challenges and opportunities; 2) in the case of organizations, to restructure itself to respond; and 3) to alter standard operational procedures to respond more effectively and efficiently in ways that have a tangible positive impact on the ground - for example, in ways that enhance fairness, equity, "even-handedness," and accountability, and transparency.
- What were/might be the obstacles to a positive peace-building impact?
- How might the beneficial effects be amplified/made more sustainable both during and following the project.?

Military and Human Security

- Did/will the project affect the individuals sense of security?
- Did/will the project affect the military/paramilitary/criminal environment - directly or directly, positively or negatively? If so how?
- Was there/will there be tangible improvements in the political, economic, physical, food, security? If so, what are they, and to whom do they apply? If so, which groups? To what degree? How and why?
- Did/will the project deepen our understanding, or increase the capacity to address the non military irritants to violent conflict - e.g. environmental degradation, resources scarcity, political manipulation, disinformation, mobilization and politicization of identity, etc.?
- To what extent did/will the project contribute to the "demilitarization of minds"? For example, through the dismantling of the cultural and socio-psychological predisposition of individuals and groups to use militarized violence as a first, rather than last, resort. More generally, what was/might be the impact of the project on: 1) the decreased prominence of military weapons in social, political, and economic life; 2) the gradual delegitimation of a gun culture; and 3) the evolution of non-violent modalities of conflict management.

Political Structures and Processes

- Did/will the project help or hinder the consolidation of constructive political relationships within and between state and civil society? For example, how did/will the project affect the understanding, composition and distribution of political resources within and between state and civil society?
- Did/will the project have an positive or negative impact on formal or informal political structures and processes -either within the formal arena of institutionalized state politics (e.g., constitutional or party politics) or within the informal arena of civil society (e.g., traditional authority structures)? If so, how? Did/will the project contribute to the development of the capacity of individuals/collectivities to participate constructively in democratic political processes? Did/will it contribute to increasing the transparency, accountability? representativeness? and appropriateness of political structures?
- Did/will the project influence policy processes or products? If so, in what ways?
- Did/will the project help defuse inter-group tensions? If so, how?
- What was/what will be the impact of the project on human rights conditions within a country or region? (e.g., awareness, legislation, levels of abuse/respect?)

Economic Structures and Processes

- To what extent did/will a project contribute to or detract from efforts to "re"-construct damaged economic and social infrastructure? Specifically? in the following areas:
  high level of debt;
  unsustainable high military budgets;
  skewed distribution of wealth, income, and assets;
  resettlement of displaced populations;
  environmental degradation - particularly that which inhibits economic productivity.
- To what extent did/will the project
  assess damage to social and economic infrastructure;
  provide technical assistance for rehabilitation and reconstruction;
  rehabilitate and reconstruct economic infrastructure;
  reactivate smallholder agriculture;
  rehabilitate the export sector;
  rehabilitate key industries;
  up-grade employment skills;
  stabilize the national currency and;
  rehabilitate financial institutions.

Social Reconstruction and Empowerment

- Did/will the project contribute to the development or consolidation of equity and justice, or the means of providing basic needs?
- Did/will the benefits of the project get shared equitably?
- Did will the project include members from the various communities affected by the conflict? How? With what effectiveness? What criteria for effectiveness?
- Did/will the project seek explicitly to benefit or build bridges between the different communities? If so, how? Effectiveness? Criteria of effectiveness? Did/will it help foster an inclusive - rather than exclusive - sense of community? Did/will it facilitate the ability of individuals and groups to work together for there mutual benefit?
- Did/will the project facilitate positive communication/interaction between and within groups? Is this sustainable?
- Did/Will it provide/generate the skills, tools, capacity for individuals and communities to define issues/problems to be addressed, formulate solutions to those problems, or resolve those self-defined problems?
- Did/will the project take into consideration the history/legacy of conflict in its design? For example, did/will it consider the specific impact on children, women and other vulnerable groups such as displaced populations, and the politically, socially and economically marginalized.
- Did/will the project increase contact, confidence, or trust between the communities? Will it dispel distrust? Did/will it create common interests, or encourage individuals and groups to recognize their common interests, and did/will it modify their behavior in order to attain them?
- To what extent did/will the project incorporate/privilege the views and interests of affected indigenous populations?

Notes

1 "Evaluation" is a term, it turns out, loaded with unintended, and sometimes negative connotations. Nonetheless, it is the term which best describes a whole range of activities including information gathering, analysis, reflection, assessment, and appraisal. Providing a "grade" or pronouncing a "judgment" on the quality of implementation is perhaps the least important element of evaluation as it is understood in this chapter. Naturally, donors and implementing agencies do want to know whether a project has been a "success" or not, and to take actions to avoid repeating errors and failures, and indeed, to root out incompetence. But the more important function of evaluation, broadly construed, is to choose the best and most appropriate strategies at the beginning, to assure that they are being implemented to best effect, and to provide knowledge that can be of value in the future, both within the original context, and elsewhere. Although the word "evaluation" is not generally attached to the sort of assessment or "conflict analysis" that is undertaken prior to an intervention, it seems appropriate to address it here, as it is part of the reflective process that is essential to effective conflict prevention and conflict resolution activities.

2 This publication was produced after a four-day seminar which took place in March 1999 to reflect on peacebuilding initiatives carried out by the National Council of Churches of Kenya and the Nairobi Peace Initiative-Africa.

3 This and much of what follows is drawn from the unpublished paper entitled "A Practitioner's Reflections on the Evaluation of Peacebuilding", prepared by George Wachira for the "Towards Better Peace Building Practice" conference in the Netherlands in October, 2001. Wachira delivered a keynote address at the conference based on the paper.

4 A study that defines a broad set of criteria regarding both outcomes and processes -- drawn from the work of Mary B. Anderson, John Paul Lederach, the causes of conflict lit-

erature, as well as the prevention literature -- and then examines the performance of three types of NGO initiativs with respect to those criteria, is Lund, Michael S., et al. (2001a), *The Effectiveness of Civil Society Initiatives in Controlling Violence and Building Peace*, Management Systems International, Inc. (Viewable under www.usaid.gov)

5 Information is available online from the Collaborative for Development Action website at www.cdainc (home page), www.cdainc.com/lcpp-index.htm (Local Capacities for Peace Project), and www.cdainc.com/rpp-index.htm (Reflecting on Peace Practice Project).

6 The conference took place from October 24 - October 26 and was convened by the European Platform for Conflict Prevention and Transformation, and Kontakt der Kontinenten.

7 Barnes, Teresa. "Lessons Learned in Conflict Prevention: State of the Art". This article, which appeared in the background briefing document prepared for Better Peace Building conference, is based on presentations held at the Expert Meeting on Lessons Learned in Conflict Interventions, held from Feb. 1-4, 2001 in Londonderry, Northern Ireland.

8 Anderson, Mary B. "Reflecting on the Practice of Outside Assistance: Can we know what good we do?", in *Berghof Handbook for Conflict Transformation*, Berghof Research Center for Constructive Conflict Management, 2001. The article, available from the Berghof Center website (www.berghof-center.org/handbook/cf.htm) as an HTML or PDF document, is one of a series of articles which together constitute the excellent "Handbook for Conflict Transformation".

9 Leonhardt, Manuela. "The Coming of Age of PCIA: What have we learned? Where are we going?" (unpublished). Leonhardt presented the paper during the "Peace and Conflict Impact Assessments" workshop held during the Better Peace Building conference.

Additional remarks attributed to Leonhardt are drawn from the paper and her presentation.

10 De la Haye, Jos. "A Sectorial Conflict Impact Assessment: Guidelines for Peace Education" (unpublished, 2001). As the name suggests, De la Haye's paper and presentation during the Better Peace Building conference focuses on "sectorial" applications of the methodology, but in fact, the six steps provide an excellent overview of the PCIA approach in general.

11 Bush, Ken. Peace and Conflict Impact Assessment (PCIA) Five Years On: The Commodification of an Idea (response paper), in *Berghoff Handbook for Conflict Transformation*, Berghof Research Center for Constructive Conflict Management, 2001. Another in the series mentioned above.

12 Hoffman, Mark. "Peace and Conflict Impact Assessment Methodology: Evolving Art Form or Practical Dead End?", in *Berghoff Handbook for Conflict Transformation*, Berghof Research Center for Constructive Conflict Management, 2001.

13 De la Haye, Jos. "A Sectorial Conflict Impact Assessment."

14 Lund, Michael. "Learning Lessons from Experience: Preventing Violent Intra-State Conflicts". The paper, included in the background briefing document prepared for Better Peace Building conference, appears in altered form in *Searching for Peace in Europe & Eurasia: An Overview of Conflict Prevention and Peacebuilding Activities*, a joint publication of Lynne Rienner Publishers and the European Centre for Conflict Prevention. The book is due to be published in February 2002.

15 Hoffman, Mark. "Peace and Conflict Impact Assessment Methodology: Evolving Art Form or Practical Dead End?"

16 Leonhardt, Manuela. "Improving Capacities and Procedures for Formulating and Implementing Effective Conflict Prevention Strategies - An Overview of Recent Donor Initiatives" in *The Impact of Conflict Prevention Policy*, Michael Lund and Guenola Rasamoelina (eds.), Baden-Baden, Nomos Verlagsgesellschaft, 2000.

17 "A Practitioner's Reflections on the Evaluation of Peacebuilding." Again, this and subsequent remarks attributed to George Wachira are drawn from the published paper upon which his keynote address at the "Towards Better Peace Building Practice Conference was based.

18 Rothman, Jay. "Action Evaluation and Conflict Resolution Training: Theory, Method and Case Study. *International Negotiation.* 2:451-70, 1997.

19 Ross, Marc Howard. "Action Evaluation in the Theory and Practice of Conflict Resolution", *Peace and Conflict Studies*, May, 2001. George Mason University

20 Bush, Kenneth. "A Measure of Peace: Peace and Conflict Impact Assessment (PCIA) of Development Projects in Conflict Zones" (extracts), International Development Research Centre, Working Paper No. 1. See Appendix for the sample questions Bush includes in his discussion.

21 Anderson, Mary B. "Reflecting on the Practice of Outside Assistance: Can we know what good we do?"

22 Anderson, Mary B. "Reflecting on the Practice of Outside Assistance: Can we know what good we do?" These five lessons are described in greater detail in Anderson's paper.

23 See the Search for Common Ground website (www.sfcg.org) for general information, and specific information on the Toolbox at: www.sfcg.org/act2.cfm?locus=Toolbox

24 Lund, Michael. *Learning Lessons from Experience: Preventing Violent Intra-State Conflicts.*

25 See the CDA website at www.cdainc.com/rpp-description2.htm. These critical issues are discussed in more detail there.

26 Bush, Kenneth. "A Measure of Peace: Peace and Conflict Impact Assessment (PCIA) of Development Projects in Conflict Zones."

Further Reading

Mapping Approaches to Lesson Learning

MICHAEL S. LUND, Senior Associate, Management Systems International, Inc. Washington, D.C.

Policy Context

After the Cold War ended, international activities in developing countries that pursue post-conflict peacebuilding, conflict management and conflict prevention expanded dramatically. In response, several researchers began in the early 1990's to gather policy-relevant lessons from the actual experience with various kinds of conflict interventions. They have looked at differing varieties and scopes of such activity and examined them through quantitative, case-study and, more recently, evaluation research. More recently, donors and other funders have begun to take an interest in "learning lessons" and identifying "best practices" from this expanded activity.

Unfortunately, the findings from the accumulating studies have been diverse and dispersed, and they have not been consolidated or disseminated to the locations and people where they might be used and applied. Lessons are collecting on the shelf, but supply has not met demand in any significant way. The contribution of the present volume and the conference on which it is based is that they bring many of these scattered lessons together in one place.

Lessons and Learners

While this clearly is progress, we still have something of a bazaar, and one that is both haphazard and limited in the wares that are available. Not all the "producers" of lessons relevant to peacebuilding are represented here, and not all the "customers" who could use these and other lessons were at the conference or will read this book. One reason for the gap between the existing knowledge and its utilization for improving practice is the lack of an overall framework that sorts out and classifies the diverse accumulating findings, thus helping to direct them to particular consumers who could benefit from the lessons of this experience or that.

A few overarching lessons may apply to the world as a whole and to many actors. Busy governmental or nongovernmental practitioners may press researchers to give them, say, *the* five lessons to be learned "1, 2, 3, 4, 5." Such nostrums definitely can have some educational value, but they are often very general. Some are platitudes that provide little specific guidance ("Act early!" "Consult with those involved in the conflict!"), and some of these sometimes are even misleading for specific contexts.

The kinds of lessons that are likely to be more useful will pertain to the particular regions, individual states, or sub-state communities in the international system at which conflict intervention activity is being carried out, and/or to the particular sectoral or other units of collective activity that are operating at these various levels. So the practitioners who are potential consumers of prevention lessons actually know that they play rather different decisionmaking and implementation roles at and across each of many different levels. Headquarters-level officials and planners set general policy and oversee agency operations, for example, desk officers monitor specific country-level developments, country-level administrators run programmes, and project managers operate activities in particular communities or other sites. Thus, there are actually several sets of such lessons about what is effective or ineffective.

Given their particular stations, practitioners will naturally tend to take an interest in the results of prevention actions that are within their control, and thus in lessons that focus on their particular level for preventive action. We know from information theory that people tend to respond to information to the extent that they are already sensitized to it or searching for it. Thus, one reason why relatively little progress has been made in applying the existing experience in conflict prevention may be that the many lessons that are being generated have not been codified in a unified classification scheme that indicates where they apply in terms of these differing levels and types of activities. If so, some "index" would be useful so that the lessons can be referenced by the diverse decision-makers and practitioners who are interested in peacebuilding, as well as further cumulated by researchers. Such a catalogue would enable the many differing actors who can influence a conflict situation to find conflict intervention guidance that applies to *them*.

A Visual "Literature Review"

To illustrate a lessons-learned data-base project that is currently being developed, a learning framework is outlined in Table 1 below. It charts some of the terrain of conflict intervention activity by identifying major levels and units of conflict action at which various lessons have been or can be gathered. Examples are listed of the kinds of lessons that fit each category and that appear in this book or other sources.

Table 1 A Map of Approaches to Drawing Lessons

Types of lessons	Description and assumptions	Examples in the book or from elsewhere	Main levels of decision-making or actors that are intended audience	Some strengths and weaknesses
Normative Principles and Process Guidelines				
1. Codes of conduct	Normative rules to guide the behavior of practitioners to ensure their moral integrity and professional responsibility.	International Alert Code of Conduct	Many agencies, organizations in peacebuilding, but mainly international NGO's.	Reflect steps toward professionalism; do not necessarily correspond to effective interventions.
2. Lists of general "do's and don't's"	Broad observations about appropriate attitudes, behaviors, skills for individuals and organizations in formulating and implementing initiatives.	Chapter by Jos Havermans; Readings from Jonathan Freedlund, Dylan Matthews, *People Building Peace.*	Unspecified, diffuse, and varied actors, but many seem aimed at NGO's.	Considerable congruence among some helpful insights/guidelines. But focus is un-specified, yet often deals only with small group-interactive processes, can be too vague/truistic and mix normative and empirical.
3. International legal and political standards being promulgated and enforced vis-a-vis states and other parties.	Normative international standards set by global or regional organizations, and seek to enforce/cultivate compliance.	OSCE standards, EU accession criteria, UN human rights conventions follow-up, international humanitarian law	UN, regional organizations collective bodies (e.g., UN Human Rights Commission)	Important, understudied area of intervention, but is often not based on empirical analysis or political realities.

Types of lessons	Description and assumptions	Examples in the book or from elsewhere	Main levels of decision-making or actors that are intended audience	Some strengths and weaknesses
Impact Evaluations Of Specific Interventions Nature of the evaluated interventions (units of analysis):				
4. Constitutional arrangements allocating authority among parts of governments	Federalism, decentralization, autonomy, partition structures, etc.	Donald Horowitz, *Ethnic Conflict*	National governments and international funders	Focuses on structures that shape particular actors incentives; but slights the political processes required to adopt the various options
5. Generic policy instruments used in multi-actor intervention	Seeks to characterize typical performance of main alternative policy types of intervention in the overall "toolbox" shared by many actors (e.g. mediation, elections, peace education)	*Options for Negotiators* book (IDEA), other sources,[1] categories of peacebuilding in reading from Catholic Relief Services.	Heads of agencies, policy planning level	Uses "If x, then y" method to cumulate generalizations from study/ comparison of multiple cases of applications, goes beyond interactive approaches. But lacks consistent typologies, varies in impact criteria, is technocratic.
6. Particular actors' programmes in one or more sectors; individual programmes; role of certain groups	Evaluates various results of donors' activities or certain groups peacebuilding efforts, such as women, religious leaders, elders, business community.	Studies cited in chapter by Jim Wake, case-studies of OECD DAC Task Force on Peace, Conflict and Development.	Programme and project level	Limited to donor development interventions; but lack of typologies of interventions makes it difficult to cumulate findings; tend to focus only on post-conflict.

Types of lessons	Description and assumptions	Examples in the book or from elsewhere	Main levels of decision-making or actors that are intended audience	Some strengths and weaknesses
7. Conflict-wide, multi-actor interventions	Looks for key ingredients (actors, timing, instruments, conditions) found in multi-instrument intervention "successes" versus "failures"	Reading from Jentleson book.[2]	Top decision levels of intergovern-mental bodies, foreign and aid ministries	Includes many potential conflict cases (prevention), vague impact criteria.
8. Individual projects	Studies diverse national/local initiatives of donors and NGO's.	Collaborative Development Action, Inc. Local Capacities for Peace projects, such as described in Mary B. Anderson *Do No Harm* book[3]	Local or national project administrators, implementers	Multiple diverse cases, systematic, range of explicit impact criteria, but development tools and individual project "micro" focus.

Notes

1 See Ben Reilly, Michael Lund, et. al., *Democracy and Deep-Rooted Conflict: Options for Negotiators* (Stockholm, Sweden: Institute for Democracy and Electoral Assistance, 1998). Some instruments such as mediation, negotiations, and sanctions have received libraries of attention, although not usually from a prevention perspective. An exception is William Zartman, ed. *Preventive Negotiations* (Rowman and Little field, 2001). But little has been done on other preventive measures. This includes Cortright, David (ed.), *The Price of Peace: The Role of Incentives in International Conflict Prevention*, Rowman & Littlefield Publishers, Lanham, MD, 1998); Esman, Milton J., „Can Foreign Aid Moderate Ethnic Conflict?" *Peaceworks*, no. 13, (Washington, D.C.: US Institute of Peace, March 1998); certain chapters in Carment, David and Patrick James, eds. *Peace in the Midst of Wars:Preventing and Managing International Ethnic Conflicts* (Columbia, SC:University of South Carolina Press, 1998).

A study under the Greater Horn of Africa Peacebuilding Project at Management Systems International, Inc. (MSI) evaluated the peace and conflict impacts of peace radio, traditional local-level peace processes, and national „track-two" political dialogues in five countries: Lund, Michael S., et. al. (2001a), *The Effectiveness of Civil Society Initiatives in Controlling Violence and Building Peace*, Management Systems International, Inc. (viewable under www.usaid.gov). Earlier efforts to apply various criteria to diverse prevention policy instruments are found in *Preventing and Mitigating Violent Conflicts: A Guide for Practitioners* (op. cit.) and Lund, "Impacts of Development Aid as Incentives or Disincentives in Reducing Internal and Inter-state Conflicts: A Review of Findings from Documented Experience," Unpublished report to the Development Assistance Committee (DAC), Task Force on Peace, Conflict And Development, (OECD), 1998. Some products are putting assessments of such instruments into forms that can be used by country desk officers and other practitioners. See, for example, the brief assessments of election observers, human rights observers, and other instruments in Lund and Mehler, et. al., *Peacebuilding and Conflict Prevention in Developing Countries* (op. cit). A manual of UN „preventive measures" such as fact-finding missions, humanitarian aid, and local community economic development was prepared for the Framework Team in the UN Secretariat: Lund, Michael S. et. al., (2001), *Applying Preventive Measures: A Manual For United Nations Practitioners in Situations of Potential Conflict* (Prototype), submitted to the Framework Team, United Nations Secretariat.

2 See, for example, Hugh Miall, *The Peacemakers: Peaceful Settlement of Disputes since 1945* (New York: St. Martin's Press, 1992); Gabriel Munuera, *Preventing Armed Conflict in Europe: Lesson from Recent Experience* (Paris: Institute for Security Studies, June, 1994); SusanWoodward, *Balkan Tragedy: Chaos and Dissolution after the Cold War* (Brookings Institution, Washington, D.C., 1995; Lund, *Preventing Violent Conflict* (U.S. Institute of Peace, 1996); Peter Wallensteen, ed. *Preventing Violent Conflict: Past Record and Future Challenges* (Uppsala: Uppsala University,

Department of Peace and Conflict Research, 1998); Lund, Rubin and Hara, "Learning from Burundi's Failed Democratic Transition, 1993-96: Did International Initiatives Match the Problem?" in Barnett Rubin, ed. *Cases and Strategies of Preventive Action* (Century Foundation Press, 1998); Vayrinen, et. al., *Inventive and Preventive Diplomacy*, (Notre Dame, Indiana:Joan Kroc Institute, University of Note Dame, 1999); Lund, " 'Preventive Diplomacy' for Macedonia, 1992-1997: Containment becomes Nation-Building," and other chapters in Bruce Jentleson, ed. *Preventive Diplomacy in the Post Cold War World: Opportunities Missed, Opportunities Seized and Lessons to Be Learned* (Lanham, Maryland: Rowman and Littlefield, 1999); Lund, "Why Are Some Ethnic Disputes Settled Peacefully, While Others Become Violent? Comparing Slovakia, Macedonia, and Kosovo," in Hayward Alker, et. al. Eds. *Journeys through Conflict* (Lanham, Maryland: Rowman and Littlefield, in 2001).

3 See the case-studies in Do No Harm: *How Aid Can Support Peace - Or War* (Lynne Rienner, 1999) and subsequent studies organized and analyzed by Mary B. Anderson and her associates at Collaborative for Development Action, Inc.

The following overview derives from the publication *Conflict-Sensitive Approaches to Development- A Review of Practice*, by Cynthia Gaigals with Manuela Leonhardt, of Saferworld and International Alert, *2001*. In this overview, the authors give an indicative summary of several ways in which PCIA has been conceptualized by different authors and institutions. Key features of these frameworks are outlined and so are their strengths and weaknesses. Although it is recognized that a lot of these approaches share things in common, it gives valuable insights in the projects related to PCIA so far. The publication is also available on-line: http://www.international-alert.org/publications

Frameworks for Conflict Impact Assessment

Author/ Aqency	Purpose	Rationale	Root causes Indicators	Methodology	Comments
Luc Reychler, Conflict Impact Assessment, Univ. of Leuven, 1998	Conflict Impact Assessment (CIAs) (ex-ante and ex-post)	Aims of CIAs: • assess the positive/ negative impact of interventions on the dynamics of conflict • support more coherent conflict prevention and peace-building policies • develop tools for policy makers in order to ensure that development and peace-building efforts are more effective	Possible Conditions for sustainable peace: • consultation and n negotiation systems in place at different levels • structural measures in place (democratisation, social free market systems) • integrative moral and political climate (expectations of mutual benefits, multiple loyalties, etc.) • security (objective and subjective)	Policy level requirements: • clear vision of peace • comprehensive needs assessment • coherent action plan (actors, domains, measures, timing) • effective implementation (co-ordination, timeliness, funds) • inclusion of conflict stakeholders • target attitudes that inhibit the constructive transformation of conflicts **Project level:** • integration of project into regional peace policy • assess impact of conflict on project and vice versa • generate alternative options and decision-making (modifications to raise 'peace added value')	**Strengths** • stress on peace as development objective • structural and attitudinal conflict factors used • indicators for project appraisal and monitoring included **Weaknesses** • little indication of how CIAs tool could be implemented in practice

Author/ Aqency	Purpose	Rationale	Root causes Indicators	Methodology	Comments
Kenneth Bush, A Measure of Peace, IDRC, 1998	Peace and Conflict Impact Assessment (PCIA) (ex-ante and ex-post)	**Conflict issues:** • development projects impact on conflict and peace environments • projects need to be measured according to developmental and peace-building criteria • indicators should reflect different perspectives on peace-building	**Central question for all PCIA:** What is the impact of the project on structures that enhance peaceful co-existence? **Main areas of impact:** • Institutional capacity to manage or resolve violent conflict and to promote tolerance and peace. Military and human security. Political structures and processes • Economic structures and processes • Social reconstruction and empowerment	**Criteria for performing PCIA:** Project location in area with a history of violent conflict or in disputed territory Pre-project PCIA • Environmental risk assessment: location, timing, political and economic context, legal and security structures, infrastructure • Project-related considerations: support, trust and participation of community and political structures, resources, flexibility, staffing **Post-project PCIA** *Conflict-relevant changes in:* • access to resources • socio-economic tensions • food security and material subsistence • political, economic or social systems	**Strengths** • consideration of unintended impact of project • indicators for both ex-ante and ex-post assessment **Weaknesses** • little indication of how PCIA could be implemented in practice

Author/ Aqency	Purpose	Rationale	Root causes Indicators	Methodology	Comments
DFID/ Michael Warner, Discussion paper, 1999	Conflict Impact Assessmen t (CIA) (ex-ante, monitoring, ex-post evaluation)	• to mitigate the negative impact on conflict • to exploit peace opportunities	**Conceptual framework for CIA** • projects can have an impact upon conflict and vice versa • projects can support structural and moral/political capacities for peace	**Framework methodology for CIA** *Strategic conflict analysis:* • country and location specific study to identify risks and opportunities *Screening* exempt low risk projects from detailed CIA • assume that projects are planned within a peacebuilding framework *Preliminary conflict impact assessment* • checklist of indicators *Detailed CIA* in co-operation with stakeholders, prioritising options, setting up a conflict management plan, organising capacity building programmes, focusing on consensual negotiation processes	**Strengths** • most elaborate approach in terms of the practical integration of a CIA system into project cycle • open-ended approach, provides scope for decision-making based on contextual knowledge **Weaknesses** • largely conceptual framework

Author/ Aqency	Purpose	Rationale	Root causes Indicators	Methodology	Comments
Mary B. Anderson, Do No Harm, Local Capacities for Peace Project, 1996, 1999	"Do No Harm" and "Supportin g local capacities for peace" (monitoring)	• to identify humanitarian and/or development assistance that helps people to disengage from fighting • to develop structures to peacefully resolve conflicts	**Negative side effects of aid:** *Resource transfer* • resource transfer to warring parties through theft, taxation or diversion of aid • governments may focus resources on the military • control of food allows manipulation of people • distortion of local economies • introduction of scarce resources can reinforce rivalries *Implicit ethical messages* • acceptance of terms of war Bestowing legitimacy on warriors • Undermining peace values • Reinforcing animosity	**Conflict-related issues on policy level:** • systems for delivering food aid • choice of local partners • interagency co-ordination • aid agency criteria for "success" (reflecting external rather than local priorities) **Conflict-related issues on project level:** Need to strengthen "local capacities for peace" at the levels of • systems and institutions (legitimate and responsible local leaders) • attitudes and actions (cross-cutting contacts, co-operation in areas of mutual concern) • Shared values and interests (reinforce inclusiveness and intergroup fairness) • Common experiences (memory of mutual respect and sympathy)	**Strengths** • valuable focus on the modalities of aid delivery • valuable focus on strengthening "local capacities for peace" **Weaknesses** • checklist of indicators rather than open-ended approach • little indication of how proposals could be put into practice

Author/ Aqency	Purpose	Rationale	Root causes Indicators	Methodology	Comments
Anne-Marie Laprise, Programming for Results in Peace-building CIDA, 1998	Performance Indicators for Peace-building (ex-post)	• to provide a framework for evaluating peace-building programmes, linked to Results Based Management (RBM) principles for development agencies	**Main areas for measuring peace-building:** • Domestic capacity and propensity for peaceful conflict resolution • Resolution of ongoing and prevention of new conflicts • Political, legal, security and civil society structures supporting a lasting peace • Recovery of the country or region from the damage inflicted by war • Women fully contribute to and benefit from peace-building and post-conflict reconstruction • Understanding of and support for peace-building, at home and abroad	**Challenges of evaluating peace-building;** • lack of clear approach to peace-building • need for realistic objectives, accounting for high risks, defined in Log-Frame • establishing causality • data availability **Project-level evaluation:** • measuring results according to Log-frame • indicators identified by those responsible for producing results • directional indicators for long-term processes **Policy/Programme-level evaluation:** • inappropriate to ascribe macro-changes to a single programme • identification of the link between intervention and societal changes and projects	**Strengths** • comprehensi ve discussion of the methodologi cal issues linked to monitoring and evaluating peace-building **Weaknesses** • innovative indicators, but very complex and still prescriptive • fails to address the problem of monitoring unintended project impact

Author/ Agency	Purpose	Rationale	Root causes Indicators	Methodology	Comments
Angelika Spelten, Crisis analysis, German Ministry for Economic Co-operation, 1998	Crisis analysis (early warning)	**Support development planners** • to assess the risks of violent conflict • to identify measures which contribute to long-term stability • to reach decisions • on actions when conflict escalates	**Conflict factors:** *Structural conflict factors* • structural disparities, social awareness of conflict, legitimacy of state institutions, external influences *Accelerating factors* • pressure for modernisation, policy changes, structural adjustment, land reform, resettlements, environmental conditions, resource competition, collectively perceived threats *Triggering factors* • polarisation within society, individual actors change political strategy, increasing use of force and violence	**Set-up of conflict analysis:** Using three sets of conflict factors, countries are classified into three conflict-relevant categories: • *Stable potential for conflict* recommended action: attentive watching • *Potential crisis escalation* recommended action: rigorous evaluation of development measures concerning potential negative effects • *High potential for crisis and violence* recommended action: fundamental redirection of development aid **Conflict-related project monitoring:** • External environment • Conflict recognition and flow of information • Planning process • Impact of development co-operation on conflict	**Strengths** • focus on risk assessment • useful indicators for monitoring conflict trends **Weaknesses** • prescriptive checklist approach • no provisions for identifying peace-building opportunities • no guidance for positive action

Author/ Agency	Purpose	Rationale	Root causes Indicators	Methodology	Comments
Milton Esman, Can Foreign Aid Moderate Ethnic Conflict? 1997	"Ethnic impact statement" (ex-ante)	Conventional development projects can have distributional effects that generate or exacerbate societal conflict based on perceived or real injustices.	**Comprehensive country or regional background analysis** • main ethnic communities (demography, identity, values, political power, economic roles, internal divisions) • interethnic relations (stratified/ segmented, recent history, cross- cutting affiliations) • relations with government, politicisation **Estimates of project impact on ethnic relations** • identification of complementary measures or modifications for projects	**Define clear "allocation formula"** in dialogue with all stakeholders. **Options:** *Common interests:* • "positive sum outcomes for all the parties concerned and mutual confidence that benefits and costs are equitably shared" **Divisibility:** • equal territorial spread of aid measures, involvement of local people in project design and management **Interdependence:** • "division of labour between ethnic communities rewards co-operative rather than competitive behaviour" **"Ethnic conditioning" for aid policy** • respect for ethnic minorities and just distribution of aid precondition for co-operation with strongly discriminating governments	**Strengths** • includes problem of "distributional effects" of aid • provides decision-making options about distribution **Weaknesses** • controversial proposal of aid conditionality for minority protection

Author/ Agency	Purpose	Rationale	Root causes Indicators	Methodology	Comments
FEWER, Manual for Early Warning and Early Response, 1999	Early warning and response development (ex-ante)	• to collect and analysis of information about potential and actual conflicts • to provide peace promoting policy options to influential actors	**Steps for early warning:** *Context analysis* • descriptive analysis, geographic and historical factors, key actors and agendas *Identifying conflict indicators* • political, economic, socio-cultural, institutional *Analysing the situation* • classifying indicators: structural factors, accelerators, triggers, synergies and mitigating factors *Identifying opportunities for peace* • windows of opportunity in terms of events, mediators, facilitators, options and agenda items	**Steps for response development:** *Identifying instruments for conflict prevention* • political, economic, socio-cultural, at international, regional, and local level *Analysing potential peace actors and institutions* • appropriate to identified conflict prevention tools *Transforming the situation by stages* • establishing a timeframe for suggested actions and actors *Towards viable and sustainable responses* • check response options in relation to potential impact, position of key actors, alliance configurations, likely organisational or political changes, enhancing opportunity structures	**Strengths** • strong methodologi cal approach for conflict analysis and developing positive action, relevant also for development programming **Weaknesses** • needs to be adapted for development work

Author/ Agency	Purpose	Rationale	Root causes Indicators	Methodology	Comments
Chris Roche, Impact Assessment and Emergencies, Oxfam 1999	Guidelines for impact assessment of emergency assistance by NGOs (ex-post)	• NGOs need to improve the analysis of humanitarian assistance • Positive effects need to be advocated	**Developing impact assessment indicators** • emphasis on monitoring and "impact tracking" • differential impact on groups (gender, age, class) • flexible use of indicators to account for changing circumstances capturing negative and unintended changes including mortality/morbidity, protection and security, sustainability and link with longer-term issues	**Impact assessment process** • to clarify purpose and scope of study • to clarify assumptions about how change happens • to choose appropriate methods **Issues arising from the use of participatory tools** • possible manipulation by powerful groups • need to respect people's time, priorities and trauma • need for clear standards for research process including confidentiality and cross-checking **Policy and institutional assessment** • ethical analysis (duty- bound or goal-bound ethic) • organisational practices (accountability, staff support, analysis, co-ordination, participative planning, gender integration, security)	**Strengths** • tool kit for impact assessment in conflict regions, based on empirical research • innovative focus on policy and institutional assessment **Weaknesses** • potential impact of projects on conflict not directly addressed

Author/ Aqency	Purpose	Rationale	Root causes Indicators	Methodology	Comments
Emery Brusset, Verifiable Conflict Indicators, 1999	Verifiable Conflict Indicators (ex-ante and ex-post)	• indicators as operational descriptions of conflict related changes • allowing the assessment of impacts of actions as well as contextual factors	**Indicators** *Sovereignty* Discourse on existential threats to state sovereignty *Resources* Governmental and societal resources to counter threats to sovereignty and identity. E.g. arms, control of infrastructure, land rights. Note: Only perceptions of "existential" threats are regarded as security risks.	**Recommendations for the "verification" of these indicators** *Micro-level* Monitoring identity and resource indicators in historical perspective, possible by long-term resident personnel (e.g. aid workers, international monitors, anthropologists) *Macro-level* Monitoring identity and sovereignty indicators on level of political discourse, e.g. by diplomats, economists, journalists. Low reliability of macro-economic statistical data.	**Strengths** • valuable development of indicators for conflict "triggering" factors **Weaknesses** • focus on proclaimed attitudes and intentions of major conflict parties • neglect of local capacities for conflict managemen t and peace-building

Author/ Agency	Purpose	Rationale	Root causes Indicators	Methodology	Comments
Luc van de Goor, Suzanne Verstegen, Conflict and Policy Assessment Framework, Clingendael , 2000	Integrated approach that includes predicting and understanding conflict escalation, as well as guidelines for policy intervention. (conflict analysis, policy analysis, planning assessment and decision making, implementation)	• early warning for policy context • response oriented integration of conflict analysis and policy analysis • linking conflict and policy analysis to processes of policy planning and implementation	• partial or newer democracies are more fragile and more prone to state failures than long-lived democracies • material living standards: efforts to improve the overall level of material living standards are a significant way to reduce risks of state failure • involvement in int. trade is associated with a lower risk of state failure	**Procedural approach for designing conflict-related policies** • country profile • conflict analysis in risk countries • policy analysis • planning, assessment and decision-making • implementation	**Strengths** • applicable for a wide range of foreign policy interventions **Weaknesses** • very state focused • questionabl e assumptions concerning the causes of conflict

Author/ Aqency	Purpose	Rationale	Root causes Indicators	Methodology	Comments
Canadian Peace-building Co-ordinating Committee, Towards a Lessons-Learned Framework for NGOs in Peace-building 1999	Learning framework for peace-building by NGOs (ex-post)	• to promote shared analysis, the developmen t of practical tools and best practice for NGO peace-building work	**Definition of peace-building:** • peaceful interventions based upon the removal of root causes of armed conflict • intervention-criteria: impartial, culturally sensitive, convertible to follow-on initiatives, amenable to implementation in partnership with the recipients	**Issues related to successful peace-building** • *Descriptive* Type of activity, goals, funding, context and history of conflict, timing, main actors • *Process* Contribution of different actors, project history • *Relational* Relation to other peace-building activities in the area (complementarity, interference) • *Evaluative* Self-evaluation (reasons for success and failure, unintended outcomes, control over outcomes, differential impact on men, women and children, external factors) • Prescriptive Integration into wider peace-building policies, lessons learned for other efforts	**Strengths** • basic tool of potential use for NGOs, based on principle of self-evaluation • focus on interaction between the project and its environmen t and its influence on outcomes **Weaknesses** • focus on evaluation without paying sufficient attention to planning

This chapter derives from Simon Fisher et al, *Working with Conflict: Skills and Strategies for Action*, Zed Books, London, 2000. It contains interesting approaches and models to conduct evaluation within one's organization. RTC provides training and resources for individuals and organizations working in situations of conflict. More information about RTC's work can be found at www.respond.org or by contacting Responding to Conflict, 1046 Bristol Road, Selly Oak, Birmingham, B29 6LJ, UK. Tel: +44 (0)121 415 5641, Fax: +44 (0)121 415 4119, Email: enquiries@respond.org

Working with Conflict: Evaluation

"Nature has given us two ears, two eyes and but one tongue; to the end we should hear and see more than we speak." (Romanian expression)

Evaluating an activity or programme is an important step in the cycle we have introduced as the framework for this book. In formal settings, evaluation is part of a defined procedure aimed at comparing the achievements of a project with its intended objectives, as well as determining how effective the process of implementation has been. However, evaluation can also be an informal practice to inform you of the result of an activity you have undertaken, and to help you learn and to use that learning to improve your practice.

Whether formal or informal, evaluation is crucial in helping you to understand the results of your intervention. It provides a moment for standing back and reflecting on what you have done and what the consequences have been, whether intended or unintended. It addresses fundamental questions, such as:

- What is the overall vision behind this project or action? Is it a shared vision?
- What are the goals? Whose goals are they? Are they being achieved?
- Are these the goals that ought to be promoted? Are they appropriate to the situation?
- Are there structures in place to support the work? Do structures at different levels work well together?
- What are the objectives of the specific project or action?
- What is this project or action contributing to the overall peace process?
- Is this intervention making any difference? What difference is it making?
- Are the changes positive or negative, or some of each?
- Would these changes have occurred without this intervention?
- Are there other factors, or other stakeholders, contributing to the changes?
- What is the impact of this project on the community as a whole and on the different individuals within it?

- Are there unanticipated impacts? What are these? Are they positive or negative?
- Is the programme cost effective? Is it worth the investment of funds, resources, and time?
- What does success mean for the different stakeholders, or constituencies?

Each constituency will have its own perception or interpretation of the questions:
- *The community* wants to know: Are these programmes or activities helping us or are they making things worse? Are all sections of our community benefiting? How can we support and encourage the good work, and help to change what is not right?
- *Funders / sponsors* want to know: Are the funds and resources that we contributed helping to improve the situation or making it worse? Are we supporting the most effective ways of working and in the most useful way? Do the benefits justify the costs?
- *Workers / intervenors* want to know: Do our efforts have good results? Is this the most effective way to use our time and energy? Are the risks that we are taking worth it? Do our efforts combine with and strengthen those of others, or are we actually in competition with them? Are we addressing all the problems at all levels?
- *Governments* (the authorities) want to know: Is the programme making the situation more or less stable? Does it support or undermine the authority of government? How can we encourage the best efforts, and reform or curb those we regard as destructive?

Each of these stakeholders has their own aims and their own style of evaluation, and each needs to be included in the process. A key question is *who?* Who conducts the evaluation, directs the process and decides its shape? Who funds it and on what basis? Where is the power? Another question is *how?* The process of evaluation is as important as its outcome. These questions raise dilemmas that should be dealt with at an early stage.

However, it is easier to pose the questions than to find the answers. There is, as yet, no agreed and effective methodology for the evaluation of work for development, peace and justice in general, and programmes of conflict transformation and peacebuilding, in particular, present specific challenges. Programmes that are intended to address conflict have some distinctive characteristics which may require special approaches in order to evaluate them. Conflict is caused by many factors at different levels and requires a corresponding variety of interlinking interventions in response. No single activity, person or group can build peace alone. So, just as the work of conflict transformation has to be built on a comprehensive understanding of the context, so evaluation needs to be equally broad in its examination of the levels of activity, the range of actors involved and the interconnections between them.

Rupert Taylor's attempts to evaluate the impact of particular interventions in the South Africa conflict led him to the conclusion that the programmes could not sensibly be evaluated individually, in competition with each other. On the contrary, he found that the actual impact was cumulative: one web of organisations influenced other webs of organisations, all of them interconnected with shared founders and memberships. The interconnectedness of conflict transformation organisations themselves, and their close relationships, yet distinctiveness, from development and welfare agencies on the one hand, and political organisations on the other, led to their having an enormous impact on the situation itself.[1]

Assessing the impact of a particular piece of work on conflict is made all the more difficult by the assumptions underlying any approach that aims to be both long-term and sustainable:

Working Assumptions[2]

- Peacebuilding is about seeking and sustaining processes of change, it is not exclusively, or even primarily about sustaining outcomes. Rebuilding societies torn by violence and war involves rebuilding relationships and finding new ways of relating. What you are trying to measure is therefore not a static outcome but a dynamic process.
- Peacebuilding requires changes across multiple levels and perspectives. You must understand, create, and sustain the space for change along a continuum that includes personal, relational, structural and cultural dimensions.
- Pursuing such a range of changes in a society torn by war requires vision and a design for attaining that long-term goal. The design of any process of change is built on some understanding of how change works and what produces it. A concern for evaluation suggests that you need, therefore, to be explicit about your own often-implicit theories of change which are inherent in the designs and proposals you carry forward.
- Social conflict is based in relationships. Societal change within a framework of strategic peacebuilding can only be accomplished through sustained initiatives that promote vertical and horizontal integration of people and processes.
- When you approach evaluation, you need to think about the longer-term context as well as the immediate conflict episode and its dynamics.
- Responsive evaluation needs a continuous cycle of action and reflection.

In a conflict situation you are often working in a context of permanent emerging crisis and constant intervention. Work on conflict should have the capacity to be short-term responsive and intensive, and at the same time have a long-term vision. This means that as you act on the immediate crisis you should build in time for reflection that helps your learning and informs you about change, as necessary. The following diagram attempts to capture and clarify this understanding:

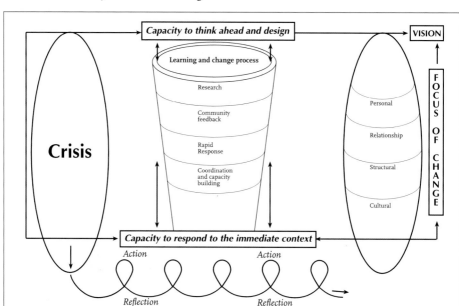

An Ongoing Process Of Action And Reflection

Evaluating "Working with Conflict"

"A fall into a ditch makes you wiser" (Chinese expression)

By its nature this work takes place in situations that are unstable, where changes happen fast and violence is never very far away. These changes take place in settings where emotions are charged and violence has been experienced by many. Building peace is itself a change process and one that is often highly political. Evaluation is not a neutral activity, but takes place in an environment that is rife with power dynamics. It may easily be perceived as an overtly political exercise by actors who are otherwise trying to appear impartial. There may be negative consequences not only for the process, but also for the wider community.

It is essential, therefore, for those who are evaluating interventions in conflict to understand both the forces at work in the present context and the previous history of the conflict, including the differing interpretations of that history. The causes of a conflict are multifaceted and complex. There are many issues involved and different stakeholders may have widely differing perceptions.

Evaluation of RTC

RTC commissioned its own evaluation in 1998, from an external consultant, to address the central question: Have we made any difference after six years? The methodology aimed to identify the explicit links between RTC's actions and the intended outcomes, and to search for the implicit links: specifically, consequences that were not planned. As this was a genuine attempt to discover what was happening, rather than an exercise to satisfy funders, the process of learning amongst RTC staff and trustees was seen as important as the final evaluation document.

In terms of wider impact, the report highlighted three main areas for development:

- It identified a gap that had emerged between individual change (which RTC courses and consultancies often promote) and change at organisational level, where, amongst policy makers especially, incomprehension and even suspicion about work on conflict can create obstacles. This has led RTC to look for ways to strengthen partnerships with particular organisations in order to complement the relationships we have with individuals, and to work more deliberately with policy-related staff.
- It said that RTC risks being preoccupied with action at the expense of reflection and learning. While this may have been necessary in the early stages, any organisation has to strike a balance between these two poles if the work is to prosper in the longer term, and contribute to the development of the field as a whole. A new post has since been established which incorporates organisational learning as a major activity. It is still proving difficult, however, to ensure that time is allocated for the reflection to take place.
- Also the report recommended that a strategic process is needed to give shape and coherence to the many activities RTC undertakes, both those it initiates, such as international courses and the programme of video case studies, and those where it is responding to others' requests. We have now developed a strategic framework, and are seeking to marry up the sense of purpose it gives with the messy reality of everyday demands and urgent requests.

A full report of this evaluation is available from RTC.

Many agencies still see evaluation as a one-off exercise - a snapshot of how things are going at a specific moment, although awareness is growing of the need to link evaluation with ongoing monitoring and to involve the people affected by the programme in these processes.[3] In our experience evaluation needs to be a continuous process. Conflict situations are dynamic; changes happen, often quite rapidly. It may be difficult to establish a moment for evaluation. Because of this, evaluation should be regarded as an engagement in a process of continuous self-reflection. It is an opportunity for learning rather than an examination or a judgement, and the learning from evaluation needs to feed back into the programme as well as to those with managerial or funding responsibilities.

A programme that works on conflict is process-oriented, addressing both people and their relationships as well as what they aspire to achieve. So an evaluation should be people-centred, and involve all the stakeholders from the original conception of the project to the setting of indicators, monitoring, managing, and evaluating. All of these factors present a challenge to the more traditional forms of evaluation.

The Evaluation Wheel[4]

The impact of any specific activity in terms of peace and conflict can, of course, be evaluated in isolation: Does this initiative work, or not work? Is this programme of peace education changing the attitudes of pupils? However, in the light of the discussion above, it makes more sense to set your evaluation in the wider context of the situation. If the peace education programme has been implemented in local schools in response to gang warfare in the neighbourhood, and after five years the number of violent incidents has not reduced, it would still be possible to evaluate the programme as a success in terms of popularity, perhaps, and change of behaviour within the school. However, the wider context remains apparently unaffected. The following questions and diagram may help you to conceptualise how to set your evaluation in the wider context:

1. What is the vision of the project?
2. What are the values that guide and inform it?
3. What are the activities undertaken?
4. Are the values and the vision reflected in the day to day activities?
5. What are the levels at which the activities are undertaken?
6. What is the focus of change? Is it happening? If not, what needs to happen now?

Participation

People's participation is the foundation of sustainable work to build peace, and the evaluation of these processes needs to fully acknowledge that. There are many techniques that can be applied to evaluation, such as Participatory Rural Appraisal, which will increase the level of community participation. One project paying particular attention to the evaluation of peace and conflict activities is the Action-Evaluation Project.[5] A number of other initiatives are underway to test different approaches and methodologies for evaluating conflict resolution/transformation activities and programmes, and, as their results become known, more and better choices should become available. The methodologies, however, should not obscure the importance of involvement and ownership by those who have most to gain and to lose in action to address conflicts.

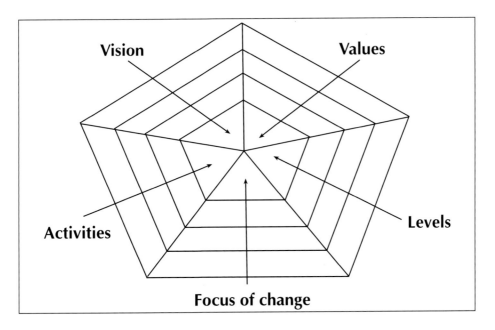

Impact Assessment

"The fly is small, but it is big enough to make one sick." (Turkish expression)

When assessing the effect of a project to, for example, rebuild a bridge, it is clear at the end whether or not the planned physical impact has been achieved. With work on peace and conflict the question of assessing impact is more complex, but equally vital.

Our understanding of impact assessment includes two components, the impact on peace and the impact on conflict. [6]

The term *Peace Impact* includes those effects that foster and support the sustainable structures and processes which strengthen the prospects of peaceful coexistence and decrease the likelihood of the outbreak, (re-)occurrence, or continuation, of violent conflict.

The Term *Conflict Impact* includes all social, economic, and political effects that increase the likelihood that conflict will be dealt with through violent means.

The aims of peace and conflict impact assessment are:

1. To assess, over a period of time, the positive and negative impact of different kinds of intervention (or lack thereof) on the dynamic of the conflict;
2. To contribute to the development of a more coherent conflict prevention and peacebuilding policy: and
3. To serve as a sensitising tool for policy shapers and policy makers, helping them to identify weaknesses in their approach (such as: blind spots, incoherence, bad timing, inadequate priority setting).
4. Peace and conflict impact assessment can be a tool that assists development and humanitarian organisations in analysing situations of (potential) conflict, identifying strategic opportunities for conflict prevention, and monitoring the impact of their activities.[7]

An impact assessment exercise will capture the essence of a situation at a particular moment in time. However, as conflict is highly dynamic and there may be rapid change, it is important to have a means of ongoing observation, monitoring and analysis of these changes, both for programme planning and implementation and also so that the moment of evaluation can be set in context.

Indicators

"You can tell a ripe corn by its look." (expression from Southern Africa)

An important component of assessing impact is indicators, which can suggest whether the project is leading toward the intended goal or not. Indicators are helpful in setting standards against which achievements will be judged. Particularly in this field of work, it may never be clear that objectives have been fully attained. Have we reached perfect peace? Even if there is not perfect peace, the indicators are a way to check whether things are headed in the right direction.

For sustainability of the project, the indicators should be set where possible by the beneficiaries, so that their standards are used to judge impact and so that they understand and "own" the results. This will also enhance community participation in both the activity and the evaluation, and make it possible for the community to monitor its own situation, celebrating improvements and acting quickly if the situation worsens.

What constitutes peace and conflict is complex and variable. To assess the impact using peace indicators or conflict early warning indicators, you need to consider various aspects both of the situation and of the programme. Below, we offer an example which includes some possible indicators in different categories. These are not prescriptive or exhaustive, but may give you a starting point for identifying possible indicators in your own situation.

The following table is adapted from a community workshop in Wajir, northeast Kenya.

PEACE INDICATORS	CONFLICT EARLY WARNING INDICATORS
Physical and psychological health indicators • Low population mortality • Few injuries / death caused by weapons • High nutritional status • Refusal of acts of violence • Participation in society's affairs	**Physical and psychological health indicators** • Population mortality • Injuries and death caused by weapons of war • Desire for vengeance • Prevalence of depression
Environmental Indicators • Inter-communal management of natural resources • Inter-communal sharing of natural resources • Normal patterns of cultivation and livestock-tending	**Environmental Indicators** • Refusal of access to natural resources • Burning of grass
Security indicators • Refusal of incitement to violence • Free assembly of people • Creation of community peace structures	**Security indicators** • Presence of army • Riots and demonstrations • Disappearances • Political detainees
Social indicators • Freedom of thought, belief, religion, speech, and media • High level and varied types of social interaction • Intermarriage	Social indicators • Censorship, spying, religious persecution, self-censorship, silence • Low level of social interaction • Sectarian organisation, polarisation
Political indicators • Cross-communal political parties • Fair and free election • Freedom of movement	**Political indicators** • Sectarian political parties • Emergency rule or martial law • Deprived of one's nationality, exiled, or internally displaced
Judicial indicators • Human rights legislation • Equality under the law • Repeal of discriminatory laws	Judicial indicators • Political interference in the Judicial Process • Use of discriminatory laws • Use of mechanisms of informal justice
Economic indicators • Progress in addressing economic grievances • Reduction in level of poverty and unemployment	**Economic indicators** • High level of poverty • Unfair distribution of land, goods and services

The whole area of impact assessment is constantly being developed and updated. It is another key policy area where the experiences of practitioners, working on the ground, need to be captured so that they can influence and inform the direction of research and methodology.

An example from the International Development Research Centre in Canada
where Dr. Kenneth Bush has been leading work on Peace and Conflict Impact Assessment (PCIA). He suggests some specific questions that need to be asked when beginning a programme of peacebuilding activities.[8]

At the planning stage:
• Are the minimal political, legal, security and infra-structural conditions in place?
• Is there sufficient political support for the activity, on the ground and at other key levels?
• Is the opportunity structure opening or closing?
• Is the timing right?
• Does the proposed activity have the right mix of resources?
• Does the lead organisation have experience on the ground?
• Are the expected positive impacts achievable?
• How will these be assessed?
• Might the activity aggravate violent conflicts?
• What precautions are proposed?
• Will the activity be sustainable?

At the monitoring and evaluating stages other questions are important. These include:
• Has the activity created or exacerbated violent conflict?
• Has it reduced the level of violence and fostered reconciliation?
• Has it led to sustainable processes, which enhance prospects of peaceful coexistence?
• Has it led to substantial changes on issues underlying the conflict?

Key issues in Evaluations

1. Recording
It is important to record the proceedings. This can be done using tape recorders and other electronic means, provided that all the people involved understand and accept this form of recording. While it is important to record everything, sometimes the evaluator's reliance on equipment can be counter-productive.

People may give more candid answers if the proceedings are being recorded by them, for their benefit, and using methods familiar to them. This may include not only written records, but the designation of one person to act as the oral memory of the event. Community involvement in documentation also makes it more likely that records can be retrieved later. All of this simply

This is an example from a rural Kenyan village.
Mr. Elias an Education Officer was given a task of evaluating the effectiveness of a school management committee. He went to interview the various stakeholders, including the school management committee itself. Mr. Elias had a series of focused discussions with a group of elders. He got permission to use audio-tape to record the proceedings and started the dialogue. Everyone participated and told him everything, and Mr. Elias felt very satisfied with the meeting. He then checked his tape and realized the battery had run flat and he had no spare, so he told the committee to proceed with the meeting. One of the committee members was happy that Elias was not recording anything: "Well", he said, "Now that you are not recording on tape, we can tell you the real story."

emphasises that the evaluation is done primarily, not for the purposes of the evaluator, but for the stakeholders and the community.

2. Reporting
Amongst the problems in this type of work is the lack of data. A lot of successful peace initiatives happen off-the-record, with no minutes or reports kept. This can pose a difficulty for the evaluator. But we must remember that peacebuilding represents sensitive, delicate and very confidential work where lives are on the line and affected by what is reported. The work itself is more important than its assessment. While reporting is important to the donor for the purpose of accountability and transparency, it should be done in way that enhances the work and is not counterproductive.

Questions to consider include the following:
- Who writes reports? Who sees them before they are widely distributed?
- Who receives reports, and in what order? How is this decision made?
- How / when are results fed back to: (a) the community, (b) beneficiaries and other stakeholders of the programme, (c) staff of organisations involved, and (d) those actually interviewed as part of the evaluation process?

An example from Central America
During the years of repression in Guatemala and Nicaragua in the 1980s, the keeping of written records was potentially life-threatening if the records fell into the wrong hands. One agency carried out all its activities in an oral tradition. Verbal reports were made to the relevant committees, and nothing was committed to paper that could have been dangerous for those concerned. When the danger receded, the agency funded a major study to record and evaluate the programmes which had been supported. A wide range of individuals, groups and organisations were consulted and interviewed and the results analysed, shared, recorded and then published.

3. Team composition

Just as an approach to conflict is best undertaken by multidisciplinary teams, so too is an approach to evaluation. In a contested situation, it is an advantage to have a team with diverse perceptions, experiences and regional/gender/ethnic/linguistic identifications, which may make more people comfortable in giving their views. Since evaluation is itself an intervention into an ongoing process, the team should be equipped with conflict-handling skills, such as mediation, facilitation, listening and negotiation. These are important because sometimes an evaluation can trigger painful memories which need to be handled with care and sensitivity.

4. Contested results

Because these are situations of conflict, there is no single interpretation of events. An evaluation, including its objectives, process, and results, will be contested, as everything is contested. For this reason, evaluation of work in conflict, like the direct work on the conflict which is being evaluated, should exhibit the characteristics mentioned so often in this book. Evaluation should be:

- Inclusive,
- Participatory,
- Balanced,
- Honest, and
- Transparent,

Evaluation and learning are both crucial to a dynamic and sustainable process of change. A thorough and ongoing process of evaluation, analysis and reflection, that captures the learning from our actions, and informs the direction we take, will make us increasingly effective as we struggle on towards our vision.

When I was a boy of fourteen, my father was so ignorant I could hardly stand to have the old man around. But when I got to be twenty-one, I was astonished at how much he had learned in seven years. Mark Twain 1835-1910.

Notes

1 Rupert Taylor, *The Role Of Peace & Conflict Resolution Organizations In The Struggle Against Apartheid* (forthcoming publication).

2 Adapted from John Paul Lederach, *Building Peace: Sustainable Reconciliation in a Divided Society*, United States Institute of Peace, Washington, 1997.

3 See *ONTRAC*, No 13, September 1999, the newsletter of the International NGO Training and Research Centre (INTRAC).

4 Adapted from material by CDR Associates, Boulder, Colorado.

5 The Action-Evaluation Project is located at the McGregor School, Antioch University, Yellow Springs, Ohio, USA, and directed by Dr. Jay Rothman. It has a website at www.aepro.org which includes an online sample evaluation process.

6 See Luc Reychler, "Conflict Impact Assessment (CIAS) at the policy and project level", 1998:3, CPRS, University of Leuven.

7 From "Peace and Conflict Impact Assessment Project", a paper by Manuela Leonhardt for International Alert, 1999.

8 IDRC Workshop Report, A Measure of Peace: Peace and Conflict Impact Assessment (PCIA) of Development Projects in Conflict Zones, Ottawa June 1-2, 1998

Part 2
Lessons Learned in Peacebuilding

Lessons Learned from Ten Years Experience in Conflict Prevention

"Every Conflict is Unique, and so is its Solution"

There is no overall recipe for ending or preventing conflicts, because every conflict is unique. But there are general conclusions to be drawn, and communal lessons to be learned, from ten years of experience with conflict prevention. The 'lessons learned' may help the field, and the people working in it, move forward. *By* JOS HAVERMANS

Practitioners of peacebuilding have learned a remarkable variety of lessons from their experience with stopping or preventing conflicts over the past years. In this rich variety, some lessons stick out. When asked what major lesson they learned from their peacework, the most frequent answer practitioners give is that there is no blueprint for building peace, that every conflict is different and, as a consequence, that what may work in one situation may not in another. This may come as a shock for those looking for common denominators and references to go by when embarking on peace efforts. At the same time, it gives evidence to the adventurous nature of peacework. Values such as inspiration and risk-taking seem to be as relevant as the more academic, rational notions underlying efforts to build peace.

Most practitioners and organizations use the lessons they learn within the scope of their own activities. An organization that focuses on working with grass-roots groups on the village level, will learn from its mistakes and successes in the past in adapting its design of new projects in similar settings. Applicability will not be an issue in these circumstances. But it is clear that the lessons learned by such an organization may be the complete opposite of those learned by another organization working on a different level. The Institute for Multi-Track Diplomacy, for instance, said that it has learned, from efforts to set up a dialogue between opposing groups in Cyprus, that transparency is of crucial importance. Being totally open about what is being discussed at community meetings, and literally keeping the door open to all citizens to attend, has turned out to be of crucial importance for building trust between the local communities. Yet, it is obvious that this kind of transparency and openness to the general public would have been counterproductive in many other instances, especially for peace initiatives on the official level. When it comes to brokering peace between political leaders, confidentiality is usually an indispensable requirement for success. The need for confidentiality is an important 'lesson learned' from the Oslo talks on the Middle East conflict. Had it not been for the absolute seclusion and confidentiality of the first overtures, this process might have irreparably stalled in the very early stages.

Despite the irreconcilability of some lessons learned and a good amount of contradiction or paradoxes among them, it makes sense to look for common lessons. A need is felt to assess where we are currently standing in the field of conflict prevention. What has been learned so far, in the most concrete terms? Where should we look in order to find clues to improve peacemaking practices?

Increasing awareness about the kind of lessons learned is expected to contribute to improving the practice and profession of peacebuilding. Knowing what approaches and lessons other practitioners found most compelling, can make peacemakers feel more confident about the approaches they chose in areas and other conflicts new to them.

Many projects, conferences and seminars held over the past few years on the subject of conflict prevention and peacebuilding have resulted in lists of lessons learned, but few efforts have been made so far to add them all up and identify the most recurrent conclusions and observations. One of the exceptions is *Mapping Approaches to Lesson Learning* developed by Michael S. Lund.[1] Lund classified several types of lessons, derived from activities at different levels, in varying regions of the world, into one framework to be helpful in choosing an approach to drawing conclusions from peace efforts. One of the characteristics of Lund's efforts is that he seeks to take into account who the target audiences for lessons learned are and what purpose the lessons and conclusions are supposed to serve.

In this chapter a number of lessons are discussed that have been mentioned most frequently by professionals in the field of conflict resolution. There is, no doubt, a good degree of incongruity among them. Awareness of the diverse background and context in which lessons were drawn is, therefore, of essential importance. Lessons are drawn from engagement in peacework by widely varying categories such as women's groups, grass-roots initiatives, government undertakings, religious communities or even the military. In addition, the lessons these actors brought forward, may each be connected to different stages of a conflict, such as the pre- or post-conflict stages. Than there are different qualities of involvement playing a role: early warning, prevention, mediation, or reconciliation.

Another factor that needs to be mentioned here is that the lessons that have been drawn over the years are coming from different sources. The most significant difference here is that some are drawn from academic analysis done by scholars, others from day-to-day experiences that peaceworkers have gone through. These practitioners may have been local volunteers, totally

Michael S. Lund, Management Systems International Inc., USA, key-note speaker

immersed in the conflict themselves, others, professional outsiders working for NGOs or governments. All this accounts for the undoubtedly highly subjective quality of the lessons discussed in the next paragraph. Yet, when the hundreds of lessons drawn over the past decade are sifted, a number of larger, recurring lessons emerge. They may be helpful, informative and instructive for both experienced peaceworkers and newcomers in the field of conflict prevention and resolution.

Lessons Learned

The terrorist attacks on New York and Washington on September 11, 2001, seem to have had a big impact on people working in the field of peacebuilding. Some professionals, such as a staff member of Search for Common Ground working in Macedonia, expressed disillusionment. Acknowledging he now felt doubt about the relevance of conflict prevention, Search for Common Ground's Eran Fraenkel said: "What sense does it make for me to get up every morning and work for peace if a few individuals are able to come in and destroy everything?"

No one in the field, however, seems to have turned their back on the goals and ways of conflict prevention because of what happened on the 11th of September. Most people, including Mr Fraenkel, seem to believe the attacks

Kevin Clemens, International Alert, United Kingdom, key-note speaker

and its aftermath are all the more reason to reflect on where the field should be heading. They want to try to improve practices of peacemaking. A remarkably large number of peacemakers since '9/11' called on their colleagues to be more imaginative in developing ideas and strategies that can make non-violent conflict resolution more effective.

Dozens, if not hundreds of lessons can be drawn from ten years of experience with conflict prevention. Many are related exclusively to a specific situation, at a specific time. But there is a lot of similarity between a number of the lessons learned. Experience with seeking peace in totally different conflicts, spread far apart over the world, seem to have led to similar conclusions. The lessons discussed below have been retrieved from a wide variety of conference reports and seminars as well as findings and conclusions brought forward by attendants of conferences, including the latest and biggest meeting on the subject, 'Toward Better Peace Building Practice', held in Soesterberg, the Netherlands, in October 2001.

There Are No Blueprints
The most marked conclusion drawn from years of experience with conflict prevention is that there are no overall recipes for ending conflicts. "There are no blue prints", was lesson number one among twelve presented by Kevin Clements, Secretary General of International Alert. Clements stressed that "The uniqueness of all conflicts" needs to be kept in mind all the time. "There are no overall recipes for solutions. However, I believe we do need a code of conduct and shared values", he said.

The working group on early warning at the same conference emphasized this as well: there is no blue-print for early warning. All methods that have been developed may work everywhere, provided they be adapted to the needs of end-users and the specific context of the countries or region involved.

People who are active in setting up networks of organizations working toward peace also came up with the same message: there is not one ultimate, omnipotent model. The shape of a network would have to vary according to certain national or regional circumstances, they say. For NGOs in Sweden, for example, it may be very acceptable to include government agencies in a network aimed at propagating reconciliation in a foreign conflict. But in conflict regions themselves, NGOs are often seen by the government as dangerous opposition forces. Networking with the government may be the last thing these NGOs would want to do.

Conflict Prevention Works
Based on case studies, a group of scholars contributing to a Carnegie Commission study, *Opportunities Missed, Opportunities Seized. Preventive Diplomacy in the Post-Cold War*, concluded that conflict prevention is a realistic, viable strategy. As the scholars put it: "It can be done".

Bruce Jentleson, who edited the study, concluded that "Preventive diplomacy is not just a noble idea, but is a viable real world strategy". The study also pointed out that despite the fact that many conflicts may have deep historical roots, they are not inevitable, nor predestined. They are much more the consequence of conscious calculations than historical determinism, thus there is room to influence the course of events.

Even people living in a conflict area who come in touch with foreign peacemakers believe preventing conflicts or reducing tension by non-violent means is viable, despite their initial skepticism about what outsiders could do to prevent further escalation of "their" conflict. "Although we feel that we are more experienced experts on what war entails than many of the people coming to our region to support reconciliation, we do believe that programs offered by peacebuilders make sense", said Slavica Slavnic, representative of a multi-ethnic civic organization in the Republika Srbrsca. "The ethnic groups should talk to each other as much as possible and we welcome efforts that help facilitate this."

Avoid Becoming a Pretext for Inactivity
NGOs should try to avoid their role in peacemaking from becoming a pretext for governments not to do anything. The effectiveness of NGO work in the field of peacemaking has increased dramatically, but it should not become a replacement for government action. A multi-track approach is often more effective than either a government or NGO approach on its own. The successful intervention of the Roman Catholic Italian Sant'Egidio in Mozambique in the early 1990s proves a case in point. Sant'Egidio closely co-operated with the Italian ministry of Foreign Affairs in getting the Mozambican government and rebel movement Renamo to talk to each other.

Be Aware of the Limitations of Conflict Prevention
Many professional peaceworkers say that there is a need for a sense of proportionality of what outsiders can do. There are limitations, some of which are of a practical character, as Kevin Clements pointed out. "The US in the fall of 2001 earmarked forty billion dollars for the fight against terrorism," he explained. "There will undoubtedly be less money for us now, while the needs are enormous for cure and prevention".

To a certain extent, peaceworkers say, preventive activities may show their effectiveness only in the long term. This is another notion of modesty peaceworkers should keep in mind: a quick reward is unlikely. Sometimes, results of peacework seem very limited. "We didn't stop the war, but we did get our message across," a professional working on the production of what is called 'inter-ethnic programming' in Macedonia reported. "For us, making someone stop in their tracks to think about what they are doing was a positive outcome", she added.

Awareness of the limitations of conflict prevention is an opening to acknowledging that even limited successes can make preventive efforts worthwhile. As Bruce Jentleson noted in the acclaimed study *Opportunities*

Missed, Opportunities Seized: in some cases the success of conflict prevention may not be a total resolution of the dispute, but the prevention of a conflict escalating into mass killings. Jentleson also points out that some successes may prove to be transitory. Some conflicts, such as in Congo, finally developed into war, despite efforts to defuse tension that were in themselves, successful at the time. "However", Jentleson says, "unless it is demonstrated that the principal reasons for eventual failure were integral to the initial success of prevention, as an analytic matter such an eventuality would not totally negate the earlier success."

Jonathan Freedland, a reporter for *The Guardian* newspaper, made the point that even peace talks that seem to have failed, in most cases save lives. "For all its flaws, the Northern Ireland effort can claim to have saved nearly six hundred lives", he wrote in the summer of 2001, when the Northern Irish peace process was going through another setback. "Until the IRA cessation in 1994, approximately one hundred people were killed per year. (...) With more than hundred dead since 1994, that leaves close to six hundred saved in seven years", he wrote. Freedland also mentioned that the collapse of the Middle East peace process in 1999 resulted in about seven hundred deaths until late 2001, strengthening him in his belief that "talk saves lives" and that "whatever else happens, peace processes have to keep on." "Don't stop" is Freedland's simple and clear recommendation.[2]

Make Sure to Take Enough Time for Dealing With Conflict

This advice may seem too obvious, but early-warners in particular often find they have to do too much in too little time. Michael Lund, for instance, was commissioned to assess the potential for conflict in Zimbabwe and a few other African countries; "I did not have enough time to gather information on covert diamond trading in which the elite is supposed to be involved in certain countries. Some subjects are hard to get into, even though they are essential for understanding politics," Lund said.

Long-Term Commitment

Peacebuilding and reconciliation should be seen as a process, rather than a goal with a clear-cut ending in time. Peace can only be built up over a long period of time. Preferably, long-term relationships are built across the dividing lines of conflict in a society. Sustainability of interventions is therefore of essential importance. When interventions of outsiders are over, their action should, ideally, have left behind the capacity for continued interventions in the conflict by local actors.

Early warning experts stress that for early warning to be successful, it is necessary to link quick "go and look" efforts to structures and organizations that are engaged in continual, on-going monitoring. These monitors could provide timely information to the experts making the final early warning

Susan Collin Marks, Search for Common Ground, USA

assessments on which to act. "Early warning cannot be practiced ad hoc," they say.

A slow steady process of trust-building is often necessary before official negotiations can start. Successful examples of this approach are the activities of the Lutheran World Federation in Guatemala or the Lebanon Conflict Resolution Network. It took years of incubation before these groups entered a concrete process of conflict resolution and reconciliation.

Many practitioners belief that NGOs are very well positioned to guarantee the kind of long-term commitment required. "NGOs may be better equipped for long-term engagement than governments who tend to take a short term view, for instance because they need to be re-elected every four years," Susan Collin Marks of Search for Common Ground said.

According to Freedland, trying to reach finality in a peace process could even be detrimental. "Do not seek finality," he wrote in the article in *The Guardian* referred to earlier. He pointed out that Israeli prime minister Ehud Barak during peace talks in 2000 wanted PLO leader Yasser Arafat to declare an end to the Palestinian-Israeli conflict and for their deal to be comprehensive. "Such a goal is laudable, but incompatible with the pragmatic, piecemeal business that is peacemaking," Freedland commented.

Pay More Attention to Conflict Dynamics
More attention should be paid to conflict dynamics. How do conflicts change over time? Practitioners should try to discern changes over time in order to see when a certain type of intervention is needed. Early warning experts came to the same conclusion: "It is important to be aware of the changing nature of conflict when doing early warning analyses", was one of their major conclusions.

Build a Theory
Many practitioners and academics believe it is necessary to build a new theory of peace to work with.

"What is our theory? What vision do we have? We need a vision of a just world. Answers to questions such as how to find space to exchange visions, aspirations, dreams without doing harm to the dreams and aspirations of others. I believe we need to be more explicit of what we do and want", says Kevin Clements. Clements is among those practitioners who want to design a wide-ranging theory on which to build their approach to making peace. He believes conflict resolution is a new political philosophy that should be defined in more detail. Clements: "I am in favor of developing a new political philosophy, geared toward a more collaborative way of policy making and some reduction of military solutions."

Norbert Ropers supports Clements' view: "It is important to improve the capacities of our fields to reduce the suffering of those drawn into conflicts. But is it enough?" he asked. "I believe that we should not just be a service-providing movement. We should also be a political movement. Let's not limit ourselves to just doing social work on a global level. We also want to transform the world. Where is the agenda of our field? I believe that we should connect to political movements who discuss these issues."

Building a theory underlying the work of conflict prevention touches on sensitive political questions. Simon Fisher, of the British organization

Simon Fisher, Responding to Conflict, United Kingdom, conference facilitator

Responding to Conflict, suggested that people working in the realm of conflict prevention may have to decide what their priority is: peace and stability, or justice. Fisher: "We need to make a choice: who are we working for?", he asked at a seminar on Lessons Learned in Londonderry, February 2001. "Are we in the conflict resolution field acting as unwitting accomplices of inequality - protecting the rich but thinking we're doing the opposite? Are we helping the non-violent transformation of the world in the direction of more disparities?"

Roberto Ricigliano, an American scholar who formerly worked for the Conflict Management Group, thinks practitioners should reflect on their work more often at the outset. Ricigliano proposes working with other fields in order to become engaged with people who think differently; different, that is, from workers in the field of conflict prevention. "I want to work on developing an integrated approach. Lets not isolate ourselves in our field", he says.

Some experts working in the field of early warning put the relevance of a new theory in perspective: "It is necessary to use theory as a guide for analyses, but let's not get bogged down in frameworks that are too strict and may cloud knowledge gained from new experiences," said one practitioner.

In direct response to the wish to develop a theory and world vision fundament at conflict prevention, many practitioners emphasized the need for room for imagination and intuition. In assessing the factors and events that are responsible for a possible escalation of a specific conflict, theories do not always work, Sue Williams points out. "Sometimes it is your gut feeling that tells you where things will go," she said.

Cultural Understanding

Given that there are no blueprints for solving conflicts, it makes sense to gain insight into the uniqueness of any individual conflict. This includes, experienced peace makers say, sensitivity to cultural heritages. "What works positively in one setting can be totally ineffective in another. It is important to have good understanding of cultures", was the conclusion of women working in gender projects from Sudan, Macedonia to Nepal.

Awareness of cultural and traditional customs may result in recognizing new openings in a peace process. Tapping into traditional means of dealing with conflict especially, can be very meaningful. Peaceworkers in West-Africa recommend explicitly seeking to tailor intervention programs on traditional approaches embedded in the local culture. The West African Network for Peacebuilding, based in Ghana, in particular believes that there is still a lot to gain from paying more attention to traditional peacebuilding practices. It called for a study into African traditional peacebuilding methods in order to enable outsiders to build on what has been developed over decades in conflict regions themselves.

Cultural differences should also be taken into account among peace organizations working together. Different cultures and procedures of government agencies and NGOs, and among NGOs themselves, should be taken into account if alliances or networks are forged to work on a specific conflict.

Keep the Regional Scope in Mind

Most early warning activity still focuses one-sidedly on conflict within the boundaries of a state. There should be more and better account taken of regional dimensions, say practitioners and academics. Keeping an eye on regional conditions also make sense because research has shown that the likelihood of concerted efforts to preventive diplomacy is higher in cases in which a potential regional impact is clearly demonstrated, said Jentleson.

The message is that the field should think more about the relationships between conflicts instead of treating them as unrelated. The conflicts in Burundi and Congo, for instance, were clearly interconnected. Practitioners therefore should think in terms of "systems of conflicts".

Put Effort into Mobilizing Local Actors

Engaging local actors is of crucial importance in order to create local capacity in peacebuilding and early warning. "Capacity building is extremely important," people gathered in an early warning working group said, "because even if people may say they want to work with you, the question remains: will they do it? Sometimes it is lack of capacity building that keeps them from taking initiatives."

"We should stand alongside local peacemakers," International Alert's Clements said. "Give them a safe place for dialogue. We should accompany peacemakers and show solidarity with the poor and oppressed. If you feel you come in with a solution, you probably bring deception."

Strengthening local capacities for peace may take many forms, including education and training, nurturing the volunteer spirit in society and highlighting the work of local peaceworkers in the media. Focus on local capacities may also result in tapping into traditional peacemaking processes effectively. Identifying what local traditions could do for making peace, along with respect for certain cultural traditions, will enhance the chance of success. Somali people, for example, place high value on poetry, which in nomadic society is as important as radio or television. Traditional elders, who became engaged in efforts to defuse tensions in the country in the late 1990s, therefore brought in poets as well as religious leaders to reconcile warring clans; with good results.

Early warning specialists also stressed that more attention should be paid to giving the general public access to early warnings. In doing so, a lot of energy might be unleashed that will be directed towards politicians, aimed at putting pressure on them to take measures that defuse tension. "Mobilizing the general population in order to put pressure in policy makers is not fully used yet," the Early Warning working group at the Soesterberg conference concluded.

Acknowledge the Importance of Irrational Factors

Getting warlords or villagers to change their attitudes from hatred and an inclination to violence to attitudes of reconciliation and openness to dialogue it is, apart from instances of cool calculation, about changing people's hearts. No matter how vague these processes may seem, they are mentioned as an essential part of many successful cases of conflict prevention or conflict resolution. It is, therefore, crucial to develop and maintain a good amount of sensitivity to the direction people's attitudes are heading and to the places where people may find inspiration for a of change of hearts. The Oxford Research Group said it was surprised to find that nearly half of the interventions it studied were carried out by people with some spiritual basis for their activities.[3] The most important factor named by participants engaged in peacemaking was a sense of direction inspired "by some connection with a source of strength greater than their own ego".

The importance of emotions and inspiration is also mentioned frequently in connection with working through women's groups to make peace. Women have frequently been found to offer the ingredients essential to make peace, particularly in addressing the feelings involved. Examples in this regard are the Mothers of the Playa del Mayo, and the Wajir Peace Group. "Most of what was accomplished was done by people with a heart for peace, rather than training in conflict resolution," Dekha Ibrahim Abdi, member of the Wajir group, said.

John McDonald, a former diplomat active in the field of conflict prevention (see Box), confirmed that irrational factors are of crucial importance, but official institutions often find them hard to grasp. "You cannot change the way people think about their enemy without touching their hearts," he pointed out, "but this is difficult to accept for institutions such as the World Bank or the State Department. I once spoke to an economist of the World Bank who told me his institution had built three hundred houses for displaced people in Bosnia but was appalled that they were not being used. I told him it was out of fear that people had not returned to these villages. He had never worried about fear, he tended to think in measurable things like numbers of houses or roads built. But you have to think about emotions like fear."

A Holistic Approach Suits Best

Practitioners in the field of conflict prevention stress that effective prevention is derived from a variety of activities, addressing all aspects of society and all relevant actors. Working to just bridge ethnic gaps or defuse socio-economic tension is usually not enough. The whole scale of human activities and dimension should ideally be engaged in the process. Clements, of International Alert: "We need a holistic view, encompassing conflict resolution, development and democratization. There will be no peace without justice, democracy and development. We need to include this in mechanisms for dealing with conflicts non-violently."

"No one group - be it a government, a group of citizens or an international NGO - can bring peace alone. That is the lesson, I think, we've got to learn", John McDonald, founder and chairman of The Institute for Multi-track Diplomacy, said. The need for what it called a "multi-disciplinary approach" was put forward independently by the West African Network for Peacebuilding, based on its experience with peacework in West Africa, as well as by many other organizations and individual peaceworkers.

Efforts to include a broad scale of approaches require networking, because it is clear that not all individual organizations are able to develop knowledge and

Shoulder to Shoulder

Theo van de Broek works for Justice and Peace in West Papua, or Irian Jaya. He runs a small Justice & Peace office in the Indonesian province's capital city that has been operating as a watchdog on human rights for three years. "Our main goal is to give a voice to the local population," he said. "There is a large silent majority we seek to represent. The people we work with have lived a life of about 30 years of oppression. At the best, they were the objects of some Indonesian development policy. They themselves felt they didn't count."

Justice & Peace is now working as an intermediary between the indigenous population and migrants who have come to Irian Jaya over the past decades from other Indonesian islands. "We tell them why the Papuans stage protests. We explain to them that Papuans are dissatisfied with the fact that they never enjoyed the right to self-determination. This is their major trauma," Van de Broek explains.

Van de Broek's organization tries to prevent Papuan protesters from embarking on actions whose consequences they may not recognize. "They have a strong pro independence movement, but its leadership is weak," Van de Broek says. "They talk with a loud voice but appear to be ignorant of political processes. The movement sent a delegation to Jakarta to tell the government it wanted to secede from the republic. This led to a very strong reaction among the local population in Papua. People thought independence was now imminent. They also falsely believe that independence, as a force by itself, will bring prosperity. They stopped working their lands."

Justice & Peace decided to start offering courses at the local level in remote areas to discuss the situation with the people. We want them to gain some control over their situation and to better understand what is happening. We try to leave behind small groups of people who continue to discuss the independence issues. They can also get in touch with us in case something happens, an outburst of violence for instance. This is important: they now know their voice will be heard in Jayapura, the capital of Irian Jaya/West Papua. They sometimes attack police posts believing they are on the verge of independence and kicking out the Indonesians. This is a dangerous situation."

"One important lesson I've learned is this, says Van de Broek: "We have to be there; be in close contact with people on the local level. We do not support a specific program. Our only goal is to help the people develop their own program and to make them heard, to show they are there and to call for fundamental respect for them. We try to give room for their own traditions, while we also seek to make them aware of the fact that life is changing and that they cannot continue their life as usual."

Van de Broek continues: "My major lesson is that this type of activity has more impact than any of my previous activities here, which were focused on development. For years, I worked on development projects. But they were so remote and aloof from these people. Now I feel that we are standing shoulder to shoulder with them and we see that they feel empowered, they get the idea that they can do something themselves. They have better understanding of the situation they're in. This is the only thing we can do for them. A very important lesson is that the church should continue to be sensitive to these kinds of needs and activities: To respect and build on positive aspects of the local traditions."

capacity in all relevant fields. "We have to work together in order to be able to do justice to the complexity of the issue at stake," stated professionals reflecting on the needs of national, regional and global conflict prevention networks. A well functioning network of conflict prevention organizations can give assurance that a wide range of possible approaches is looked at when trying to keep a specific conflict in check. However, bringing different NGO sectors together in a network has been identified as one of the major hurdles of establishing a holistic approach. "Reservations and barriers between various NGO sectors and milieus is one of the main problems to be overcome," said network members. The main driving forces in the field of conflict prevention are often conflict resolution, research and human rights organizations, while NGOs working in the fields of development and humanitarian assistance often hesitate to join, not least because they fear they might lose part of their funding from government budgets to conflict resolution newcomers.

A holistic approach could also entail combining official and non-official forces to work for peace. Multi-track efforts, as these approaches are usually called, can only be effective if the exchange of information between official and non-official actors occurs frequently and for the long-term, a condition that is not often met.

Build a Network
"Networking is critical for coordinating peacebuilding efforts," peacemakers in West Africa and other conflict regions concluded. Be it a formal network, supported by a secretariat and regular meetings, or a loose set of contacts, using the knowledge, information and insight of a larger number of people is enriching and improves the quality of peacemaking efforts. A network often provides a database of experts and practitioners who can be contacted. (see also: Holistic Approach Suits Best)

Look Actively for Chances for Peace
In early warning activities most attention appears to be devoted to trying to assess what developments contribute to the escalation of conflict. There is little analyses and data collection about available capacities and chances to stop conflict, or prevent it from escalating. "The early warning industry is really at risk of making mistakes because it always tends to look at factors that may cause conflict, but it does not focus on the capacity for peace," Michael S. Lund said. "This may lead to unbalanced assessments. Early warning people tend to ignore informal mechanisms regulating conflicts, for instance. You look at the ability of actors to make trouble, much less on their ability to make things change things for the better," he pointed out.

Give Both Sides Something to Lose
If moves towards peace and reconciliation are rewarded with economic help or other valuable gains, then there is less chance of a backlash in the peace

process. As soon as people feel they have something to lose from returning to violence they are less likely to do so. This point has been raised most strongly by *The Guardian* journalist Jonathan Freedland, as he compared the peace processes in Northern Ireland with the Middle East. "The most glaring difference between the Middle East and Northern Irish peace processes is economic. Huge investment has flown into the province (...) ensuring the next generation has an interest in maintaining tranquility. (But) Palestinians' standard of living has declined since Oslo, leading to abject poverty in Gaza and soaring unemployment in the West Bank. Young Palestinian men might as well take up violence; they have nothing to lose," Freedland wrote in an article published in *The Guardian* August 8, 2001.

Coordinate Development and Peacebuilding Programs

Many conflicts occur in developing countries, and are often perceived as being at least partly rooted in poverty. Paying attention to the relationship between conflict resolution and development is a must. Firstly, the field of conflict prevention has been calling on governments and other professionals in the developing aid area to assess whether aid programs may negatively affect stability in a society. Secondly, building up trust between groups engaged in a conflict is made a lot easier when moves are made towards improving the socio-economic conditions for all. Therefore, development issues are very relevant for peace and reconciliation, especially in the post-conflict stages. This is why the West African Network for Peacebuilding, to give one example, has urged NGOs and governments to integrate development programs into peacebuilding.

Become More Media Savvy

NGOs working in the field of conflict prevention need to acquire skills about how to give their cause publicity. Some practitioners feel that peaceworkers are being surpassed in being media conscious by war mongers and others betting on violence. "Even terrorists have very good PR these days. They develop smart publicity campaigns, create media events and are good to the media," an NGO representative observed. "As a civil society organization you have to have people who know how media works."

Peace organizations should acquire basic skills such as how to organize a press conference and write a press release at the minimum, practitioners in the field say. Other practitioners remarked that media savvy is increasingly important as it is becoming harder and harder to get stories from peacemakers into the mainstream media. Many required skills seem very accessible, such as writing concise reports on an organization's activities. "Uniform structured reports help end-users to locate information. The concise nature of reports makes sure that the most important information reaches the end-user and does not get lost in lengthy and cumbersome write-ups. No one reads long, tedious reports," emphasized a practitioner active in early warning.

Conflict Prevention Needs Good Public Relations

Many practitioners believe strongly that there is need to improve the image of working for peace among the general public and politicians. Some observers, such as Luc Reychler, professor at Leuven University, Belgium, stated that "there is a real need for marketing people" to help peaceworkers boost the status of their work. "Peace has a bad name," Reychler said, "it should be presented as something enticing and positive." Professionals feel that it is important to communicate "best practices" and "success stories" of conflict prevention initiatives. Good PR and providing accessible information on activities is essential in order to gain support from a wider audience and funding institutions. It may well also boost morale among people active in the field.

In this regard the use of "the bookkeeping argument" was recommended: more focus could be put on cost-analysis in order to push actors to realize that prevention is cheaper than humanitarian assistance after a conflict. It is important to always keep in mind the answers to simple, and legitimate questions put forward to practitioners of conflict prevention; such as: why should western countries give money to contain a conflict in a remote area on the other side of the world? The answer should include reasons such as: 'to enhance security in the globalizing world and to prevent economic disruption.'

Another suggested argument is what Bruce Jentleson has called the "Humpty Dumpty Problem". Putting severely shattered societies back together again is enormously difficult, hugely expensive, very risky and in some cases just not possible. This makes a strong point for embarking on preventive initiatives.

There are several studies that provide figures that could be used to accompany these arguments. The Oxford Research Group has pointed out that the maximum costs of bringing representatives of warring factions together amounts to several dozens of millions of dollars. In one case, in Sierra Leone, a conflict resolution initiative brought peace in a region of the country, probably saving dozens of lives, for just 2,700 US dollars. NATO's bombing of Serbia in 1999 cost approximately four billion US dollars, in addition to more than thirty billion dollars needed for post-war reconstruction.

In addition to being aware of the way the media can respond to conflict, it is of great importance to realize that the media can also be used as a direct tool for peace. Organizations producing television and radio shows that spread a message of reconciliation and peace, say their work has shown that the contribution of media can be effective. Media can help change the attitude of a community. For instance, an evaluation of a television show run in Macedonia by Search for Common Ground, showed 60 per cent of children who watched the first eight editions said they would invite kids from other ethnic groups to

John McDonald:
"Put your ego behind you"

A former US diplomat, John McDonald, director of the Institute for Multitrack Diplomacy in Washington, has experienced more than a decade of "alternative" efforts to boost peace and reconciliation. Being a good listener and putting your ego behind you are among the most important lessons he says he learned during his years as a peacemaker.

McDonald: "One of the major personal lessons I've learned is that people embarking on peace processes, especially diplomats, should be much better listeners than they usually are. I have remarked earlier that American diplomats were the most arrogant in the world, the poorest listeners and the most impatient people in the world. If you put all three together - arrogance, impatience, poor listening - you're not going to be a very good diplomat, not a good representative of your country, and not a peacebuilder. I am absolutely convinced that these characteristics haven't changed since I retired as a diplomat. But at least they are all correctable. And if you would correct them, you would become more effective when you work in other parts of the world.

The other thing that I learned is that you have to put your ego behind you, and not in front of you. Every diplomat, every politician, almost every leader puts his ego out in front and says "Here I am and I'm here to make a difference". But when you relate to people who are in pain and suffering, you have to put your ego behind you and don't worry about that image. And you never take credit for what happened. You always let somebody else have the credit. You're goal is to build a peace process, not to build your ego."

"One of the surprises for me is what we learned during the upheaval of 1989 and afterward: that an individual can make a difference. This is a powerful lesson. Most of the developing world waits for the government to act or not act, and the people there don't realize that they can act themselves. This has now changed, because people have shown that it is possible to change the system by raising their voices to demonstrate, activities that we call peace activism. Look what happened in Jakarta where students managed to change the system. Look what happened in Yugoslavia. For five years the West had been trying to get rid of Milosevic. But it was the people of Belgrade and surroundings, who marched against the flaw of elections, who finally made the difference. That's fantastic. Most governments and most people underestimate people power. I believe this is a whole new area that we have to recognize. There can come a point when people get fed up and they will risk their lives to express their anger and frustration. It happened in Ivory Coast and happened in other countries. It will continue to happen because governments don't hear, they don't listen."

their homes. This figure went up progressively during the course of the series. The powerful role of media is being acknowledged by most practitioners.

Evaluate

Look back on what you did and reflect on what could have been done better or what went wrong. Many professionals in the field, as well as academics, feel that peacemakers tend to neglect reflection on specific activities. In many cases they may not even have the time to write down a report on what they've tried in a specific conflict. Reflection is of essential importance to maintain the professional level and effectiveness of peacemaking interventions.

Jos Havermans is a free lance journalist, based in The Netherlands

Literature

Opportunities Missed, Opportunities Seized. *Preventive Diplomacy in the Post-Cold War World*, by Bruce W. Jentleson (ed.). Carnegie Commission on Preventing Deadly Conflict, Carnegie Corporation of New York. Rowman & Littlefield Publishers, New York, 2000.

Towards Better Peacebuilding Practice: On Lessons Learned, Evaluations Practices and Aid and Conflict, by Anneke Galama and Paul van Tongeren. ECCP, Utrecht 2002.

Lessons Learned in Conflict Interventions. Report of the Expert Meeting, February 1-4, 2001, Londonderry. INCORE/European Platform for Conflict Prevention and Transformation, Londonderry, 2001.

Lessons Learned on Peacebuilding. Working Document International Conference on Prevention and Management of Violent

Conflict and Building Peace, Gripsholm, Sweden, May 1-4, 2001. Peace Team Forum/European Platform for Conflict Prevention, s.l., 2001.

War Prevention Works: 50 Stories of People Resolving Conflict, by Dylan Matthews. Oxford Research Group, 2001.

Reaching for Peace. Lessons learned from Mott's Foundation's conflict resolution grantmaking, 1989-1998. Charles Stewart Mott Foundation, Flint, Michigan,1999.

Towards Better Peace Building Practice. Working Document for International Conference Towards Better Peace Building Practice, Soesterberg, The Netherlands, October 24-26, 2001. European Centre for Conflict Prevention, Utrecht, 2001.

Notes

1 See: Michael S. Lund, *Mapping Approaches to Lesson Learning*, Part 1 of this publication.
2 See: Jonathan Freedland, *Ten Steps to Peace*, The Guardian, Part 2 of this publication.

3 See Dylan Mathews, *What Lessons can be Learned?*, in: War Prevention Works, Oxford Research Group, 2001, Part 2 of this publication.

The European Centre for Conflict Prevention would like to continue collecting and disseminating lessons learned by organizations and institutions. Therefore, if you have any ideas or suggestions, please contact us at info@conflict-prevention.net

Further Reading

The following list of lessons, published in The Guardian, August 2001, contains some perhaps quite obvious reflections on peace processes. However, they also show that these 'simple' lessons often are *not* implemented by the various actors involved.

Ten Steps to Peace

JONATHAN FREEDLAND, THE GUARDIAN AUGUST 8, 2001

What makes some peace processes work while others fail? What magic ingredient has kept the peace, however precariously, in Northern Ireland while bloody war has resumed in the Middle East? Why, just this week, did Albanians and Macedonians seem on the brink of a deal, only to falter at the last minute?

Plenty of people are asking the question. Last month the BBC broadcast Norma Percy's masterful *Endgame in Ireland*, an oral history of the secret talks, midnight conversations and brinkmanship that led to the Good Friday agreement.

Why some negotiations fail while others, however feebly, stay on track depends on following the rules.

At the same time, the New York Review of Books published a insider's account - extracted on these pages - of what really happened last summer between Israel's Ehud Barak and Yasser Arafat at Camp David. Meanwhile audiences at Stratford can witness the diplomatic effort to resolve an imagined ethnic conflict, in David Edgar's new play, the Prisoner's Dilemma.

So what does it take to stop two sides killing each other? Maybe it's time to learn from these very different conflicts and draw up a cut-out-and-keep guide, to be used by negotiators, diplomats and weary warriors: ten steps to peace.

1: Get Foreigners Involved
The most successful peace processes are always nurtured by outside powers. The 1993 Oslo accords between Israelis and Palestinians were brokered by Norwegian diplomats, and co-guaranteed by Washington and Moscow. They held while the US stayed involved. But when Bill Clinton was replaced by George Bush, who wanted America shot of the whole mess, the peace effort unraveled into war. A diplomatic vacuum has been left and violence has filled it.

Northern Ireland, by contrast, has observed the rule admirably. Besides Clinton, a former US senator, a Canadian former general, a Finnish ex-president and a veteran of the ANC have all got stuck in. The entire process has been supervised by the governments of Britain and Ireland - each of which is regarded by one of the combatants as foreign.

Similarly, Macedonia's progress this week towards an accord with ethnic Albanian rebels has been nudged along by envoys from the US and the European Union, and the promise of British-led NATO troops to enforce any deal.

All this outside engagement forces once-warring parties to keep at it, lest they lose face before the whole world. It also gets round the problem of distrust: they may not believe in each other, but they can both trust the outsider standing between them.

2: Honor All Previous Commitments
Robert Malley, the former Clinton official writing in the New York Review, says the atmosphere of suspicion at Camp David last summer was born of Israel's failure to implement previous promises - on troop withdrawals and the like.

In Northern Ireland, the chief nationalist and republican grievance has been London's failure to honor in full Chris Patten's report on police reform. Unionists, meanwhile, say republicans have failed to come through on arms.

Broken promises are bad news in peacemaking. They fuel skepticism about the value of politics over violence, strengthening rejectionists over moderates. The Israeli peace movement was all but destroyed by the widespread belief that Palestinians had broken their Oslo promise to stamp out terror.

3: Ensure Both Sides Can Deliver
Camp David was fraught because neither Arafat nor Barak could act without looking over their shoulder, weighing up what their own constituency back home would tolerate. David Trimble has similar trouble with the hardline unionists who deny him a mandate to say yes.

On this score, Sinn Fein is the luckiest kind of peacemaker. Republicans are a tightly disciplined (some would say undemocratic) and relatively small movement: what their leaders decide at the table comes with a copper-bottom guarantee, partly because they tend to promise only what they can deliver.

4: Give Both Sides Something to Lose
The most glaring difference between the Middle East and Northern Irish processes is economic. Huge investment has flowed into the province, much

of it American, ensuring the next generation has an interest in maintaining tranquility: businesses and jobs they will lose in a return to war.

Palestinians' standard of living has declined since Oslo, leading to abject poverty in Gaza and soaring unemployment in the West Bank. Young men might as well take up violence; they have nothing to lose.

5: Take it Slow
The genius of Oslo was that it envisaged a gradual building up of trust. Every change was phased in over time, years not months. Barak's great error at Camp David was to demand the whole process be crunched into a matter of days: a summit that would resolve all outstanding issues at once.

The Northern Ireland effort has got this right. It may be painful to watch, but the process there has been sensibly gradual, advanced by a series of confidence building measures. The two governments' blueprint, released last week, proposes just such a series of "quid pro quos" for the final heave toward peace.

6: Do Not Seek Finality
Barak wanted Arafat formally to declare an end to the Palestinian-Israeli conflict and for their deal to be comprehensive: such a goal is laudable, but incompatible with the pragmatic, piecemeal business that is peacemaking.

Better to climb up the mountain step by step than try to leap to the top: you may stumble, but you won't fall to your death.

7: Don't Ask your Enemy to Say the Unsayable
Ensuring no one has to swallow his pride is the art of good peacemaking. Here linguistic creativity is useful, forging euphemisms that make everyone a winner and ensure no one loses face. Trimble's insistence on "actual decommissioning" makes that concession less, not more, likely to happen.

8: Pick the Right Issue
If you have a bottom line, make sure it's the right one. History may show that unionists erred by making such a fetish of decommissioning: they may well get their way on IRA arms, but at what price? In return for bowing to the unionist demand for weapons, republicans seem to have got their way on almost everything else, from demilitarization to policing.

9: Don't Raise the Bar
Once you've made a final demand, you can't make another one. The Macedonian deal fell through because, at the last minute, the government wanted a timetable for rebel disarmament. (Sound familiar?)

Yesterday Trimble suggested his return as first minister was conditional not only on IRA decommissioning but also SDLP support for the province's new police force. That kind of ploy plays only to the republican skeptics who say unionists are, at bottom, hostile to sharing power with Catholics and will find any way to avoid it.

10: Don't Stop

Whatever else happens, peace processes have to keep on. For all its laws, the Northern Ireland effort can claim to have saved nearly six hundred lives: until the IRA cessation in 1994, approximately one hundred people were killed in each of the thirty years of the Troubles. With more than one hundred dead since 1994, that leaves close to six hundred saved in seven years.

In Israel and Palestine, by bleak contrast, the peace process has broken down for a year - and 691 people have died in that short time: nearly six hundred alive, more than six hundred dead. Maybe that is the most golden of all golden rules: talk saves lives.

The Oxford Research Group published in 2001 *War Prevention Works: 50 stories of people resolving conflict.* The stories collected tell what people worldwide are doing to stop war and killing, armed only with integrity, stamina and courage. These stories show how powerful non-violence can be. The stories are divided along five categories: before any violence, escalating violence, full-blown violence, contained violence and after violence. Here you will find the chapter *What Lessons Can Be Learned?* For more information and to order the publication please visit http://www.oxfrg.demon.co.uk/wpwhome.html

What Lessons Can Be Learned?

What leaps out from the pages is how personal are the processes which bring about peace. How slow, and painstaking they are, how unglamorous and undramatic. The stories repeatedly describe people who, full of suspicion and trepidation, finally agree to get together in workshops or meetings, and talk to people whom they hate or fear. They describe the methods and techniques that worked - brainstorming sessions, training in communication, mediation techniques, role-plays, dialogue and just plain listening. Not the stuff of high drama. *By* DYLAN MATHEWS

Yet under conditions of war, these actions require courage of a high order. The initiatives recorded here are exactly those, which under a regime of terror, are reason enough for abduction, torture or murder. In 1993 in Colombia, for example, six key members of the Committee for the Defense of Human Rights were assassinated, simply for defending the rights of activists. In the story of Brazil, Paolo had been teaching poor people how to stick together, and within 48 hours was abducted, tortured and killed. Yet it is perfectly ordinary people who do these extraordinary things, often with no training, usually making it up as they go along.

The lessons we shall draw here do not pretend to be an academic evaluation; they are simply a common sense drawing out of some of the main points which emerge.

1. To meet and talk about peace, when others can see only violence as the solution, is no wimpish activity. To sit down with the enemy can be an act of extreme bravery, and even to carry out the preparations to enable that to happen requires equally the conquering of personal fear. Although not much is said explicitly in these pages about the personal struggles of individuals, the proof of those struggles is abundantly evident. The Dinka and Nuer chiefs in the Sudan listened to each other's stories for three full

days "as though they were peeling back layer upon layer of pain and discovering afresh that at their core they are from one family". The women of Wajir had to overcome even the killing of a member of their own family in their commitment to keeping the peace committees going. In the Lebanon, it was youth activists from Christian and Druze villages at war who overcame their skepticism to enroll other youngsters to come to a workshop. Key figures in the Tajikistan civil war agreed to meet, "to listen carefully, to speak from the heart and respect the sensitivities of others".

2. The support of outsiders is often critical in ensuring the physical and psychological survival of those who dare to do this work. The witness of international NGOs like Peace Brigades International was essential to those in Colombia who were willing to risk their lives to defend human rights. In Nicaragua it was American citizens who volunteered their presence to deter Contra attacks.

3. Nearly one half of the interventions were carried out by people with some spiritual basis for their activities. This is remarkable, considering that in our selection process religious or spiritual affiliation played no part. Yet again and again, the factor named by participants as being central to their effectiveness is a sense of direction inspired by some connection with a source of strength greater than their own ego. The approach of Moral Rearmament, for example, is explicit; it is to "engender a heightened spiritual sensitivity in both parties and to thereby induce them to enter into a genuine and deep dialogue".

4. A slow steady process of trust-building is often necessary before official negotiations can start, if they are to succeed. The work of the Vatican in the Beagle Channel dispute is a good example of this, as is the Dartmouth Conference Regional Conflicts Task Force in Tajikistan, the Lutheran World Federation in Guatemala, the Lebanon Conflict Resolution Network, and many others.

5. Business has a powerful role to play. In two examples from South Africa it was industrialists who provided both the incentive and the techniques to enable violent opposition groups to work towards ending the killing. Business leaders in El Salvador organized a 'goods for guns' scheme, which was so successful that by the end of the second weekend almost $103,000 worth of vouchers had been given out when the organizers had only $19,500 in the bank. The President intervened to provide enough money to continue and expand the program.

6. Traditional processes can be of key importance in peace making. Somali people for example place a high value on poetry, which in a nomadic society is as important as radio or television, addressing all aspects of Somali life.

The traditional elders therefore brought in poets as well as religious leaders to reconcile warring clans.

7. Women frequently offer the ingredients essential to the establishment of peace, particularly in addressing the feelings involved. This is implicit in several of the stories, and explicit in the cases of the Liberian Women's Initiative, the Mothers of the Plaza del Mayo and the Wajir Peace Group, where Dekha Ibrahim Abdi says: "Most of what was accomplished was done by people with a heart for peace, rather than training in conflict resolution."

8. For this work to be extended, far more evaluation needs to be done. Even the best funded organizations don't write up what they do. Robert Ricigliano, CEO of the Conflict Management Group, wrote to us: "Reflecting on our work is something we do too little of ...we are much better at doing it than documenting what we have done." Chris Spies, a local peacemaker in South Africa says: "My dreams of writing usually are put on the back burner to make way for income generating work." We recommend therefore that grant-makers explicitly build evaluation, or at least write-up costs, into grants.

9. The effectiveness of NGO work in this field has increased dramatically, but it should not become a replacement for government action. A multi-track approach can often be more effective than either a government or NGO on its own. The case of St Egidio in Mozambique, and the 'Norwegian model' used by FAFO in its work with Israelis and Palestinians, are good illustrations of this point. Likewise in Mali the Norwegian government funded an NGO that knew what it was doing through a long-term involvement in the area.

10. The interventions described in this book are extraordinarily cost-effective. The maximum cost is $4 million for a series of meetings bringing together thousands of senior figures from France and Germany after World War II, laying foundations for the unification of Europe, and the minimum is $2,700 for community level conflict resolution bringing about peace in an area of Sierra Leone. When we compare this to the cost of military intervention, the result is stark. NATO's bombing of Serbia in 1999 cost approximately $4 billion, in addition to the $20-$30 billion then needed to rebuild what was destroyed, and leaving the problems of Kosovo and the dictatorship of Milosevic unsolved. The issue however is not simply the level of funding accorded to non-violent initiatives, but the way in which it is disbursed, to make sure it reaches those who are competent, well organized and determined.

For every one of these successful interventions, many others failed for lack of funds or resources. It is for that reason that the Oxford Research Group is setting up a fund to link grassroots groups at the cutting edge of conflict with each other, and with sources of support. This initiative is called "Give Peace a Bank". It will enable those in strife torn areas to learn what has been successful elsewhere, instead of re-inventing the wheel. It will provide simple invaluable resources like mobile phones and photocopiers. It will enable effective initiatives, such as those described in these pages, to be multiplied.

In 'People Building Peace' - a publication of the European Centre for Conflict Prevention - 35 stories of successful peace building from around the world are described and analyzed. Out of this, a list of sixteen lessons learned resulted. Here they are, in summary.

In Short - 16 Lessons Learned from People Building Peace

Involve as many people and sectors as possible in peacebuilding
It is an obvious point, but one that is nevertheless frequently overlooked: it is essential that as many sectors as possible are included in any peacebuilding process.

Strengthen local capacities for peace
If efforts to prevent, resolve and transform violent conflicts are to be effective in the long-term, they must be based on the active participation of local civil groups committed to building peace.

Strengthening such 'local capacities for peace' may take many forms, including education and training, nurturing the volunteer spirit in society and highlighting the work of local peacemakers in the media. Granting basic human rights such as freedom of speech and press, and freedom to organize oneself are prerequisites for including the different civil organizations in the peace process.

Conceive peacebuilding and reconciliation as a process
Peace is not an abstract goal but a process. It must be built up over a long period of time. Building peace must be organic process, growing at all levels of society. Peace cannot be built just through exclusive conclaves of the leaders of the conflicting parties. The idea of "historic agreements as a stepping-stone to peace" has proven to be wrong on too many occasions. Long-term strategic relationships should be built which reach across the dividing lines of conflict in society.

Change and transform the conflict pattern: create hope
A common feature of many stories of successful peacebuilding is that they succeeded in breaking the logic of war. Successful initiatives create hope and stimulate people to disengage themselves from war. By inspiring others these initiatives have an extremely important spin-off effect.

Create dialogue

Stimulate a feeling of interdependence, emphasize common identities and help people to understand the other side's position. Private peacemaking should focus on 'humanizing the enemy'. The most effective dialogue often occurs when each side forcefully advocates its position and then listens to its opponent. It should be recognized that people can communicate with each other, but may not be ready for a dialogue. Much creativity is needed to bring the parties together for a first round of talks.

Promote education and enhance professionalization

Educational programs should stimulate the universal awareness of coexistence, tolerance, and reconciliation. Those involved in the peace building process must be thoroughly prepared and trained. Professionalization of peacebuilding can enhance its effectiveness.

Exchange experiences

Promote international exchanges between peacemakers from conflict regions. Learning from each other's experiences inspires innovative approaches.

Include local authorities

The decentralized approach of grassroots and community-based organizations has resulted in many successes.

Strengthen coalition building between civil organizations

The effectiveness of civil activity is often hampered by a lack of coordination between groups operating in similar fields. As a result, scarce resources are wasted through duplication of tasks and failure to achieve synergy. There is great need to create civil networks and /or platforms that promote coalition- and constituency building.

Institution building

To sustain building and reconciliation, institution building should be stimulated at all levels of society and at the international level.

Make 'Conflict Impact Assessment' a requirement

In order to maximize the benefits of development aid, dispensing bodies - governmental, intergovernmental, and private - should be required to assess and report on the likely impact of their development aid policies in terms of whether they will heighten or reduce the risk of violent conflict.

Role of the corporate sector

The potential role of the corporate sector in peacebuilding is still not widely recognized. However, just as business can exacerbate tensions and fuel conflicts, so it can contribute to building peace and security.

Role of donors
The role of donors can extend beyond the simple provision of financial support for projects. Donors can provide an extra impulse in the peacebuilding process by stimulating conferences, agenda setting, and developing directories.

Prioritize Early Warning and Early Response
That prevention is better than cure is a truth, which needs to be better observed in practice. Civil organizations, governments and intergovernmental bodies should dedicate much more attention and resources to prevention, as opposed to reacting to violent conflicts. In particular, this should include generating the political will needed for early responses to potential conflict situations both present and future.

Promote an integrative approach to peacebuilding and reconciliation by using a combination of approaches
The construction of a stable peace in the northern part of Mali was not the result of any single action. It followed from a complex of efforts to rebuild trust, to address legitimate grievances, to reward combatants who chose to give up the fight, and to build incentives into the peace process that would assure the continued commitment of people on both sides of the conflict. An integrated framework towards peace building should include:
- a coherent and comprehensive approach by all actors;
- partnerships between, and the co-ordination of, the various members of the international community and the national government;
- on a broad consensus on a strategy and related set of interventions;
- careful balancing of macroeconomic political objectives, and
- the necessary financial resources.

Mainstream multi-track diplomacy
Peace processes should combine official as well as non-official approaches. Official diplomacy is usually most effective when it is linked to official processes and channels. For this, contacts as well as the exchange of information and experiences between both approaches should be frequent and structural.

Note
This 16-point list was also based on an outline of guidelines and principles from the Institute for Multi-Track Diplomacy, as well as the 'Agenda for Peace and Justice for the 21st century' of the Hague Appeal for Peace and the Strategic Plan developed by the Coexistence Initiative of State of the World Forum.

Part 3
Aid and Conflict

Feeding Armies and Militias or Supporting a Path to Peace?

Several weeks after 'September 11', US airplanes engaged in the fight against terrorism began dropping high explosive bombs on Afghanistan. At the same time, other planes were dropping high altitude 'food bombs' in an effort to feed the hungry population fleeing the violence. The reaction of aid and relief organizations to this mixture of warfare and food aid was extremely negative. They considered it a violation of the 'humanitarian mandate', with dangerous implications for their own work on the ground. Their reaction illustrates a wider problem. It is now generally accepted that it is impossible to be a neutral external actor providing aid and resources in a conflict situation. But although the necessity for development agencies to accept, analyze and apply the relations between aid and conflict is clear, the question remains, 'how exactly should this task be implemented?' Incorporating conflict prevention into an agency's thinking and practice is more easily said than done. *By* Hans van de Veen

The doctor had been sent by a humanitarian aid agency to a hospital in an area affected by armed conflict. It wasn't his fault that he got killed. He was a competent doctor and did his utmost to save the life of his patient. Nobody told him after the death of a particularly important patient that he should leave the place as soon as possible. The patient had suffered severe gunshot wounds and the doctor was unable to save his life. Two days after the death of the patient, two armed gunmen entered the hospital and killed the doctor. Local inhabitants wondered why the doctor had not left the place earlier. Apparently, he had failed to realize the seriousness of the warnings. Nobody had made him aware that this was the rule of the game.

There are many more - also less harrowing - examples that illustrate how essential it is to engage the right staff in conflict situations, says Thania Paffenholz, who works for the Swiss Peace Foundation. In her opinion, the personal skills of people working in the field are as important as their professional qualifications. "Good attributes are commitment, openness, flexibility, self-confidence and the ability to adapt. Also the ability to work in a team is essential. Professional qualifications are a necessary precondition, however without these personal skills, a fieldworker will not be able to cope with the difficult situation of working in or around an existing or potential conflict setting. Merely to rely on professional qualifications, while leaving personal skills to chance, will minimize the likelihood of success and may put field staff at risk."

Executive summary: It is now widely accepted that all aid given in the context of a violent conflict becomes a part of that conflict. As a result of recent experiences in the many post-Cold War internal conflicts, and thanks to some excellent case studies and reflections, we now have a far better understanding of the specifics of this linkage. But what are the implications for NGOs (and donors, and governments), what options do they have? How should they deal with conflict if their primary mandate is to stay neutral and supply aid to people in need? There are stimulating examples of organizations who have succeeded in expanding their humanitarian mandate into peacebuilding and conflict resolution. Nevertheless, looking at the whole, a significant shift in attitude and actual working, is barely noticeable. Aid agencies advance numerous arguments in favor of carrying on as before. Resistance towards change (at field level as well as at headquarters) and a lack of funding seem to be the real problems. For this, both agencies and donors need to improve on conflict analysis. Also, cooperation with local partners is essential.

However, even the highest professional qualifications are insufficient if a relief worker simply is not aware of - or fails to understand - the mechanisms of war and conflict, as well as the impact of their own humanitarian work in those situations.

Better training seems to be the obvious answer. Without exception, all participants of the working group on Humanitarian Aid and Conflict at the Soesterberg conference agreed on this. One can discuss for many hours ways to include peace-building efforts in humanitarian aid, the most practical step to be undertaken is to ensure that field workers and staff at headquarters receive conflict training. Training in conflict dynamics, analysis, indicators etc. will provide them with the tools to recognize the factors feeding a conflict, and raise their awareness of the potential impact of their actions. Without such tools and understanding it is impossible to incorporate peacebuilding elements into the work. At the same time, awareness building in relation to the cultural background of the country of assignment, is seen as tremendously important.

Obvious as this may seem, in practice the resistance towards this kind of training for humanitarian field workers and their staff is enormous, as confirmed by representatives of organizations which have been through the process of adaptation to conflict situations in past years. Says Jane Backhurst of World Vision: "The necessity of linking in planning and practice between aid and conflict is clear now within my organization, but many people failed to see the 'why' for a long time. There was much resistance to looking at issues of justice and advocacy. When the process of incorporating a focus on conflict was started, people would say: 'Oh no not another issue we have to

Thania Paffenholz, Swiss Peace Foundation/Centre for Peace Building, Switzerland, conference facilitator

mainstream into our work!' They had already been asked to mainstream first ecology, then gender, and they could not cope with yet another trend."

South-African Jaco Cilliers is Peacebuilding and Justice advisor at the Catholic Relief Services (CRS), a humanitarian organization which rethought its role after the 1994 genocide in Rwanda and got involved in peacebuilding. CRS was confronted with fierce internal resistance to this shift. Cilliers: "From a humanitarian NGO perspective, the field of peacebuilding is seen as just spending money, without actually contributing anything concrete. It is difficult to show results. Peace builders do not build houses, the results are not concrete."

Nick Lewer of Bradford University was asked by Oxfam GB to study how to introduce the concepts of peacebuilding into its work in Sri Lanka. Field officers had resisted earlier efforts in this direction, arguing that they already knew what the conflict they were confronted with in their work was about. Lewer: "One of the lessons learned so far is the crucial role of the individual. It is normal to find that some people are more open towards change than others. In the humanitarian field there seem to be many of those who are reluctant to adapt. It is obvious why: peacebuilding is a long-term job, which contrasts sharply with the short-term nature of relief work. For relief workers, the introduction of a new element like conflict awareness within their organization in practice means at least two weeks of extra training. They hate that. 'I don't need another thing to complicate my life,' they say."

Organizations need to understand the feelings of their people in the field, says Lewer, and give a pragmatic response to this. "Oxfam has understood this. The organization is careful not to impose a new attitude on their people." As a researcher though, Lewer - while making clear he is not speaking about Oxfam specifically - fails "to understand how it is possible that NGOs that work for thirty years or so in a conflict, have so much resistance towards analyzing their own role and refuse to make a proper conflict analysis."

As much as their colleagues in the field, many staff at the headquarters of development and relief organizations seem to resist change. But there must be more, and better explanations - such as a lack of knowledge. Although the necessity for humanitarian and development agencies learning to accept, analyze and apply the relations between aid and conflict is clear, the big question remains how exactly should this task be implemented. Incorporating conflict prevention into an agency's thinking and practice is easier said than done. The concept is not easy to grasp and to translate into explicit activities. Because of this, many development- and humanitarian NGOs and workers have so far rejected the 'mainstreaming' of conflict prevention in their organization's daily routine.

Understanding the Lessons Learned

Over the past decade, the mandate of aid has been extended significantly. To understand this, one has to go back to the 1980s, when the end of the Cold War brought about far-reaching political changes that culminated in a great increase in the number of civil wars, especially in Africa and the former Soviet Union. While traditional diplomacy was unable to cope with these kind of conflicts in remote areas, characterized by deep social divisions and weak governance, many non-governmental relief and development organizations made their entrance. The international community, desperately looking for possibilities to promote democratic and peaceful changes in those same regions, enthusiastically supported the enhanced role of NGOs. As a result, humanitarian assistance and development aid were confronted with a long extension of their mandate, under increasingly difficult conditions.

Within a few years, a fierce debate emerged on the consequences of the growing importance of humanitarianism and the new role of relief and development NGOs. While working with the best intentions, they were accused of fueling war economies, undermining social contracts and feeding the killers, etc. Humanitarian relief in complex emergencies was being

Box 1 **Stories from the Field**

'I would like to mention one more anecdote, which influenced my thinking about people working in the field. The story concerns a donor agency that had funded a cholera hospital in an area of armed conflict. A monitoring mission from the donor agency was sent to the region because the cholera epidemic could not be brought under control despite the emphasis that had been put on the need for preventative measures such as chlorinating of wells. The mission discovered that the implementing agency, a prominent European NGO, had been conned by the local subcontractors. The contractors took the money for chlorinating the wells, but never performed the work, because they had no interest in reducing the cholera rates. No cholera, no income, simple as that! The aid agency staff, which was changed every three to six months, never understood this situation. During the flight back to the neighboring country, I had an opportunity to talk to one of the doctors from the hospital. He had just finished his six-month term and was moving on to another assignment. He was 24 years old, had graduated from medical school one year previously and this was already his second assignment in a war zone. He explained to me that he loved emergencies, "because you have a clearly defined task to perform in a limited amount of time: cholera breaks out, you treat the cholera and off you go to another place". He also mentioned what satisfaction it gave him to work so efficiently. I tried to mention the failure regarding the preventative measures, but his mind was already set on his next assignment. Was it Afghanistan or Sierra Leone? He was not quite sure but that didn't really matter, he ended the conversation.'

Source: Peacebuilding - A Field Guide, edited by Luc Reichler and Tania Paffenholz, Lynne Rienner Publishers, Boulder/London, 1999

described as a "fig leaf", covering the disinterest of the international community to seek lasting solutions to political crisis in countries that hold little strategic value for Western powers. Within the humanitarian community itself there was much debate regarding such issues as core humanitarian principles (e.g., neutrality, impartiality) and military-humanitarian relations (e.g. protection). All this debate led to a rethinking of the role of NGOs and more generally, of the role of humanitarian and development assistance in areas affected by chronic political instability.

Donors invested in research and development policies which make a more explicit link between poverty, conflict and aid. New criteria, policies and, on occasion conditionalities were introduced. In 1997, the OECD's Development Assistance Committee (DAC) adopted the *Guidelines on Conflict, Peace and Development Co-operation*. This contained the crucial statement that "to work effectively towards peace, development agencies need to work alongside partners in developing countries before, during and after the conflict." The OECD Guidelines are "one of the clearest and most authoritative statements on the new

Box 2   **Aid, Conflict and Peacebuilding in Sri Lanka**

Should an international humanitarian relief and development organization working with people affected by violent conflict attempt to proactively engage with issues of conflict reduction and peacebuilding? What might such a program look like? What resources would be required and what changes would be necessary? What are the challenges that would have to be met?

A few years ago, these were the questions facing Oxfam GB in Sri Lanka. Today, Oxfam's operation incorporates a conflict reduction and peace-building perspective through its 'Relationship Building Programme'. The program aims to add value, sustainability and impact to a process of community-based analysis and action that seeks to maximize the practical grass-roots peace-building and conflict-reduction potential of such activities.

How successful this new approach will be remains to be seen. The need for a change however, was obvious. Sri Lanka has traditionally been one of the highest per capita recipient countries of aid. At the same time, after almost 40 years, the conflict in the country now dominated society to such an extent that violence has become a means to attain legitimacy, wealth and protection. Prospects for peace in the near future are remote. This was the reason for aid donors and agencies working in Sri Lanka to rethink their past achievements and acknowledge the need for change in future strategies. The DFID-report mentions three main issues that are particularly important in designing and implementing this new approach.

- Donors should undertake more political analyses in order to better understand the working of political systems and incentives of political actors in Sri Lanka. Who gains and who loses from certain programs or strategies and for what reasons? Knowing the answers to these questions is crucial before a strategy is designed.
- A lot of conflict-sensitive approaches have a limited impact as they do not link up to other projects and/or policies. For example, there is a wide gap between national and strategic levels on the co-ordination of aid programs in the north and in the south. In the north the aid programs are quite tightly linked as the conflicting parties are determining the activities of the aid-agencies, and in the south, where the conflict is less pronounced, the programs tend to be less connected.
- Donors and operational agencies should develop long-term, strategic engagement plans. The crux of the problem is that short-term thinking and mandates based on short-term funding are being used to react to long-term problems and needs. The report concludes that an important constraint on current policy and practice is the lack of a methodology or framework for agencies working in Sri Lanka. Based on this observation, Oxfam's new approach (including peace and conflict impact assessment tools - PCIAs - was developed.

Source: Aid, Conflict and Peacebuilding in Sri Lanka (DFID, November 2000). The case-study Oxfam in Sri Lanka: Operationalising Conflict Reduction and Peacebuilding is published as a paper in the Working Paper Series, Centre for Conflict Resolution, Department of Peace Studies, University of Bradford, UK (http://www.bradford.ac.uk)

mandate of aid", in the words of Peter Uvin, research professor at the Watson Institute for International Studies, Brown University, US. As a follow-up to the publication of the guidelines, Uvin headed a research process on 'incentives and disincentives for peace' - the way humanitarian aid and development aid can be used to promote dynamics of peace in recipient countries.

In the wake of the OECD initiative, other donors adapted their own policy. UNDP-director Gus Speth advised that development assistance should never be stopped during a conflict, whenever possible. "From a development perspective, we must have preventive development before the crisis. We must have ameliorative development during the crisis. And we must have curative development after the crisis." The EU rethought its policy on structural stability in countries going through a process of transition, while the World Bank created a special post-conflict unit. The Bank also made 'peace and social harmony' an integrative objective for its initiatives. A number of bilateral donors such as CIDA (Canada), SIDA (Sweden), DGIS (Netherlands) and DFID (UK) also developed guidelines for conflict sensitive aid.

Several humanitarian and development NGOs nowadays are also addressing this linkage by developing new mandates and policies for their projects. In Sri Lanka for instance, DFID and Oxfam have been working together to design strategies to enable aid and relief to be delivered more effectively in conflict affected areas, including a preventative capacity. (See box 2)

A general consensus seemed to grow that NGOs working in conflict situations had to choose between either sticking their heads in the sand or confronting the issues directly. Says Jacco Cilliers of CRS: "Depending on the nature of the conflict, using a variety of means, NGOs can contribute to the avoidance of conflict or violent conflict spiraling into full blown crisis. They can support local communities and civil society organizations to work for peace and strong ties across social groups. At the international level NGOs can lobby their home governments and international organizations regarding pending violent conflict. There are no easy answers regarding the role of NGOs in preventing deadly conflict, but we can be certain of one thing if conflict prevention is not successful: the inevitable destruction of all that we and the communities we serve have worked to achieve."

If, as has been argued, peace is the pre-requisite for development, human rights and justice, then humanitarian and development organizations should develop a much greater share of their resources to the fight for peace, first and foremost, to prevent as well as to put an end to deadly conflict. But what would that fight look like?

Some experience in various aspects of 'peace programming' by the humanitarian community was acquired through the Local Capacities for Peace

Box 3   *Lessons learned through the Local Capacities for Peace Project*

1. When international assistance is given in the context of a violent conflict, it becomes part of that context and, thus, also of the conflict. Although assistance agencies intend to be impartial in relation to who wins and who loses in a conflict, the actual impact of their aid is never neutral regarding whether the conflict worsens or abates. In conflict settings, aid can reinforce, exacerbate and prolong conflict. However, it can also help to reduce intergroup divisions and support people's capacities to find peaceful options for solving problems.

2. Conflicts are characterized by two types of factors: A. Dividers/Tensions: Conflicts are always characterized by intergroup divisions and tensions, and B. Connectors and Local Capacities for Peace: Conflicts, perhaps surprisingly, are also characterized by a number of things that link and connect people even though they are at war. This is especially true of conflicts that occur within societies, where people recently lived and worked (and worshipped) side-by-side; went to school together and, in some cases, intermarried.

3. When aid comes into the context of conflict, it inevitably affects the Dividers/Tensions and the Connectors/Local Capacities for Peace that exist in the context. By the way in which aid is provided, it either feeds into and worsens intergroup tensions and divisions, or it reduces them. By the way in which aid is given, it either ignores or bypasses existing connectors and peace capacities and, thus, weakens and undermines them or it supports and reinforces them.

4. The LCPP found that the resources transferred by aid agencies into conflict areas affect conflict in five predictable ways:
    a. Aid resources are often stolen by warriors and used for their purposes to support armies or to buy weapons.
    b. Aid has market effects through its impacts on wages, prices and profits; through these, aid either reinforces incentives for continued warfare or incentives for peace.
    c. Aid has distributional impacts in that it targets some groups and not others; when aid is directed toward one of the subgroups in conflict, it can exacerbate intergroup jealousies and tensions.
    d. Aid can substitute for local resources that, without aid, would have been required to support civilian life; this, in turn, frees up local resources for the pursuit of conflict.
    e. Aid can legitimize some people and some activities and delegitimize other people and other activities; insofar as its effects legitimize warriors and warfare, it can reinforce conflict.

5. The LCPP also found that aid delivers "messages" as well as resources. How aid is given, how staff interact with local people, how protection is arranged and the like all convey messages that either reinforce the modes of conflict or reduce them. There are seven patterns of these "implicit ethical messages."
    a. When aid agencies hire armed guards to protect either their goods or their staff, one implicit ethical message can be that it is legitimate for arms to determine who

gains access to food, health care and other aid services. Warlords also use arms to determine who gains and who does not gain such services.

b. When international aid agencies refuse to cooperate with each other and, instead, compete for partners or beneficiaries in the field, the implicit ethical message is that, when one disagrees with others, it is not necessary to cooperate with them. This is one of the fundamental modus operandi of conflict.

c. When international aid workers use aid resources for their own personal pleasure (as, for example, when they take the agency vehicle to the mountains for the weekend even though petrol is in short supply), the implicit ethical message is that people who control resources may use them for their own purposes without accountability to others who might need them more. This, again, is one of the ways that warlords often act.

d. When international aid agencies have evacuation plans for emergencies which ensure the withdrawal of expatriate staff but leave local staff behind, the implicit ethical message is that different lives have different value. This is one of the messages of war.

e. When international aid agency staff deny responsibility for the impacts of their aid claiming to be "only one small actor in a complex situation" and "subject to the rules of my headquarters or my donor," the implicit ethical message is that individuals who work in complex environments do not have to accept accountability for the outcomes of their actions. People in warfare very often also deny accountability; they claim that "someone else made me kill or fight."

f. When aid workers, who are nervous about conflict and their own safety, approach every interaction with local people with fear, suspicion and belligerence, they reinforce the atmosphere of aggression and provocation that persists in conflicts.

g. When international aid agencies rely on gruesome pictures for their fundraising and publicity, the implicit message is one of demonization, on one side of the war, and innocence on the other side. Warriors can use such publicity to further their cause in the international arena and, furthermore, war is seldom so simple. Guilt and innocence are present on all sides and aid agencies have a responsibility to educate and interpret complex situations with more respect, subtlety and accuracy.

6. It is in the details of aid programs that the impacts are conveyed. That is, the timing (when and for how long) of a program; the location; the staffing (both expatriate and local); the selection of partners and of "targets"; the decisions about what and how much external resources to supply. All these affect whether aid feeds into Divisions and Tensions or supports Connectors and LCPs. Finally, and most important of all, it is in the "how" of aid programs (what kind of distribution system is chosen, how the terms of access to goods are defined and enforced, etc., etc.) that aid's most direct impacts are felt

Source: Do No Harm: How Aid Supports Peace - Or War. Mary B. Anderson, Lynne Rienner Publishers, Boulder and London, 1999

Monique Mekenkamp, European Centre for Conflict Prevention, The Netherlands, and Mary B. Anderson, Collaborative for Development Action, USA

Project, conducted by the American NGO Collaborative for Development Action. Begun in 1994, the project is a collaborative effort involving over a hundred international and indigenous NGOs, several UN agencies and a number of donor countries. The project was intended to help aid agencies learn how to provide humanitarian or development assistance in areas of conflict in ways that, rather than feeding into and prolonging war, helps local people disengage from fighting and establish alternative systems for dealing with the problems that underlie their conflict. Lessons learned from the many case studies and workshops were published in Mary B. Anderson's book, *Do No Harm: How aid can support peace - or war* (see Box 3). "All of the donors and agencies involved in the LCPP agree that these lessons learned are useful in helping us understand past experience about how aid and conflict interact," says the CDA's Marshall Wallace. "When these phases of the Project were complete, however, the question remained about how to use the lessons in ongoing programs in areas of conflict."

To find an answer to this question, the LCPP initiated a series of Pilot Implementation Projects, partnering with operational NGOs that already had active programs in twelve different conflict zones in the world. The LCPP provided a liaison to work with the field staff of these agencies on a regular basis over an extended period of time (up to three years total) to "try out" the LCPP approaches. The experience has produced a number of practical ideas about how to adopt, adapt and use the LCPP in real time and real space, as well as raising further issues.

"Among the issues raised in the course of the implementation phase", says Wallace, "two have encouraged further work by the LCPP. First is the question regarding the implications of the LCPP and the 'Do No Harm' approach for donors and NGO headquarters. What roles and responsibilities do donors and NGO headquarters have when aid is delivered in the context of conflict? And second, how do aid agencies 'mainstream' ideas? Once something has been identified as important, how do agencies respond and how do they move concepts into practical application?

Independent studies have led other scholars to very similar conclusions. Collecting lessons as such is not difficult, rather, it is the implications of these lessons that complicate the issue. How should one respond to the realization that aid can do a lot of harm? What does that recognition mean in practical terms for humanitarian aid workers distributing food to refugees in conflict areas? Further, the concept of conflict prevention is not easy to grasp and to translate into explicit activities. For this reason, development- and humanitarian NGOs and workers have, so far, been reluctant to implement the lessons in their daily routine.

Although the necessity for development agencies to accept, analyze and apply the relations between aid and conflict is clear, the question remains how exactly should the task be implemented? Lewer and Goodhand argue in their paper *Potential and challenges for NGOs in mainstreaming conflict prevention* (2001) that mainstreaming conflict prevention is easier said than done. How far should this issue be incorporated into the agency's thinking and practice? And how far should the mainstreaming be extended? Should development NGOs change into peace-building organizations as well? The authors argue that NGOs should indeed try to tackle the roots of the conflict, by working 'on' conflict, but also that they should develop a linkage between the conflict and their work, i.e. develop a conflict sensitive approach, or learn to work 'in' conflict (see Table 1).

However, Lewer and Goodhand warn that, when deciding to expand their mandates, NGOs should guard against exceeding their responsibility and engaging themselves in the conflict dynamics as such. This warning is coupled with a second caution: before policymakers decide on the actual agenda of development NGOs, the voices of those actually engaged in the conflict should be heard. What are the experiences of and views on the conflict reality they are faced with in their every day lives?

Table 1

Approach	Working around conflict	Working in conflict	Working on conflict
Assumptions	• Conflict is a 'disruptive factor' over which little influence can be exercised • Development programs can continue without being negatively affected by the conflict	• Development programs can be negatively affected by, an have a negative impact on the dynamics of conflict	• Development programs can exploit opportunities to positively affect the dynamics of conflict
Strategy	• Withdraw from or keep out of conflict affected areas • Continue to work in low-risk areas on mainstream development activities	• Reactive adjustments are made to programs in medium and high-risk areas • Improve security management • Greater focus on 'positioning', i.e. neutrality and impartiality • Cut back on high input programs	• Refocus programs onto the root causes of the conflict, e.g. governance, poverty alleviation, social exclusion • Attempt to influence the incentives for peace and disincentives for violence • Focus on protection of human rights

Source: DFID Guide to Conflict Assessment: Third Draft (internal document), J. Goodhand, London, DFID, 2001, p. 21

A number of agencies and programs have been experimenting with new approaches. These include Oxfam GB in Sri Lanka and NCA in Mali (see boxes). At the organizational level agencies have implemented re-skilling through training workshops, co-operated with research programs, and undergone re-alignments of aims and objectives. It has been shown that introducing peace-building elements into daily practice can be achieved in two ways:
• Top-down efforts: identified by headquarters and then disseminated downwards (like Oxfam GB identifying conflict reduction as a regional strategic change objective);
• Bottom-up efforts: identified by people in the field - pressure from below, based on experience, working with local partners and consultation with beneficiaries.
The most effective way of mainstreaming conflict prevention into aid and relief work involves a combination of top-down and bottom-up efforts, conclude Goodhand and Lewer.

Ongoing NGO experience shows that they have tried to mainstream the issue of peacebuilding by:
- adding it to the management responsibilities of the staff
- appointing conflict advisors
- forming a special conflict unit
- investing in training and capacity-building of staff.

Box 4 **Preliminary NGO checklist**

Development and relief NGOs planning to incorporate peacebuilding and conflict prevention into their programs need a perspective and determination which:
- regards conflict and peace as multi-factorial dynamic processes, often moving in and out of phases of peace and violence, and with actors who change over time. This means conflict is not linear and predictable.
- whilst seeing particular conflicts as unique and specific, looks at the experience of other violent situations and learns from peacebuilding and conflict resolution attempts in those places. A mix of appropriate 'Western', and 'non-Western' methods should be utilized, wherever possible incorporating local and traditional conflict resolution and peacemaking processes.
- gives equal importance to relational influences as well as structural factors of conflict when designing programs (especially psychological, social and cultural factors).
- incorporates in-depth surveying, analysis and understanding of the social fabric and relationships within a community where a 'peace' related program is planned. Ensure that the disadvantages do not outweigh the benefits of such an intervention.
- engages and involves local people at the beginning of CP mainstreaming peace-building projects and program design, and identifies indigenous sources of social energy and leadership.
- ensures that interventions are contingent and complementary with other official and non-official initiatives. Co-operative and co-ordination mechanisms should be established, and peace-building networks supported.
- is clear about 'normative views' of society, about positions on human rights and justice, and encourages discussion of possible tensions between advocacy work and 'peace' related work like conflict resolution and peace-building programs.
- trains and prepares their staff and those of their partners in non-violent conflict resolution methods and techniques appropriate to local conditions (an elicitive approach).
- views peacebuilding as a long-term process. This has implications both for funding and longitudinal research and evaluation plans.
- is not afraid to take an eclectic approach, and draw freely on different disciplines. Building peace requires creative thinking and a need to break out of rigid conceptual and theoretical frameworks.

Original source: International Non-Government Organizations and Peacebuilding - Perspectives from Peace Studies and Conflict Resolution, by Nick Lewer. Working Paper No. 3, Centre for Conflict Resolution, Department of Peace Studies, University of Bradford, October 1999.

Based on these early experiences, Lewer and Goodhand developed a preliminary NGO checklist for development and relief NGOs planning to incorporate peacebuilding and conflict prevention into their programs (box 4). They also stipulate however that these are still early days - there are few tools and models for the operationalization of mainstreaming. "A strong theoretical and practical base for NGO mainstreaming does not yet exist."

Towards a Strategic Framework for Peacebuilding

This lack of tools and models is confirmed by the experiences of several organizations which have already been through the process of expanding their humanitarian mandate. "We came to the conclusion that there is no single strategy for doing this," says Jane Backhurst of World Vision. "The capacities for peace lie in the continuum of relief - development - rehabilitation. So, peacebuilding is not an add-on. Rather, it means we need to look at our work from a certain perspective: then we can incorporate peacebuilding."

"Having principles is one thing, but actually applying them is another story," adds Jacco Cilliers of Catholic Relief Services. His organization first formulated its principles and lessons learned in the field of peacebuilding back in 1996, but it still finds it difficult to integrate these into its daily practice. "The formulation of these principles challenged us to deepen our understanding of the root causes of the situations in which we work. For many CRS staff who work in the midst of violent conflict situations however, this takes them only so far. It does not provide a comprehensive framework that can effectively channel agency energy and resources towards what is most needed and desired by those whom we serve: the right to peace."

Peacebuilding is not new to the CRS (see box 5). However, these activities have been carried out in an ad hoc fashion with little cross-regional and cross-agency exchanges and benefit, according to Cilliers. "A common agency-wide approach based on a peace-building strategic framework would draw disparate activities into a comprehensive whole and provide a peace-building identity for the agency."

According to Cilliers, conceptual shift in the CRS's humanitarian action to one of peacebuilding requires first and foremost "increased attention to and investment in humanitarian action in general. Humanitarian crises will not go away in the years to come, and the potential for them to become even more complex is real. If CRS intends to continue to work in humanitarian crisis environments, then we must increase agency attention to such action. We suggest that CRS needs a structure that can effectively link the actions needed for the immediate response with the longer-term activities that could contribute to peace."

Box 5 **Norwegian Church Aid: Extending the humanitarian mandate**

The Norwegian government encouraged the inclusion of peacebuilding in the policy making of development NGOs after it broadened its own focus on conflict prevention. One reason for this, according to Stein-Erik Horjen of Norwegian Church Aid (NCA), is the limited resources the Norwegian government has available for this field of policy. "There are only a few people in my country working in this field. So we need to be creative and co-operate, government and NGOs."

The NCA incorporated peace-building activities into its mission statement. For this purpose, a special Department of Policy and Human Rights was established within the organization in 1999. The NCA's involvement in this field grew 'organically' out of its long-term commitment to the development of the areas where it worked.

The NCA' s approach to peace work can be best seen in its involvement in Mali. When a violent rebellion broke out in the 1990s, the NCA (which had already been active in the area for several years) decided to stay although most other agencies left. After the tragic death of five NCA employees who were accused of partiality, an NCA representative decided to use official means in order to re-establish the role of the NCA. He started diplomatic talks with government representatives while at the same time other NCA people set up unofficial and informal dialogues with the main actors in the conflict. Slowly and carefully people were also brought together in more local settings. The purpose of these meetings was to encourage local communities to establish immediate practical and transparent methods for resolving local inter-group conflicts without violence. More than 37 such meetings were held, most of them with positive outcomes.

According to Horjen, the reason why the NCA has been able to set up successful peace-building activities alongside its development projects is primarily the high degree of mutual trust between NCA staff and local people and politicians. Also, concrete and visible development work has given the NCA a positive image of really taking care of the people's material welfare. Another reason for its success identified by the NCA-staff is their church-based identity. Horjen: "Churches can play a significant role in organizing negotiations, a role governments mostly can't play."

Individuals in field sites give other interesting explanations why they were able to put so much trust in the work and approach of the NCA. Local people felt they still owned the process entirely as the NCA did not lead, only facilitated the peace-building initiatives. They provided first class tickets for people who, at the invitation of the Norwegian government, held negotiations in Norway. In providing these 'frames' for peacebuilding, people from conflict areas felt they were taken seriously which encouraged them to continue their dialogues and efforts to seek solutions to the conflicts.

Horjen: "I feel that the NCA has successfully extended its humanitarian mandate. It has done this not by losing its commitment to providing basic support to people affected by war, but by creating ways and means to provide peaceful long-term solutions to the conflict context as well."

Box 6   *Peacebuilding Activities of the CRS*

- In Rwanda the 'Peacebuilding among Rwandan Youth Project' aims to establish an environment conducive to national reconciliation. The project targets 26,000 young people and promotes peacebuilding through peace education in schools and solidarity camps.
- In Mindanao, the CRS is supporting a Philippines Bishops-Ulama dialogue forum that encourages inter-religious dialogue between Christians and Muslim leaders. Local NGOs are also supported to promote 'a culture of peace' through various workshops and activities. The Mindanao Peacebuilding Institute also offered courses in peacebuilding to participants from Southeast and South Asia.
- In Colombia, the CRS and Colombian church representatives are working together to support and strengthen US/Colombian Church collaboration and create greater awareness of the conflict. They also support advocacy on US/international policies, which supports peace processes.
- In Croatia, trauma assistance or response training has been provided for doctors, teachers, attorneys and social workers.
- In Pakistan, inter-religious seminars and workshops support exchanges on the social teachings of Islam and Christianity on forgiveness, peacebuilding and reconciliation.
- In Jerusalem, West Bank and Gaza, the CRS supports organizations that focus on conflict resolution, domestic violence and the promotion of interfaith dialogue as well as summer camps and an 'open house' where religious groups can meet and socialize together.

In order to achieve this organizational transformation, the authors say, the CRS must be structured in a way that both maximizes the agency's existing capacities and creates new capacities. "Adopting a peace-building strategic framework for CRS's work in complex emergencies requires the capacity to think strategically on an agency-wide basis, to develop strategies that cut across HQ departments, and link HQ with field programs and other organizations. Moreover, a true commitment to peacebuilding means that CRS will strategically invest resources to empower communities to transform their conflict situations. Strategies must be developed to target funding and strengthen local peace-building initiatives at all levels to ensure they can be supported and sustained over time."

Coupled to these organizational changes, the boundaries of what the organization does in complex emergencies should be pushed. Assistance - the organization's primary focus - is only one of many activities that can be understood as contributing to peacebuilding. Cilliers: "A new agency-wide approach to conflict should however not only include assistance activities on the ground, but peace-building activities in the wider context, including protection, advocacy, lobbying, conflict transformation, reconciliation, information sharing, dialogue and policymaking."

Donor Education as a Key Element

Many of the suggestions made for an effective extension of the CRS's humanitarian mandate were also heard during the several workshops and plenary debates at the Soesterberg conference related to the issue of aid and conflict. One element specifically stressed in a workshop organized by VOICE, Voluntary Organizations in Cooperation in Emergencies (the largest humanitarian network in Europe), was the different positions of development and emergency organizations. VOICE's Jennifer Tangney observed that, "as development NGOs have largely taken aspects of peacebuilding on board, the pressure is now on humanitarian NGOs to seriously examine the potential in their sector for such undertakings." There is great interest in the promotion of a continuum between emergency and development, Tangney stressed, so at the very least, humanitarian NGOs must evaluate the work of development NGOs and analyze the potential to adopt suitable aspects of their policy in favor of peacebuilding. Nevertheless, she stressed, "one must always bear in mind the special nature of humanitarian aid whose over-riding aim is that of lifesaving and primary aid in emergency situations. There may well be difficulties in adapting the approach being taken by the development sector in the humanitarian field." However, Tangney says, the need for a reasonably integrated approach is beyond question given the close links between the work of both sectors.

There was remarkable consensus on the proposition that humanitarian (and still many development) organizations no longer have any excuse to continue in their old course, no matter how difficult implementing a peace strategy in their work might be. One excuse commonly heard is that the time constraints under which many humanitarian NGOs operate reduce their ability to plan conflict strategies. This is no longer acceptable, said Gianni Rufini, director of the Italian NGO Intersos: "Humanitarian aid is commonly operating in conflict theatres and therefore must take its impact into account. The majority of contemporary conflicts are predictable."

Apart from the pressure for a fast response, there are other, more decisive factors hampering humanitarian NGOs from including peacebuilding in the planning and projects, it was concluded in a workshop on Humanitarian Aid and Peacebuilding. The big challenge for many organizations is to build in long-term thinking. It's a slow process, many participants stressed, getting engaged in peacebuilding means thinking a decade ahead. Apart from the inevitable internal problems this involves, the big problem is how to get funding for this slow process of change. In addition, conflicts can also change over time, so the work of relief and development organizations must change as well. Again, this is difficult to explain to donors.

The lack of financial resources in terms of staff and training etc. makes it difficult to undertake appropriate action and this seems to be a crucial factor. More funding is also needed for better evaluation, Wolfgang Heinrich of the Collaborative for Development Action argued. "Our work can be more effective if we can learn from our own experience. However, there is not enough financial support available for these evaluation practices."

Donor education was seen as the key element in the introduction of peacebuilding aspects to humanitarian aid and ensuring that aid is "responsible". Just 0.5 per cent of ECHO (the humanitarian relief organization of the European Union) funding is earmarked for training of humanitarian personnel. This is despite calls from ECHO for improved quality of staff. It reflects the difficulty that NGOs face when attempting to increase staff capacity, as funding for such activities is extremely restricted.

Consequently, it was recommended that humanitarian NGOs need to become more articulate in explaining to donors why peacebuilding should be included in programs and the types of training, which may be appropriate. Moreover, it was recognized that behind the donors are politicians who influence donor policy. Political lobbying and advocacy need to be undertaken by these NGOs in a more coherent, cohesive fashion to ensure that the necessary changes are made at the donor level. Therefore, the working group recommended:

- Better inter-NGO communication to recognize shared needs;
- Political advocacy as a means of influencing donor policy;
- Public awareness campaigns regarding conflict and humanitarian aid - to raise public support for the inclusion of longer-term goals in relief contexts;
- Donor education about the importance of peace-building activities for the impact of the aid, staff security, Linking Relief, Reconstruction and Development (LRRD), etc.;
- Finally, it was agreed by all, that the most practical step to be undertaken at present was to ensure that field workers and HQ personnel receive conflict training, as without the tools to recognize the factors feeding a conflict, or an awareness of the potential impact of their action, it is impossible to discuss in a real sense the inclusion of peacebuilding efforts in humanitarian aid. This point is intrinsically linked to all of the above points as it relies on a dispensation in favor of peacebuilding, funding, donor policy etc. Without support, humanitarian NGOs will not be able to take even this most basic step.

Local Ownership

Another crucial condition for successfully integrating peace-stimulating elements into the humanitarian field that was frequently emphasized at the Soesterberg conference is the need to build peace from the inside. As the CDA's Wolfgang Heinrich said: "There are always local capacities for peace. We should work as facilitators of change."

Emmanuel Bombande, West African Network for Peacebuilding, Ghana, conference facilitator

Before policymakers decide on the actual agenda of development NGOs, the voices of those actually engaged in the conflict should be heard. What are the experiences and views on the conflict reality they are faced with in their every day lives? And what is their view on engaging development NGOs in the peacebuilding activities?

Pierre Barampenda, who gave a presentation on the ways his organization, ActionAid UK in Burundi, implemented peace-building aspects in their humanitarian work, illustrated this. His principal message was that the use of local capacities (academics, specialists, workers etc.), local methodologies and local participation are linchpins to peace-building efforts. This way, the tendency towards paternalistic practices by western humanitarian NGOs can be addressed.

Emmanuel Bombande of the West Africa Network also stressed this point for Peacebuilding (WANEP), saying that on too many occasions, Western concepts of intervention have tended to weaken capacities for peacebuilding in Africa rather than strengthen them. "Every time a form of intervention fails to recognize the existing local capacities for peace, the programs of intervention are short lived. Within the African worldview, intervention from outside to resolve conflict is understood as imposed, even if there is tolerance and receptivity towards the interveners," Bombande explains. "Secondly, outside intervention that does not take into account critical partnerships that build and enhance capacity at local levels does not offer space for communities to become their own peacemakers and thereby consolidate their own culture of peace. Outside intervention that is imposed subtly encourages communities to consume alien cultures, which feeds into new conflicts."

Box 7 **Stories from the Field**

'During election monitoring missions in Africa, I witnessed many incidents: the young female observer from a European country who was arrested by local authorities because she was wearing a miniskirt, for example. And there was the case of another observer, who was unable to figure out why he never received proper information from the local communities about threats to members of opposition groups. However, it emerged that he always asked people in public whether they had had any problems with the ruling party, so that it was hardly surprising that nobody told him anything. During an internal debriefing, he heard about the interviewing techniques of other colleagues and was astonished how they knew about these methods. When asked, some told him that they had simply handled the situation with common sense, while others conceded that they had gone through extensive training.'

Source: Peacebuilding - A Field Guide, edited by Luc Reichler and Thania Paffenholz, Lynne Rienner Publishers, Boulder/London, 1999

The Field Diplomacy Initiative in Belgium published a book by Luc Reichler and Thania Paffenholz, *Peacebuilding - A Field Guide*, which, in its second section - Working in the Field - reflects on the challenge of linking aid and peacebuilding. It covers such issues as community mobilization, enhancing the local capacity for peace and the use of participatory action-oriented research. In his article, Vivien Erasmus describes how the efficiency of aid delivery could be hugely improved by involving the local communities in decision-making and project planning.

Thania Paffenholz describes the need for organizations to look for as many local actors as possible. "While working in Somalia I found that external actors, be it aid or conflict resolution organizations, tended mostly to involve the local actors that were familiar to them. Many aid organizations involved only the community chiefs, while most conflict resolution NGOs involved the local human rights or peace activists in their work. Neither involved for instance the business community. And yet, if one talked to the business people themselves, a very different perspective emerged. They as a group were closely involved in rebuilding Somali society, and as such had a stake in development and peace. This potential however, was never explored by the external actors."

Box 8 **ActionAid's Perspectives on the Prevention of Conflict, Humanitarian Aid and Development**

1. Understanding the background causes of a conflict including those which are difficult to resolve such as: historical context, prejudices, action and behaviour.
2. Identification and recognition of local institutions which have a traditional role in the peaceful resolution of conflict, the reestablishment of respect and good governance.
3. Understanding the effects of conflict on social relations between populations, including women, children and the poor. The interactions between, for example, parents, students and teachers are vital to respond efficiently to needs.
4. Integrative and participatory approaches are important to understand future orientation. Firstly, one must work with separate groups such as men, women, the poor, in order to allow them to express themselves and to develop confidence.
5. The founding of organisations through the linking of populations based on an awareness of their rights, responsibility for their social protection and support with a view to recovering their previous family life.
6. The creation of space for expression to allow the population to articulate and to make itself heard is a key element to the resolution of conflicts. This could be done through national or regional peace talks, or at regular intervals within communities or groups.

Source: Peacebuilding in Africa, Case Studies from ActionAid

Hans van de Veen is a free lance journalist based in The Netherlands

The European Centre for Conflict Prevention would like to continue facilitating the debate on aid and conflict through collecting and disseminating publications and reports on this issue. Therefore, if you have any ideas or suggestions, please contact us at info@conflict-prevention.net

Literature

Anderson, Mary B.: *Options for Aid in Conflict - Lessons from Field Experiences*. Local Capacities for Peace project/Collaborative for Development Action, Cambridge, USA, 2000.

Bouta, Tsjeard and Georg Frerks: *The Role of SNV in Development Countries in Internal Armed Conflict*. Netherlands Institute of International Relations 'Clingendael'. The Hague, 2001.

Goodhand, Jonathan and David Hulme: *Peace Building and Complex Emergencies*. Working Paper Series, Paper no. 12. Final report to the Department for International Development, IDPM, University of Manchester, March 2000.

Goodhand, Jonathan and Nick Lewer: *Potential and Challenges for NGOs in Mainstreaming Conflict Prevention*. Bradford University. Unpublished paper.

Oxfam in Sri Lanka: Operationalising Conflict Reduction and Peacebuilding. Paper in the Working Paper Series, Centre for Conflict Resolution, Department of Peace Studies, University of Bradford, UK (http://www.bradford.ac.uk)

Lewer, Nick: International Non-Government Organizations and Peacebuilding - Perspectives from Peace Studies and Conflict Resolution. Working Paper No. 3, Centre for Conflict Resolution, Department of Peace Studies, University of Bradford, October 1999.

Reichler, Luc and Tania Paffenholz: *Peacebuilding - A Field Guide*. The Field Diplomacy Initiative, Belgium.

Reilly, Annemarie and Jacco Cilliers: Champions for Peace - The Role of CRS in Times of Violent Conflict? A paper written for the CRS World Summit.

Uvin, Peter: The Influence of Aid in Situations of Violent Conflict. OECD/DAC Informal Task Force on Conflict, Peace and Development Co-operation, Paris, September 1999.

Further Reading

InterAction is a coalition of more than 165 US-based relief, development, environmental and refugee agencies working in over one hundred countries around the world. The following executive summary is taken from one of the Disaster Response Committee's reports: *Development Relief: NGO Efforts to Promote Sustainable Peace and Development in Complex Humanitarian Emergencies, by Kimberly Mancino, Anita Malley and Santiago Cornejo, June 2001.* This report was prepared for InterAction's Transition Working Group which aims to facilitate and steer the debate on aid and conflict within InterAction's member organizations. The report provides an overview of NGO's current practices in developmental relief, including values, principles, and activities, as well as issues and challenges. The full report is available on: http://www.interaction.org/disaster/index.html

Development Relief

NGO Efforts to Promote Sustainable Peace and Development in Complex Humanitarian Emergencies

Many humanitarian and development organizations are striving to implement relief activities in ways that, in addition to addressing immediate needs, also contribute to sustainable development and peace. This type of programming is referred to as developmental relief. The Transition Working Group of InterAction commissioned this report to provide an overview of NGOs' current practices in develop-mental relief, including values, principles, and activities, as well as to identify issues and challenges facing NGOs in this area. The focus on current practices is an acknowledgement that these activities are not yet well enough understood for best practices to be identified. The information contained in this report was gathered in interviews conducted with nine NGOs between February and April 2001, as well as taken from reports, program summaries, and other documentation provided by the organizations interviewed.

Approaches, Values, and Principles in Developmental Relief
Developmental relief is a response to the need felt by NGOs to address not only the symptoms of com-plex humanitarian emergencies (CHEs), but their root causes as well. NGOs are implementing a variety of changes to improve their emergency response, including using new frameworks to analyze the causes of emergencies, pursuing new activities such as psychosocial and peacebuilding programs, and even fundamentally redefining their role in

emergency response. NGO approaches to developmental relief are unique to each organization and are closely tied to reach organization's core values and beliefs. Despite these differences, NGOs share a common set of values and principles that inform their developmental relief activities. One principle is that emergency response should be holistic, analyzing and addressing the root causes of conflict. Several NGOs use the Do No Harm approach and Local Capacities for Peace framework in their relief activities. Justice, peace, and reconciliation are other important values, as is the ability to work with all parties to a conflict. NGOs also emphasize the need for sustainable and contextual activities and accountability to beneficiaries, as well as empowerment of those affected by emergencies. Many organizations also call for long-term planning and goal-setting at the outset of emergency response.

Developmental Relief Activities

The NGOs interviewed for this study are engaged in a variety of developmental relief activities, organized here according to three broad categories of objectives:
1. strengthening local participation, capacity, and civil society;
2. economic and agricultural revitalization, and
3. peacebuilding and reconciliation.

All of the NGOs interviewed stressed the importance of local participation in program planning, implementation, and evaluation; capacity building; and strengthening civil society institutions. The emphasis on local participation acknowledges that if emergency response aims to lay the groundwork for sustainable development, NGOs must foster a sense of community ownership of the activities. NGOs are increasingly relying on local organizations to implement programs and are building local capacity. Recognizing the importance of an effective civil society to move communities from conflict to peace and development, NGOs also work to strengthen civil society associations and institutions that promote the interests of the community as a whole.

Economic and agricultural programs are seen as motors for economic revitalization and important mechanisms by which to guarantee livelihoods and hasten a community's return to normalcy. Such programs recognize the importance of productive activity to the individual's and the community's self interest; they are also viewed as a means of drawing divided communities into mutually beneficial activities and promoting group interdependence.

Peacebuilding and reconciliation activities are a relatively new focus for humanitarian assistance NGOs attempting to address ethnic, religious, and other tensions that underlie conflicts. These may be stand-alone programs or components of other programs, and are directed at both individuals and groups. Some programs do not have explicit peacebuilding or reconciliation components but are designed in ways that implicitly promote interaction, collaboration, and interdependence among groups in conflict. NGOs are increasing their awareness of how relief can hinder or promote peace and how it may cause harm as well as yield benefits.

Evaluating Developmental Relief Activities

Evaluating the developmental relief activities described in this report presents difficulties for the NGOs. Because the objectives of developmental relief activities are focused on long-term, qualitative change, NGOs are challenged to find appropriate indicators of such social impacts as empowerment, institution building, and conflict resolution. NGOs working in emergency response are used to dealing with quantitative measures, but indicators for developmental relief activities need to be more qualitative in order to detect behavioral and attitudinal change. While NGOs are very interested in and committed to identifying appropriate indicators and developing evaluation methods for these activities, much work remains to be done in this area.

Issues and Challenges in Developmental Relief

NGOs have identified a number of important issues and challenges in implementing developmental relief activities. Several challenges stem from the difficulties of promoting long-term, sustainable change in volatile situations and of balancing long-term goals with immediate needs. Activities that address the root causes of conflict through advocacy, peacebuilding, and reconciliation can be very sensitive, and NGOs must be mindful of how they present themselves and their objectives. Developmental relief activities may also present challenges for humanitarian NGOs striving to maintain impartiality and neutrality; in fact, NGOs differ in their views on the appropriateness of neutrality within a developmental relief approach. Beneficiary participation and local partnerships can pose other challenges, as NGOs must expend more energy on capacity building and gathering local input. NGOs also recognize the importance of ensuring that local partners are accountable and that they pro-mote peace rather than division within the community. Other challenges stem from resistance NGOs encounter within their own organizations from staff who feel uncomfortable with or threatened by a developmental approach to relief activities.

Funding for Developmental Relief

Several funding issues constrain NGO efforts to promote sustainable peace and development within their emergency response activities. Most NGOs interviewed noted that the structure and availability of funding from multilateral and bilateral agencies are major hindrances to developmental relief pro-grams. Consequently, many NGOs partially rely on private funds for these types of activities. Several different funding difficulties were identified, including the separation of relief and development funds, inflexible funds, and overly technical, donor-driven approaches. NGOs are advocating for changes in funding structures in order to better support developmental relief programming.

Catholic Relief Services is a large aid agency, based in the United States. The agency has addressed the linkage between aid and conflict by developing several peacebuilding programs in its projects all over the world. For CRS peacebuilding involves a holistic approach to programming that addresses and transforms the root causes of violent conflict. It includes the processes, interventions, strategies and methods used by CRS and its partners to promote a peace that is just. The following sixteen categories of activities give an overview on how CRS has implemented peacebuilding in its original mandate. Also available on line: http://www.catholicrelief.org/what/overseas/peace/index.cfm

Catholic Relief Services
Sixteen Categories of Peacebuilding Activities

1. Peacebuilding through Education, Training and Workshops
Catholic Relief Services' country programs engage in a variety of educational activities that contribute to building long-term peace. These programs range from strengthening the capacities of local organizations as part of building up a healthy civil society, to providing educational resources on peace, conflict management, justice and reconciliation, to establishing longer term educational facilities. In the summer of 2000, CRS and Eastern Mennonite University cosponsored a regional peace institute on the southern Philippine island of Mindanao. This way local peacebuilders' skills, knowledge base and networks can be increased.

2. Peacebuilding through Prevention and Early Warning
Catholic Relief Services engages in strengthening civil society through capacity building programs with community groups and non-governmental organizations, as mentioned above, as well as through improving living conditions around the globe. Both of these activities can be helpful in addressing some of the underlying causes of conflict that may lead to violence. In Morocco, CRS programs are taking an additional approach to preventing violent conflict by incorporating conflict resolution into all programming areas.

3. Institutionalized Peacebuilding and Peace and Justice Commissions
Catholic Relief Services has a long history of working with the local Catholic Church in numerous countries by supporting local Peace and Justice

Commissions. These Commissions provide one type of institutional base for activities that promote both peace and justice. An example of work being pursued by these commissions is the "East Timor Peace, Reconciliation and Dialogue Initiative." Through this initiative, CRS works with the Peace and Justice Commissions of the East Timorese Dioceses of Dili and Bacau and helps support twelve local non-governmental organizations in their peacebuilding and reconciliation efforts. A second example is CRS' work with the regional Peace and Justice Commission of Zimbabwe that seeks to promote peace and justice issues at the national level.

Catholic Relief Services also assists numerous institutions that are not affiliated with the Catholic Church. For example, agency staff in Albania work with the Albanian Peace and Justice Center in assisting families involved in disputes. In nearby Macedonia, CRS supports local non-governmental organizations like the Center for Multi-Cultural Understanding and Cooperation, which is involved in pursuing interethnic dialogues to help improve interethnic relations.

4. Women and Peacebuilding

Catholic Relief Services also works with women who are often marginalized by formal political systems and affected by violent conflicts in unique ways. In Bosnia-Herzegovina CRS' micro-enterprise and agricultural projects focus specifically on providing women with business opportunities, which involve building cooperatives across ethnic group lines. In Cambodia , the agency supported women's rights and democracy training programs as one way of helping to empower women. Also, see the example of Liberia in Peacebuilding through Trauma Healing and Psychosocial Work for another way the CRS works with women in peacebuilding.

5. Security and Peacebuilding

In 2000, Catholic Relief Services engaged in advocacy to support a cessation of hostilities in Sierra Leone, where the agency has a long history of involvement. In addition to more traditional development programs, CRS also engaged in a pilot reconciliation and healing program in 1995 in Sierra Leone.

6. Peacebuilding through Inter-Religious Dialogue

Catholic Relief Services actively supports inter-religious dialogue in a number of countries as a natural outgrowth of its Catholic identity and involvement with local and national Church bodies. For example, in the Mindanao region of the Philippines CRS works with the Bishops-Ulama dialogue forum, encouraging dialogue between high-level Christian and Muslim leaders. In Pakistan , CRS supported inter-religious dialogues in the districts of Rawalpindi, Gujrat, and Lahore, as well as seminars emphasizing the social teachings of Islam and Christianity to promote messages of forgiveness, peacebuilding and reconciliation. CRS Pakistan also sponsored a millennial inter-faith peace walk. In Cameroon, the agency supports a local Ecumenical

Service for Peace, which offers programs in citizen education, conflict resolution and peacebuilding.

7. Peacebuilding through Business and Micro-enterprise Development

Sustainability is not only a hallmark of good development work, but also a hallmark of good peacebuilding. For example, in addition to its cooperatives work in Bosnia-Herzegovina (mentioned in the Women and Peacebuilding) CRS supports multi-ethnic village banking projects to develop new business opportunities that will help rebuild the war-torn country which continues to suffer from high unemployment. Inter-communal development programs in The Philippines, such as the Myramville village bakery project, provide opportunities for interfaith interaction as well as livelihoods. Business development programming in Peru includes a focus on incorporating conflict resolution into business practices and management styles. In Macedonia, many of the community banks that CRS works with have developed a mix of people including ethnic Roma, Albanian and Macedonian members, even during the recent Kosovo crisis.

8. Peacebuilding through Media and Communications

A major part of Catholic Relief Services' campaign to achieve security in Sierra Leone involved an advocacy campaign in the US media that focused on limiting the negative perceptions and media coverage of Sierra Leone's war and encouraged actions to limit the impact of the conflict.

9. Peacebuilding through Development and Reconstruction

Destroyed buildings and infrastructures are very visible signs and outcomes of war. Reconstructing them is a natural part of Catholic Relief Services' development programming in countries such as Burundi, Yugoslavia and Bosnia-Herzegovina. In these communities, CRS strives to work with groups across traditional conflict lines. For example, in Bosnia-Herzegovina, reconstruction programming has very carefully involved multi-ethnic participation through Community Working Groups, who help identify program priorities and participants from their respective communities.

10. Peacebuilding through Advocacy and Citizen Diplomacy

Catholic Relief Services engages in advocating for better relations between citizens of countries often viewed as antagonistic to the United States.

- For example, the agency's work in strengthening the capacities of local non-governmental organizations in parts of Iran is viewed as a gesture of goodwill and symbol of hope for future inter-religious dialogue, as well as international dialogue.
- Catholic Relief Services' activities in North Korea are viewed similarly as bridge-building enterprises.
- The agency promotes more active dialogue in Vietnam between U.S. and Vietnamese representatives, engaging with church and government representatives.

- Catholic Relief Services supports citizen advocacy in Egypt.
- The agency also promotes an annual anti-violence advocacy campaign in the U.S..

11. Peacebuilding through Advocacy and Citizen Diplomacy

... The positive role played by mediation and pacification agencies should be extended to the non-governmental humanitarian organizations and religious bodies ... [to] promote peace between opposed groups and help to overcome age-old rivalries, reconcile enemies, and open the way to a new and shared future...
(Message of His Holiness Pope John Paul II on the occasion of World Day of Peace, January 1, 2000)

Given the close relationship that Catholic Relief Services has with the United States Conference of Catholic bishops and its access to Catholic church leaders internationally, the agency is often able to support the peacebuilding activities of these leaders. An excellent example is the work that CRS is doing with representatives of the Colombian church. Together, they are generating awareness and support for Colombia's negotiated peace processes within the U.S. government and public. A second example is a meeting the agency helped sponsor in 2000 that brought bishops and religious leaders from Central America and Africa together in Mauritius to initiate a south-south dialogue on conflict resolution. Other countries that CRS is engaged in some degree of higher-level diplomacy and advocacy work with include Cuba and Nigeria .

12. Peacebuilding and Research

In order to ensure quality peacebuilding programs, Catholic Relief Services believes it is important to engage in research as well. Some of the research projects the agency is engaged in include CRS Justice Case Studies, Local Capacities for Peace Project, and Reflections on Peace Practice Project. CRS' country programs involved in this research include Gambia, Liberia, Bosnia-Herzegovina and the Philippines.

13. Peacebuilding through Intervention Roles

While Catholic Relief Services staff are often in positions to mediate and facilitate inter-ethnic engagement, this activity is often not documented or traditionally considered part of CRS programs. However, some examples are emerging. For example, CRS, in cooperation with the National Conference of Bishops in Burundi, supported the work of local committees promoting peace through mutual acceptance.

14. Peacebuilding through Trauma Healing and Psychosocial Work

In addition to the visible destruction caused by war and violence, considerable invisible damage is done to people who lived through it. In Bosnia-Herzegovina and Croatia, CRS has helped develop and support psychosocial work on trauma awareness and response through training and education. These programs often complement the other development work that CRS is doing in communities. In Liberia, the agency supported an innovative project that focused on the effects of war and violence on women, such as rape, physical violence and widows as single heads of households. Trauma healing workshops that involved traditional midwives and local stories, songs and folktales helped women discuss the impact of violence and develop strategies to reduce future violence and rebuild trust in Liberia.

15. Peacebuilding through Demobilization
Once a formal political agreement is negotiated, demobilizing armed groups is a very difficult task. In 1995, Catholic Relief Services engaged in a project to help demobilize the ULIMO Liberian rebel forces in Sierra Leone, which had mixed results. This is an area of peacebuilding that continues to be difficult for CRS and other agencies.

16. Emergency Response, Post-conflict Reconstruction and Peacebuilding
Peacebuilding is often viewed as irrelevant in the immediate, short-term response to emergencies where the most important goal is to keep people alive. However, Catholic Relief Services has found there are ways to begin laying the seeds for long-term peace even in these crucial times. For example, in Bosnia-Herzegovina, Catholic Relief Services began working at interfaith cooperation during the war by working with Orthodox, Muslim, Jewish and Catholic organizations in emergency relief efforts. Similarly, in Indonesia, the agency worked with the Central Java Inter-faith Emergency Program on emergency assistance. CRS also provided staff dealing with refugees from East Timor with education on conflict resolution to help in their day-to-day activities and conflicts occurring within the camp.

Selected Literature and Reports

The bibliographies of previous chapters already provided lists of literature referring to specific issues and topics. The purpose of this list is to give further information on recent publications dealing with the broad issue of lessons learned on peacebuilding and conflict prevention. It is not inclusive or complete. Its aim is to furnish some examples of initiatives taken by donors, governmental institutions, NGOs and other actors working in the field of conflict prevention and peace building, reflecting on their policies and work in order to bring coherence to their activities and gain knowledge on the impact of their work.

Lessons Learned and Evaluation Practices

The Oxford Research Group (United Kingdom) published 50 stories of people and organizations who have initiated successful attempts to resolve conflict. The stories range from situations of latent violence, to actual violence and post-violence. The actual costs of the projects are given, demonstrating the relatively cheap price of 'peace'. The stories also show just how powerful non-violence can be.
War Prevention Works: 50 stories of people resolving conflict, by Dylan Matthews, Oxford Research Group, 2001.
For more information: http://www.oxfordresearchgroup.org.uk

The Conflict Prevention Network's Yearbook 1999/2000 aims to grasp the impact of the conflict prevention policies of the European Union. It is an interesting reflection on how projects and policies designed at governmental levels actually work on the ground. It further discusses the practice of Conflict Impact Assessment.
The Impact of Conflict Prevention Policy; Cases, Measures and Assessments, edited by Michael Lund and Guenola Rasamoelina, Nomos Verlagsgesellschaft, Baden-Baden, 2000
For more information: http://www.swp-berlin.org/cpn

The European Centre for Conflict Prevention collected 35 inspiring stories of people building peace. The stories are drawn from different actors including women, business, media and churches. The stories demonstrate the great potential of multi-track diplomacy, showing that people of all ranks in society can play a positive role in working towards peace.
People Building Peace, 25 Inspiring Stories from Around the World, A publication of the European Centre for Conflict Prevention in co-operation with IFOR and the Coexistence Initiative of State of the World Forum, 1999
For more information: http://www.conflict-prevention.net

Conflict-Sensitive Approaches to Development: A Review of Practice, published by Saferworld, International Alert and the International Development Research Centre, gives an elaborate overview of possible tools

and approaches for development organizations working in conflict situations. It introduces the Peace and Conflict Impact Assessment (PCIA) methodologies by explaining the different tools and approaches that have been developed over recent years. An especially clear overview of existing frameworks, indicating their weaknesses and strengths is to be found in one of the report's appendices. (see also part 2)
Conflict-Sensitive Approaches to Development: A Review of Practice, by Cynthia Gaigels with Manuela Leonhardt, 2001.
For more information: http://www.international-alert.org

The Nairobi Peace Initiative-Africa, Kenya held an action-reflection seminar on the peace-building activities of their own organization and the National Council of Churches (Kenya) in 1999. The aim was to create a forum for peace-workers to discuss the development of a framework and responsive tools for the evaluation of peace-building initiatives. The seminar provides a good example of how organizations like NPI address the need for reflection on their own peace-building initiatives.
Draft report on Workshop on Strategic and Responsive Evaluation of Peacebuilding: A Framework for Learning and Assessment, NCCK and NPI-Africa, arch 1999.
For more information: npi@africaonline.co.ke

INCORE (Initiative on Conflict Resolution and Ethnicity, Northern Ireland) provides the INCORE Internet Thematic Guides. Sources, articles, institutions and organizations are provided on categories such as Women and Conflict, Aid and Conflict, Religion and Conflict, Human Rights, and many more. All the sources mentioned can be found on the Internet.
For more information: http://www.incore.ulst.ac.uk

The Charles Stewart Mott Foundation (United States) published an overview of the lessons it has learned in its grant-making activities over the last decade. The Foundation asked external research institutes to evaluate the impact and output of the projects they have funded in Central and Eastern Europe. These training-based projects mainly focus on democratization processes, the resolution of ethnic differences and multicultural training.
The report is a good example of a donor organization assessing its own activities and criteria for funding.
Reaching for Peace: lesson learned from the Mott Foundation's conflict resolution grant-making, 1989-1998
For more information: http://www.mott.org

The Carnegie Commission on Preventing Deadly Conflict was established in 1994 to address the looming threat to world peace from inter-group violence and to advance new ideas for the prevention and resolution of deadly conflict. The Final Report, published December 1997, outlines the findings of the Commission's work which has now officially ended. The Final Report and

many of the essays and articles that have followed remain valuable reading. The Commission's work represents the first major attempt to measure the possible impact the international community can have in conflict resolution and peace-building related activities. The Commission has examined the principal causes of deadly ethnic, nationalist, and religious conflicts within and between states, and the circumstances that foster or deter their outbreak. The publications outline the strengths and weaknesses of various international entities involved in conflict prevention and discuss ways in which international organizations might contribute toward developing an effective international system of non-violent problem solving.
Preventing Deadly Conflict: Final Report, Carnegie Commission on Preventing Deadly Conflict, Carnegie Corporation of New York, 1997
For more information: http://www.ccpdc.org

Action Evaluation is a new method of evaluation that focuses on defining, monitoring, and assessing success. Rather than waiting until a project concludes, Action Evaluation supports project leaders, funders, and participants as they collaboratively define and redefine success until it is achieved. Because it is integrated into each step of a program and becomes part of an organization, Action Evaluation can significantly enhance program design, effectiveness and outcome. Participants emerge with a sense that the evaluation process has enhanced and improved program and organizational capacity as they achieve success. Action Evaluation has two key requirement; 'participation' and 'reflexivity'. Participation means that all stakeholders engage in the process from the beginning, articulating and negotiating their goals, their values, and their proposed action plans. Reflexivity means that all participants function as "reflective practitioners" together, reflecting and examining the interaction of goals, values and activities. These reflections are done systematically and continuously during the project. An interesting article by Marc Howard Ross, which introduces the Action Evaluation theory, can be found on the website of the institute that develops and practices this approach to evaluation.
Action Evaluation in the Theory and Practice of Conflict Resolution by Marc Howard Ross, 2000
For more information: http://www.aepro.org

Practitioners Guides

Responding to Conflict (United Kingdom) published one of the first handbooks for practitioners working in peace-building and conflict-resolution training programs. The practical tools analyzed and described in this book derive from the experiences of over 300 practitioners from 70 different countries, all involved in the RTC Working with Conflict courses. The book is divided into four parts: analysis (focusing on how to understand conflict), strategy (building effective strategies to address conflict), action (intervening in conflict and addressing the consequences) and learning. This last section

explains some useful evaluation models and addresses the key-issues and questions when evaluating the impact, success and failures of peace-building work and training.
Working with Conflict: Skills and Strategies for Action
For more information: http://www.respond.org

The Berghof Research Centre for Constructive Conflict Management, (Germany) has published a handbook for conflict transformation on the Internet. Its aim is to give practitioners and scholars an overview of currently available approaches, methods, techniques and theories of conflict transformation. The authors document and assess progress in the field as well as offer opportunities to reflect on and discuss the strengths and weaknesses of these approaches. The publication should contribute particularly to strengthening the link between practice, systematic reflection, research and theory. The topic structure of the Handbook is organized according to the conceptual preconditions, the different social levels and the various dimensions of conflict transformation.
Berghof Handbook for Conflict Transformation
Availabe at: http://www.berghof-center.org/handbook/index.html

Peacebuilding: A Field Guide, edited by Luc Reychler and Thania Paffenholz, is a concise guide for practitioners working in the areas of conflict prevention and peace building. It provides practical answers to dilemmas, issues and problems facing field workers. It focuses on preparatory processes such as conflict analysis, selecting and training staff; dealing in the field with issues such as western versus non-western approaches towards mediation, monitoring, relief and aid, media, awareness raising and security. It also covers surviving in the field with discussion of issues such as stress, moral dilemmas, effective listening and codes of conduct.
Peacebuilding: A Field Guide, edited by Luc Reychler and Thanina Paffenholz, Lynne Rienner Publishers: Boulder/ London, in association with the Field Diplomacy Initiative, Belgium
For more information: http://fdi.ngonet.be

The International Institute for Democracy and Electoral Assistance (Sweden) has produced a handbook with lessons learned and options for negotiations in conflict. The handbook shows how to structure negotiations and design democratic institutions. It provides practical advice for policy makers and political leaders in post-conflict societies. The book is one of a series of filed practice handbooks published by IDEA.
Democracy and Deep-Rooted Conflict : Options for Negotiators, edited by Peter Harris and Ben Reilly, International Institute for Democracy and Electoral Assistance (International IDEA), 1998
For more information: http://www.idea.int

Aid and Conflict

International Alert's Program on Development and Peace Building examines the relationship between violent conflict and the agents and processes of development. It aims to provide development and humanitarian actors with knowledge-based gender-sensitive policy prescriptions, best practices and tools. One of the project's latest outcomes is a report discussing the impact of peace building on international engagement. Three case studies are used - Afghanistan, Liberia and Sri Lanka - to illustrate and foster the debate on aid and conflict. The methodology of the paper is built around two schools of thought on this issue. The first is the humanitarian maximalist school which argues that new wars require an extension of humanitarian mandates, meaning a linkage between aid and other policy instruments. This is opposed by the humanitarian minimalists school which argues for deepening the mandate, which is described as the 'back to basics' approach. It is interesting to see how the authors have used and criticized these two positions in writing up both the cases and their valuable concluding remarks.
Conflict and Aid: Enhancing the Peacebuilding Impact of International Engagement: A Synthesis of Findings from Afghanistan, Liberia and Sri Lanka, Jonathan Goodhand with Philippa Atkinson, International Alert, 2001
For more information: http://www.international-alert.org

World Vision has produced an extensive evaluation report investigating the contribution that World Vision's Area Development Programs can bring to peace building, most notably in reducing the potential for, and the effects of, violent identity conflicts. The report states that 'peace building' within the development world has become ghettoized, confined to workshops or specific reconciliation programs. While at the same time, the potential of existing programs to contribute to peace processes is often overlooked. Therefore, the report tries to bridge the gap between the disciplines of natural resource management and current peace-building approaches. It is recognized that both areas of research and practicality differ in theory and practice. However, development processes and conflict dynamics both mainly derive, quite properly, from local grassroots levels. Therefore, there appears to be a linkage between effective, participatory grass-roots development and peace building.
The contribution of community development to peace building: World Vision's Area Development Programmes, Siobhan O'Reilly, World Vision UK
For more information: http://www.worldvision.org.uk

The Conflict Research Unit of the Netherlands Institute of International Relations, 'Clingendael', has analyzed the role of the *Netherlands Development Organization for Technical Assistance to Development Countries (SNV)* in conflict emergencies. The SNV's field offices are increasingly confronted with internal armed conflict. Consequently, the SNV decided to review their experiences of providing development assistance in conflict situations and explore the possibility of developing an approach to be adopted in future project planning. The report is a good example of a possible way to enter the debate on aid and conflict within a development agency. It discusses the main theories on analyzing conflict, the potentialities and dangers involved in peace building. Lastly, it also outlines some interesting practical considerations to be taken into account when SNV-staff decide to work in conflict torn societies. The report has been the basis for future debate within SNV on this issue.

The Role of SNV in Development Countries in Internal Armed Conflict, Tsjeard Bouta & Georg Frerks, Conflict Research Unit Netherlands Institute of International Relations 'Clingendael', 2001
For more information: http://www.clingendael.nl/cru/index.htm

The Development Co-operation Directorate of the OECD initiated an informal taskforce on conflict, peace and development co-operation in 1997. This has resulted in some interesting research projects and led to the DAC Guidelines on Conflict, Peace and Development Co-operation. These guidelines have recently been updated after consultative reviews and dialogue with partner countries in Africa, Latin-America and Asia. The aim of the task group is to deal with the many issues of concern to both donor and partner countries when considering the use of Official Development Assistance in countries in, or prone to, conflict. The guidelines stress the need for donors to recognize the implications of their involvement in conflict-ridden areas. They outline the dynamics of conflict and discuss the role security and development can play in ensuring peace. Also, the potential dangers of these kinds of involvement are discussed.

OECD Informal DAC Task Force on Conflict, Peace and Development
For more information: http://www.oecd.org/dac

Voluntary Organisations in Cooperation and Emergencies (VOICE) is a network of more than 90 non-governmental organizations (NGOs) throughout Europe that are active in the field of humanitarian aid, including emergency aid, rehabilitation, disaster preparedness and conflict prevention. It was created in 1992, with a Secretariat established in 1993. VOICE's essential overriding mission is to foster links among Humanitarian Aid NGOs and to make an effective contribution to the framing and monitoring of humanitarian policy, primarily at the European Union. Recently VOICE has addressed what is referred to as the grey zone, or the missing link between relief, rehabilitation and development. This debate sprung from the recognition that development policy and practice has changed insofar as these activities increasingly occur in conflict-ridden areas. This means the features and consequences of violence have to be addressed. VOICE has published some discussion papers outlining the potentialities and limitations of the European Union's and its affiliated aid agencies' in addressing the linkage between aid and conflict.
For more information: http://www.ngovoice.org

The book *Good Intentions: Pledges of Aid for Post-conflict Recovery* provides an excellent examination of the realities of post-conflict recovery and social reconstruction. In six case studies, the authors, drawn from both donor states and recipient countries, evaluate multilateral efforts to support sustainable recovery and peace building in societies emerging from protracted conflict. The timing, composition and objectives of aid pledged by the donor community are analyzed, as are the conditions that donors place on their assistance, the mechanisms they create to coordinate it, and donor performance in delivering it. The impact of aid on reconstruction and peace-building goals is also analyzed and, finally, the causes, consequences, and lessons of any gaps between pledges and disbursements are assessed. Countries studied include Cambodia, El Salvador, Mozambique, the Palestinian Territories, South Africa, and Bosnia and Herzegovina.
Good Intentions: Pledges of Aid for Postconflict Recovery, edited by Shepard Forman and Stewart Patrick, Lynn Rienner Publishers, 2000
For more information: http://www.rienner.com

The Collaborative for Development Action is a small consulting firm specializing in issues surrounding humanitarian assistance, but undertakes several impressive projects focusing on learning. CDA works in collaboration with aid agencies and governments to learn lessons about humanitarian interventions. The work of CDA is discussed and illustrated in previous chapters. The Reflecting on Peace Practice Project (RPP) is one of the main endeavours of CDA. RPP has developed 26 case studies of work on conflict. The cases are explicitly not evaluations, but rather capture the reflections of the agencies, participants, and outside observers as to the development and impact of the activities undertaken. The following case-studies can be downloaded from CDA's website.

1. Forging a Formula for Peaceful Co-Existence in Fiji: a case study on the Citizen's Constitutional Forum (Peter Woodrow);
2. An Overview of Initiatives for Peace in Acholi, Northern Uganda (Mark Bradbury);
3. International Service for Peace (SIPAZ): Promoting Peacebuilding and Non-Violent Conflict Transformation in Chiapas, Mexico (Carlisle Levine);
4. When Truth is Denied, Peace Will Not Come: The People to People Peace Process of the New Sudan Council of Churches (Hadley Jenner);
5. Part I: The Georgia-South Ossetia Dialogue Process: A View from the Inside (Lara Olson)
   Part II: Partnering for Peace: Conflict Management Group and the Norwegian Refugee Council Collaborating on the Georgia-South Ossetia Dialogue Process (Susan Allen Nan);
6. Building Peace Through Third Party Impartial Facilitation: The Story of OAS-ProPaz in Guatemala (Orion Kriegman);
7. Kenyan Peace Initiatives: Kenya Peace and Development Network, the Wajir Peace and Development Committee, the National Council of

Churches of Kenya, and the Amani People's Theatre (Janice Jenner and Dekha Ibrahim Abdi);

8. The Coalition for Peace in Africa (COPA) (Sue Williams);
9. The Cooperation for Peace and Unity (CPAU), Afghanistan (Sue Williams);
10. Extending the Humanitarian Mandate: Norwegian Church Aid's Decision to Institutionalize its Commitment to Peace Work (Mary B. Anderson);
11. Reflecting on the Christian Peacemaker Team in Hebron (Sue A. Lyke and Joseph G. Bock);
12. Local peace constituencies in Cyprus: the bi-communal trainer's group (Oliver Wolleh);
13. Weaving New Relations, A Contribution to Peace: A Case Study on Yek Ineme in El Salvador (Patricia Ardon);
14. NGO Participation in Conflict Prevention in Burundi (Lennart Wohlgemuth);
15. Explicit and Implicit Peacebuilding: Catholic Relief Services in Mindanao, Philippines and Bosnia-Herzegovina (Reina Neufeldt, Sarah McCann, Jaco Cilliers);
16. The Interreligious Peace Foundation: Christians, Muslims, Buddhists and Hindus addressing the conflict in Sri Lanka (Alexandre Bilodeau);
17. The Peacemakers: NGO Efforts in the Middle East: 1948-2001 (Everett Mendelson);
18. From Forgiveness to Reconciliation: Moral Re-Armament and the Agenda for Reconciliation (Donna Isaac);
19. PRIO/Nansen case study: the Balkan Dialogue Project (Donna Isaac);
20. Towards Reconciliation: Impact Assessment Background and General Preliminary Findings, Peace Teams, Osijek, Croatia (Jessica J. Jordan and Marina Srabalo, and Project Coordinator for Impact Assessment, Michelle Kurtz);
21. Conflict Prevention through Supporting Democratic Representation and Participation of Hungary's Roma Minority: A Case Study of Partners Hungary in Tiszavasvari. (Lara Olson);
22. Women Weaving Peace Together: A Contextual Case Study on The Leitana Nehan Women's Development Agency, Buka, Bougainville Province, Papua New Guinea (Andy Carl);
23. Preparing the Table: A Retrospective on the Centre for Intergroup Studies, 1968-1990, Cape Town, South Africa (Greg Hansen);
24. UNICEF Sri Lanka: Children As Zones of Peace (Luc Zandvliet and Orion Kriegman);
25. Peace Zones of Apartado, Colombia (Sue Williams and Phillip Thomas);
26. Conflict Transformation by Training in Nonviolent Action: Activities of the "Centre for Nonviolent Action" (Sarajevo) in the Balkan Region (Martina Fischer)

Areas Assessed

Opportunities Missed, Opportunities Seized edited by Bruce W. Jentleson is published as part of the Carnegie Commission on Preventing Deadly Conflict series. It assesses and discusses the feasibility of *preventive diplomacy*. Different case studies cover four broad areas: the Soviet Union, Yugoslavia, Africa and Korea. In each case, the possibilities for successful preventive action are outlined and opportunities both missed and seized, are discussed. Jentleson provides a conceptual and analytical framework for preventive diplomacy and comes up with a concise set of conclusions and ways forward in this area of conflict prevention. *Opportunities Missed, Opportunities Seized: Preventive Diplomacy in the Post-Cold, War World, edited by Bruce W. Jentleson, Carnegie Commission on Preventing Deadly Conflict, Rowman & Littlefield Publishers, Inc. New York, 2000* (see also Annex 1)
For more information: http://www.ccpdc.org

Accord: An International Review of Peace Initiatives is a series of publications by Conciliation Resources (United Kingdom). They provide detailed narrative and rigorous *analysis of specific war and peace processes*, combining readability with practical relevance. The publications aim to provide a practical learning resource to enrich people's understanding of the potentialities and pitfalls of 'peace building'; a primer for international readers unfamiliar with specific wars and peace processes; and insights from those directly involved or affected by peace processes, particularly local civic organizations. Examples of peace processes studied are; Tajikistan, Sierra Leone, Northern-Ireland and Sri Lanka.
Accord: An International Review of Peace Initiatives
For more information: http://www.c-r.org/accord/index.htm

The Compendium of Operational Frameworks for Peace Building and Donor Co-ordination is a publication of the Conflict Prevention and Post-Conflict Reconstruction Peace building Network (CPR) of the Peace building Unit of CIDA (Canada). The information in the compendium derives from several meetings of *bilateral and multilateral donors* who want to address the increasing need to engage in conflict prevention activities. The purpose of the Compendium is to draw together practical tools and best practices that could encourage and promote coordinated engagement in responding to violent conflict by humanitarian and development organizations. The Compendium contains operational frameworks and guidelines developed by various bilateral and multilateral organizations. The compendium is a good example of an on-going and coordinated learning process amongst donor agencies.
A Compendium of Operational Frameworks for Peace building & Donor Coordination
For more information: http://www.acdi-cida.gc.ca/cida_ind.nsf

The Swedish International Development Cooperation Agency (SIDA) has evaluated its *donor policy on supporting peace-building initiatives*. The objective of the study was to collect and analyze lessons learned from peace building, to give guidance to SIDA in developing policies and methodology, and to promote institutional learning in the field of peace building. The project has resulted in three reports: State of the Art, which is a synthesis of existing evaluations and lessons learned in the international arena; five case studies in which projects funded by SIDA are evaluated; and the Final Report.
SIDA Evaluation 00/37: Assessment of Lessons Learned from SIDA Support to Conflict Management and Peace Building, Department for Cooperation with Non-Governmental Organisations and Humanitarian Assistance.
For more information: http://www.sida.se/evaluation

The Stockholm International Peace Research Institute (Sweden) has published a report of its Krusenberg Seminar that was held in June 2000. The seminar brought together a diverse range of individuals from government, international organizations, media, business, academia and NGOs. The purpose of their interaction was to consider the factors that affect international willingness to undertake conflict prevention and to bridge the gap between *early warning and early action*. The report contains some interesting short papers and outlines the conclusions of the seminar.
Preventive Violent Conflict; The Search for Political Will, Strategies and Effective Tools, Report of the Krusenberg Seminar
For more information: http://www.sipri.se

Annexes

Annex 1

The following section derives from the concluding chapter of the book, already shortly discussed in the Reading List, Opportunities Missed, Opportunities Seized, Preventive Diplomacy in the Post-Cold War World, edited by Bruce W. Jentleson, Carnegie Commission on Preventing Deadly Conflict, Rowman & Littlefield Publishers, 2000. Six interesting lessons learned in preventive diplomacy are outlined, all based on case-studies done by the authors involved in this publication.

Opportunities Missed, Opportunities Seized
Preventive Diplomacy

We had two principal goals in this book. One was to present expert studies of major cases that challenged the preventive diplomacy capacity of the international community in the first years of the post -Cold War era. Our authors have done that, providing important analyses and insights in each of the ten cases. The other principal goal has been a comparative one, to discern and assess patterns across the cases in the successes and failures of preventive diplomacy. These patterns, and their implications for both theory and policy, are the focus of this last chapter. The argument was made from the outset in the first chapter for the realism of preventive diplomacy: that it is a viable strategy and can be done, and that it has a strategic logic and should be done. With the evidence provided by our case studies, I return to this argument and show its substantiation. I then address the requisites for effective preventive diplomacy-how to do what can and should be done. The chapter concludes with a section considering the problem of political will, the difficulty of which is exceeded only by its essentiality. *By* BRUCE W JENTLESON

The Viability of Preventive Diplomacy

The case studies strongly support the contention that preventive diplomacy is not just a noble idea, but is a viable real world strategy.

1. Missed Opportunities: *The international community did have specific and identifiable opportunities to limit, if not prevent, the conflicts. But its stagecraft was flawed, inadequate, or even absent.*
Indeed, in many of the cases it was not just one point at which an opportunity for preventive diplomacy was missed, but in fact numerous points and

instances. The errors were both of omission and commission, of the failure to act and the failure of action taken. This conclusion is drawn conscious of and consistent with the caveats concerning counterfactual analysis as discussed in chapter 1.

In the Somalia case Ken Menkhaus and Louis Ortmayer strike a sober balance as they steer "between the shoals of wishful thinking and fatalism". They acknowledge that "no amount of preventive diplomacy could have completely pre-empted some level of conflict." But they trace "a litany of missed opportunities", presenting solid evidence "that timely diplomatic interventions at several key junctures might have significantly reduced, defused, and contained that violence." They identify four distinct points at which opportunities were missed, a series of "cascading crises" through which Somalia descended into a "more violent and more intractable level of conflict".[1] They also cite instances in which misconceived actions taken by the international community "served to trigger conflict", actually making things worse.

In the Rwanda case Astri Suhrke and Bruce Jones also are able to substantiate a series of missed opportunities, including both the commissions of flawed actions and the omissions of inaction. They go back to 1989-90 when both the Organization of African Unit y (OAU) and the United Nations High Commissioner for Refugees (UNHCR) had gathered sufficient information on the increasing volatility of the worsening refugee problem (mostly Tutsi in Uganda) to seek to take a series of initiatives but got little support from the United States or Western Europe. They also stress as a key reason for the failure of the Arusha Accords the unwillingness of the international community to buttress them with tough and credible measures against violations and extremist violators. The United NationsAssistance Mission for Rwanda (UNAMIR) had "neither mandate nor capacity" to be an effective preventive military deployment. And on the eve and in the early days of the incipient genocide in April 1994, when the Hutu-dominated military still was somewhat divided, "an important factor in their decision to act was the failure of the international community to respond forcefully to the initial killings in Kigali and other regions. Given these divisions within the military, "a more determined international response against the extremists would have found allies within [the military]." This conclusion also is strongly backed by Major General Romeo Dallaire, the UNAMIR commander, as well as in other studies.[2]

Gail Lapidus makes a similar argument about the dysfunctional dynamic between the actions and inaction of the international community and the assessment of options and competition for influence among Russian elites in the Chechnya case. Here, too, while acknowledging the limits of the counterfactual, the emphasis is on the missed opportunity:

"It is difficult to demonstrate conclusively that a more active Western role in the early stages of the conflict would have altered its course. However, it arguably might have created opportunity, space, transparency, and support for a serious negotiating process and strengthened the inhibitions against the resort to force. The existence of important divisions within the Russian elite, and therefore of potential allies of appropriate conflict prevention efforts, and the interest of a number of capable regional leaders eager to find a political compromise offered opportunities to influence the policy calculus that were never utilized."

So, too, in the Nagorno- Karabakh case, we get the balanced yet significant claim from Ambassador Jack Maresca that "a number of opportunities were missed that might have led to greater negotiating progress." Indeed, this was a case in which there was a degree of early success, as the Conference on Security and Cooperation in Europe (CSCE) Minsk Group was able to bring all the main parties to the negotiating table in early 1992. But the process was allowed to "fizzle" over the course of the year, while the calculations of a number of key actors, both the parties themselves and the Russians, shifted in ways that shut the window on the opportunity for prevention.

As to Croatia and Bosnia and Herzegovina, Susan Woodward is clear and unequivocal at the very outset of her chapter that "Few, if any, deadly conflicts in recent history that have provided more opportunity for prevention than the wars that engulfed the Balkan peninsula with the disintegration of Yugoslavia in 1991." Here, too, the analysis is both of failures in the actions taken-"so many actions taken with the intent of prevention, or justified as such, [that] rebounded perversely on the idea itself of prevention"-and of the failure to act as international actors self - justified their inaction with a view of the conflict as "inevitable" and of the parties to it "as intent on killing each other no matter what outsiders did."

As to the Congo (Brazzaville), we had the intracase contrast between the 1993 preventive diplomacy success and the 1997 failure. William Zartman and Katharina Vogeli draw sharp contrasts between what was done in a timely and effective manner in 1993 and what was not done or was done highly ineffectively in 1997. They also show how the 1997 missed opportunities traced back to the failures to follow through on the 1993 seized ones, such as in not disbanding the militias, "an action that was absolutely necessary (and maybe even sufficient) to prevent the re-explosion of civil war."

2. Case Evidence of Successes: *In addition to the evidence of how the failures could have been successes, there are the successes that quite plausibly could have been failures, had it not been for preventive diplomacy.*
The counterfactual works in the other direction as well, to show why the avoidance of major conflict in cases like Macedonia, Ukraine, the Baltics,

North Korea, and at least initially in the Congo (Brazzaville) was not a given. Any or all of these could have become quite deadly in their own right-Macedonia, an - other ex-Yugoslav republic with a multiethnic mix sharing a border with Serbia; Ukraine and the Baltics, which each had their own bitter histories with Russia within which difficult issues had to be worked out; North Korea, whose hermit leadership and unpredictably aggressive track record sowed uncertainties and fears of any one of a number of possible cataclysms; and Congo, as it proved to be in 1997.

While there was some variation in the identity of the key international actors, in all of these cases preventive diplomacy had crucial impact. More of the who, what, and how from these cases will be brought out later in this chapter. For now suffice to say that we get an interesting cross-section: Ambassador James Goodby's emphasis in the Ukraine nuclear nonproliferation case on both the United States' role and the importance of a preexisting strong international regime with rules and norms of restraint; Michael Mazarr on North Korea, also emphasizing the U.S. role, although more in a carrot-and-stick bargaining context; Heather Hurlburt on Estonia and Latvia, with the focus on the CSCE/OSCE; Michael Lund on Macedonia, on a range of key international actors including the CSCE/OSCE, the United Nations, and the United States; and Zartman and Vogeli on Congo, crediting the OAU and especially Gabonese president Omar Bongo, who had an unusual combination of political and personal standing.

To attribute importance to preventive diplomacy is not to dismiss other factors, such as the roles played and decisions made by domestic actors. But as Lund puts it for Macedonia, "it is unlikely that the existing equilibria of interests and the fabric of relationships would have been able to contain serious out- breaks of violence for long without international preventive diplomacy:' More- over, in a number of cases there was an interactive effect by which domestic actors reached what l term a *cooperation calculus,* rather than a conflict one, in part because of incentives, assurances, and other support provided by international actors.

To be sure, as noted as caveats in the first chapter, any attributions of success are relative in two respects. First, the claim is not of total conflict resolution or the total absence or avoidance of violence and killing-but, yes, escalation to mass violence was prevented; the conflicts did not become horrifically deadly ones. Second, even that success can prove to be transitory, as in the Congo case, and as could have been the case as the Russian minority issue has kept coming up in the Baltics and as the 1998 Kosovo crisis pressured against Macedonia.[3] However, unless it is demonstrated that the principal reasons for eventual failure were integral to the initial success of prevention, as an analytic matter such an eventuality would not totally negate the earlier success.

3. Purposive Sources of Ethnic Conflict: *While all these conflicts have deep historical roots, the driving and dominant dynamic was more purposive than primordialist, much more the consequence of a volitional calculus than historical determinism.*

The cases strongly support the purposive side of this theoretical debate. To be sure, history has its legacies. The politics of identity-of who l am, who you are, and what the differences are between us-were driving forces in all these cases. But there was nothing inevitable about deadly conflict in any one of these cases. The conflicts were *not* strictly "these intractable problems from hell" as the prevailing Clinton administration view was expressed. They were fed, shaped, manipulated, directed, and turned toward the purposes of leaders and others whose interests were served by playing the ethnic card.

If identity were so fixed and conflict so inevitable, then one would hardly have expected, for example, for Bosnia and Herzegovina circa 1991 to have so much intermarriage (more than 25 percent) and so few ethnically "pure" urban residents and ethnically homogeneous smaller communities, as Woodward points out in her chapter. The point also is made, albeit with some hyperbole, in a statement by a Bosnian Muslim schoolteacher that "we never, until the war, thought of ourselves as Muslims. We were Yugoslavs. But when we began to be murdered because we are Muslims things changed. The definition of who we are today has been determined by our killing"[4] Suhrke and Jones could not be more unequivocal in their analysis that notwithstanding the deep historical roots of Hutu-Tutsi tensions, the Rwanda genocide was not primordialistic "mindless violence" but all too purposive: "planned ...fully prepared ...to retain political power and all that went with it" In Chechnya while giving due to the underlying legacy of antagonistic group histories and other factors inherent to the situation, Lapidus nevertheless also stresses the non-inevitability of the war, that it was "deliberately launched by the Russian leadership" So, too, in the other cases in which we also see histories of ethnic and other intergroup tensions that fostered dispositions toward conflict but that in themselves were not deterministic and required calculations, decisions, and other purposive action by leaders and other fomenters to end up as mass violence.

4. Key and Unavoidable Role of International Actors: *While not necessarily determinative, the actions and in action of international actors have major impact on whether domestic actors make a conflict or a cooperation calculus. This means most importantly that there is no nonposition for international actors.*

It follows from the previous point about the purposive nature of domestic actors that to the extent that international actors can be expected to raise the costs and risks for the violence options and/ or raise the potential for gains from more peaceful conflict resolution routes, a moderating effect on the domestic actors' calculus is possible. If there is no such expectation, the calculus is left without a major constraint and is more likely to lead to violence.

Moreover, while international actors may profess neutrality, be it limiting their involvement to humanitarian rescue or simply staying out, there simply is no "nonposition" for the international community, in the sense of no impact one way or the other. If one party to the conflict assesses that it has the advantage in military and other means of violence over the other, so long as the other cannot count on international assistance to balance and buttress, it should be no wonder that it chooses war. In some instances the choice of war is at least in part a pre-emptive one, less out of outright aggressive intentions than as a manifestation of the "security dilemma" in which warfare breaks out from mutual insecurities and fears of vulnerabilities, which credible international action could have assuaged.

Our cases are strongly corroborative. Lapidus stresses that all along Boris Yeltsin still had "a considerable repertoire of tools and strategies" for Chechnya other than military intervention but made his choices in part based on knowing that the United States and others in the international community were not going to impose significant costs for using force. In Somalia, for all the "cruel and gratuitous criminality" that clannism took on, the fact that as late as the mid-1980s this still was "a country that was remarkably free of violent crime" runs counter to the primordialist view of this violence as just an extension of historical tensions. Siyad Barre quite intentionally had politicized clan relations, and did so with U.S. Gold War-motivated support. The "conflict constituency" pattern by which General Mohalled Farah Aideed and other clan leaders pushed Somalia deeper into violence was not just an inevitability of state collapse; it was in part a consequence of international inaction and ineffective action that, how- ever unintentional, was permissive and facilitative.

In the Nagorno- Karabakh case Maresca brings out a number of ways in which the West's efforts to limit its involvement was consequential in its own right, as Russia saw that it had room to manoeuvre, and the conflicting parties on the one hand felt insufficiently reassured because of doubts about the West's will to ensure the peace and on the other hand were not constrained from "deal shopping". In Groatia and Bosnia and Herzegovina Woodward traces the numerous ways in which international actors not only failed to prevent or ameliorate the early stages of the conflict but exacerbated and worsened them. In Congo 1997 Zartman shows how the conflicting parties exploited the unwillingness of the international community to get involved in any serious way. As to Rwanda, the evidence of purposiveness and calculations of the international factor is exceedingly strong in the Suhrke- Jones chapter as well as from other sources.

5. Early Warning Availability: *Where opportunities for preventive diplomacy were seized, it was in part due to the timely availability of reliable intelligence and other early warning information.* Where opportunities for preventive diplomacy were missed, it was despite early warning availability. All told, and contrary to what often is argued, early warning was not the problem.

Goodby stresses how the Ukraine case was close to an early warning ideal type: no ambiguity as to the nature of the problem, a high-priority interest at stake, consensus on goals, receptivity to warning not impeded by problem recognition, no disincentive of having to consider military force as an option. So, too, in the North Korea case there was "detailed and relatively conclusive intelligence information about the exact character and timing of a conflict:' The early warning could have come earlier, but it was early enough, with the evidence of North Korean nuclear weapons programs beginning to mount in the mid- 1980s and having become quite "cIear" by 1989.

The timely and reliable intelligence and other information that constitute early warning was available to policymakers in every one of the ethnic conflict cases:

Rwanda: "information about the possibility of an oncoming genocide-or at any rate, civil violence on a scale that would undermine the peace process-was 'in the system' in ample quantity:'[5]
Somalia: "Throughout the 1980s the international community witnessed visible signs of a worsening political crisis...there was no shortage of information warning of a deteriorating situation:'
Congo: "no lack of information"
Chechnya: "ample early warning:' for "both the parties to the conflict and the broader international community"
Baltics: "an almost ideal early warning"
Croatia- Bosnia: "there was plenty of early warning"[6]
Nagorno-Karabakh: while "the international community did not foresee ...the strength of Russian resistance to an international intervention on the territory of the former Soviet Union;' it was "despite clear early warning signals"
Macedonia: initially "less like discrete alarms and more like general concerns" but clearer and more clarion over time, and in plenty of time for the UNPROFOR- UNPREDEP preventive deployment of military forces.

This is not to go so far as to claim that any of these warnings were strictly unequivocal or self-evident. The "signal-to-noise" problem raised by Alexander George and Jane Holl was evident in a number of cases. This is a problem that in part goes back to the indeterminacy of the sources of conflict and the difficulty of ascertaining with reliable conditional probability whether incipient tensions and low-level violence will become major conflicts. It also is inherent to issues that may be major tomorrow but have to compete with imminently pressing issues for a spot on the usually full plate of policymakers' action -oriented attention. The need for improvement in early warning is addressed later in this chapter. Still, the cases do show that early warning was less the problem than was response to those warnings.

6. Flawed Analysis, but Correctly So: *A key part of the warning-response problem was misanalysis of some or all of the following factors: the likelihood of escalation to violent conflict, the impact on national and international interests, the risks and costs of inaction, and the viability of preventive actions. The case studies show this to be more a matter of faulty assumptions, inaccurate framing, and other correctable analytical flaws than of inherent problems of unknowability.*
George and Holl make a case for the importance of quality analysis, the difficulties for achieving this, and some ways of improving the chances of doing so. This is one of the key links in the warning-response chain.

To an extent the problem was something of a first-generational one, in the sense of new types of issues bursting so quickly into the scene in a period of historical transition. Not a lot of thinking had been done before Somalia about failed states. Yugoslavia was recognized to be a less than fully stable ethnic con- federation, hut for it to descend into the mass murders, raping, and pillaging of ethnic cleansing? Or a country such as Congo, which never had had elections and campaigns before and thus provided little basis for analyzing possible scenarios and alternative strategies?

The analytic problems with these types of conflicts involved both assessments of the nature of the conflict and the probability that it would intensify and escalate. It is true that issues such as nuclear proliferation or Russian troops in the Baltics inherently have fewer analytic ambiguities and uncertainties. They also have the advantage of more apparent time sensitivity. However, we need be careful not to go from acknowledgment of the greater inherent analytic and explanations of why the analytic flaws occurred, to hands- thrown -up justification of unavoidability. The explanations tell us why analyses were flawed, but this does not mean that they had to be flawed. As Woodward writes in citing a Bush National Security Council official's lament that they "simply knew of no way to prevent this from occurring" - "this explanation is insufficient; if something matters, one finds a way to act."

It is in part the problem, as Menkhaus and Ortmayer put it, of being able "to think outside the box." This is not easy to do, and not just for analytic-cognitive reasons but also for bureaucratic and political reasons, but it is doable. Making the analogy between Chechnya and the American Civil War, seeing the repercussions in domino theory terms, accepting at face value Russian officials' "uncritically tendentious and self -serving analyses"-all are indicative of an "inadequate understanding of the situation" that, as Lapidus suggests, was not inevitable. The particular mix of these analytic problems varies from case to case. But whatever the mix, while things may not have been known correctly, they could have been.[7]

Moreover, even if the first-generational argument is accepted, its very logic also constitutes its datedness. We now have had the experience of these conflicts with their various etiologies and dynamics, and we should be expected to have learned from them.[8] Whether we have, though, remains in doubt, given the late and limited response in cases such as Kosovo. Once again the threat of concerted international action came only after the conflict had turned deadly and was more a matter of conflict management than conflict prevention.

A final point concerns the full-plate problem. This too is an explanation qua justification often made. This is a highly "inflexible" approach, as Maresca stresses: "The point is not to dispute the wisdom of maintaining such a hierarchy of priorities but rather to argue that it should be possible to maintain a sensible order of priorities and to seize opportunities related to lower-priority problems: "Given how often the full-plate justification is offered (e.g., the plate was too full in 1989-90 with the end of the Cold War to see Saddam Russein's aggression coming; the plate was too full in 1990-91 with Saddam to be able to deal with Yugoslavia or Somalia in their earlier stages; Yugoslavia was on the plate as Nagorno-Karabakh intensified), it is a problem that needs to be addressed. It is one of the reasons why policy-planning functions need to be taken more seriously and approached more systematically.

In sum, there is ample basis of the viability of preventive diplomacy. Some opportunities were seized; many others (too many) were missed. It was fit that nothing or no more could have been clone. It was that nothing, or at least not enough and not the right things, was clone.

Notes

1. Other studies of Somalia concur on there being missed opportunities even though they may differ on the specifics of what they were. See, e.g., Mohamed Sahnoun, Somalia: The Missed Opportunities (Washington, D.C.: U.S. Institute of Peace Press, 1994): "If the international community had intervened earlier and more effectively on Somalia, much of the catastrophe that has unfolded could have been avoided" (pp. xvii, 5-6).
2. See, e.g., the study convened by the Carnegie Commission on Preventing Deadly Conflict, the Georgetown University Institute for the Study of Diplomacy and the United States Army, involving an international panel of senior military leaders, which, while stressing the requisites such a force would have had to meet, generally concurred; Scott R. Feil, *Preventing Genocide: How the Early Use of Force Might Have Succeeded in Rwanda* (Washington, D.C.: Carnegie Commission on Preventing Deadly Conflict, 1998). See also reports on General Dallaire's testimony to the UN International Criminal Tribunal for Rwanda, such as Stephen Buckley, "Mass Slaughter Was Avoidable, General Says," *Washington Post*, February 26, 1998, pp. A17, A22.
3. See, e.g., R. Jeffrey Smith, "U.S. Fine-Tunes Focus of Macedonia Mission," Washington Post, April 1, 1998, p.A24; Steven Erlanger, "U.S. Is Trying to Defuse a Growing Russia-Latvia Confrontation," *New York Times*, April 16, 1998, p.A9.
4. Chris Hedges, "War Turns Sarajevo Away from Europe," *New York Times*, July 29, 1995.
5. See also Alison L. Des Forges, "Making Noise Effectively: Lessons from the Rwandan Catastrophe," in *Vigilance and Vengeance: NGOs Preventing Ethnic Conflict in Divided Societies*, ed. Robert I. Rotberg (Washington, D.C.: Brookings Institution, 1996), pp. 213-32.
6. Susan L. Woodward, *Balkan Tragedy: Chaos and Dissolution after the Cold War* (Washington, D.C.: Brookings Institution, 1995), p. 396.
7. For a similar argument, see Bruce W. Jentleson, *With Friends Like These: Reagan, Bush and Saddam*, 1982-1990 (New York: Norton, 1994).
8. On policy learning, see Lloyd S. Etheredge, *Can Governments Learn? American Foreign Policy and Central American Revolutions* (New York: Pergamon, 1985.); Joseph S. Nye, Jr., "Nuclear Learning and U.S. Soviet Security Regimes" *International Organization* 41 (Summer 1987): 371-402.

Outline of key-note speech by Robert Ricigliano (Peace Studies Program, University of Wisconsin, Milwaukee, USA) at the International Conference Towards Better Peace Building Practice.

The Need for Networks of Effective Action to Promote more Effective Peacebuilding Can't Get There from Here

Recent studies of peacebuilding have consistently reached two recommendations for improving the effectiveness of peacebuilding practice: (a) to break down the distinctions between the "peace" and "development" fields in order to promote greater integration, and (b) to promote greater coordination between the myriad of interveners on the ground in a conflict situation. While the empirical and anecdotal evidence seems to support this claim, it would be a fairly radical change in how organizations behave on the ground, how they conceive of their operating strategy, and in the broader system within which all these organizations operate. So great would be this change, one could fairly ask, "can we get there from here?"

The premise of this paper is that without fundamental shifts in how we conceive of our operating strategies and in the system of organization and funding for peacebuilding, we will see only marginal changes in or ability to achieve better peacebuilding through collaboration. This paper goes on to develop the concept of Networks of Effective Action (NEAs) as a possible vehicle for creating the kind of fundamental shifts in strategy and systemic support for peacebuilding that are needed to make more effective collaboration a reality.

Need for Collaboration

1. Some disturbing trends

Getting to peace is getting harder. The trend is toward conflicts that do not end. In their survey of conflicts in the decade from 1989 to 1999, Wallensteen and Sollenberg (2000) conclude that "comprehensive and decisive conflict resolution was very difficult in this period and appears to have become progressively more difficult."

When we try to help, we often hurt the prospects for peace. Sometimes when we try to mitigate conflict, we have the opposite effect.

Even when we get "peace", it is getting harder to sustain. Even when we get agreements, there is backsliding and breakdowns in implementation.

2. Coping with complexity

In today's world, we are attempting to manage conflicts without the ordering and conflict suppressing effects of the bi-polarity of the Cold War. Today's conflicts are characterized by a complex interplay of three main sources of conflict:[1]

a. Political factors: break downs in how individuals and groups work together and manage conflict

b. Social factors: tension, hostility in basic relationships and negative attitudes between groups in conflict.

c. Structural factors: deficits in the basic systems or institutions in a conflict situation (e.g. the lack of democratization, economic development, rule of law, etc.).

3. Barriers to Change

There are many habits and practices that can be changed on the ground to improve collaboration. More importantly, however, we need a second order change in the way we think about peacebuilding and in the system in which we operate - otherwise, our ability to cope with current trends and to create real and lasting change on the ground will be marginal.

Barriers in the way we think

Limited Theories of Action

a. Most organizations work primarily in one of the Political, Social, or Structural arenas and have developed theories of action (operating strategies, values, and assumptions) within their arena. As part of their approach to implementation, many organizations are open to or make attempts at collaboration. However, collaboration cannot be an afterthought or an extra-step tacked on to the implementation phase, but must be an integral and organic part of an organization's theory of action.

b. Each of these processes (political, social, and structural) is a necessary part of a peacebuilding — no one process is both necessary and sufficient for building a sustainable peace. Each process relies for its success on the existence of the other two processes (e.g. political processes alone cannot create a sustainable peace without social and structural processes, etc.). However, with a theory of action that is limited to one of these areas, effectiveness is compromised.

c. There is no overarching theory of peacebuilding for how the different areas, political, social, and structural peacebuilding activities, should interrelate.

Thinking in temporally defined, linear categories.
The conflict cycle offered the promise of neatly defined stages of a conflict that could provide a needed division of labor - except that it does not match, accurately enough, how conflicts play themselves out in reality. The upshot is that interveners have pigeonholed their activity in unhelpful boxes. For example, some organizations have limited themselves to working "post-conflict" only to find that in reality their effectiveness is compromised by not being involved in earlier in the conflict (e.g. in attempts at conflict settlement).

Attempts to overly centralize, order complex conflicts, e.g.
a. Use of blanket ceasefires instead of limited and localized ceasefires linked to specific projects of mutual interest.
b. Over-reliance on formal negotiations - e.g. instead of informal tracks being fortunate accidents, they should be proactively created and integrated into formal processes.
c. Over-reliance on comprehensive agreements - e.g. instead of trying to attain comprehensive agreements, intervenors should fractionate the problem and produce a series of agreements over time.

Barriers in our environment

There are lots of constraints built into the system that impede collaboration and induce competition, both financial and political. Suffice it to say that a system that is riddled with conflict is hampered when trying to assist a country in conflict.

Networks of Effective Action: a mid-term goal

Enhancing the effectiveness of peacebuilding practice through changing the (implicit and explicit) theories of action of peacebuilding organizations and fostering a system more conducive to collaboration is a long-term proposition. This is especially true given that we do not yet know what specific new theories of action or systemic framework would be most conducive to enhancing the effectiveness of peacebuilding. However, a credible mid-term goal aimed at fostering the development of a new peacebuilding practice is the formation of Networks of Effective Action (NEAs).[2] NEAs are a process-oriented approach to changing how we organize ourselves in order to promote important changes in how we think about peacebuilding on an organizational level as well as fostering changes in the system within which we operate.

Purpose

An NEA is a collection of representative actors from the political, social and structural fields concerned with peacebuilding in a specific conflict. The purposes of an NEA are to:

Enhance effectiveness through fostering a holistic approach to peacebuilding.
A more holistic approach that incorporates political, social, and structural peacebuilding activities is needed to cope with the complex challenges on the ground and to achieve sustainable peace. While no one actor will have a fully holistic approach that spans the political-social-structural spectrum, the collective thinking and efforts of a network of organizations from these different fields can produce a more comprehensive approach. NEAs would:

a. Foster entrepreneurial, opportunistic approaches. There is not a standard recipe for a peace process that will work in every situation. But creative interplay between actors with different perspectives on peacebuilding can devise new, context specific approaches. For example, a "political peacebuilder" may feel the time is not right for peace talks, but a "structural peacebuilder" might see an urgent opportunity to build rural health clinics that would address the needs of each party to the conflict. Working together they might bring the parties together to launch a health initiative that in turn set the stage for limited negotiations between the parties on other important political issues.

b. Avoid an unhelpful division of labor. Rather than bringing in development organizations (structural peacebuilders) and NGOs that deal with social peacebuilding too late in the process, a holistic approach would involve them earlier, at least for the purposes of planning and analysis.

c. Avoid over-centralization of the peace process and over-reliance on formal negotiations. An NEA would help keep the political process from getting too far out in front of the social and structural peacebuilding needs of a conflict as well as connecting formal and informal processes.

Foster the development of new "theories of action" that necessitate collaboration.
Success breeds success. Perhaps the best way to begin to alter the theory of action of an NGO, government, or IGO is to demonstrate the power of working together. NEAs can help build the trust needed to get organizations (especially track 1 and track 2 actors) to work together. Achieving success on the ground provides the positive feedback necessary to ingrain such collaboration into an organization's theory of action as well as their practice.

Principles of operation of an NEA

Operate "chaordically"
Borrowing the term from Dee Hock, the salient principles of an NEA are:

a. Shared purpose and principles. All the members of an NEA would share a

common purpose (peacebuilding) and a common set of operating
principles (rule of the road) for how the participants will conduct
themselves in pursuit if the purpose.
b. Decentralized and self-organizing. Rather than stressing command and
control, which is impossible in the field, organizations are free to make
decisions and work collaboratively so long as it is consistent with the
purpose and principles.
c. Malleable in form, empowering of its members. The NEA would exist to
increase the effectiveness of its participants and would create whatever
central bureaucracy that best serves the members.

Enable learning.
A primary function of an NEA is to supplement the limited theory of action of
any one organization by fostering opportunities for diverse organizations to
learn from one another. Further, each actor will bring different information,
contacts, and resources to the table so that together the members of an NEA
can expand the range of possible action that can be taken to advance
peacebuilding. NEAs would play an essential role in sharing information for
planning and analysis and provide opportunities for joint planning.

Value inclusivity and diversity.
There are at least three dimensions along which an NEA would promote
inclusion of diverse actors. NEAs would:
a. Bring together actors from the Political-Social-Structural areas (NEAs would
be a representative sampling from these three areas, at least, but would not
need to include every actor)
b. Integrate official and unofficial tracks (Official and unofficial actors can
complement each others work in a very powerful way, but the link needs to
be proactively created by both sides)
c. Integrate international-national-sub-national actors (Each level has its role to
play in peacebuilding - international actors can offer resources, alter
incentives, provide expertise, and extend good offices; national actors must
provide the necessary leadership, make policy, and set strategy; and sub-
national actors are the hands that build the peace on the ground.)

Systemic Support
The formation of NEAs needs systemic support. Two important
developments include:

Donor practices
Donors need to review their giving priorities to develop options for funding
that do not fuel competition among peacebuilding groups, but necessitate the
formation of NEAs.

Industry Networking

Breaking down barriers, in more than an isolated or superficial way, between different "industries" or sectors such as development, conflict resolution, and human rights is difficult. One reason for this is that competition within an industry segment (e.g. between conflict resolution organizations) can be fierce. A step toward better cross-sectoral collaboration is for organizations within an industry to break down internal barriers to collaboration within their field and then as a group to encourage better cross-sectoral collaboration. One example of this is the nascent ACRON effort (Applied Conflict Resolution Organizations Network), which is dedicated to enhancing peacebuilding through promoting collaboration within its sector and across industry sectors.

Fostering the development of NEAs: some short-term action ideas

Funders
In addition to the review of funding practices in order to reduce incentives for competition and increase the necessity of collaboration, funders can:

Support the study of collaboration.
As defined below, there have been a lot of efforts at cross-sectoral collaboration and coordination in zones of conflict. We risk repeating past mistakes if we do not do more to learn from them.

Cross-sectoral focus groups
Recognizing that "so goes the funding, so goes the field," funders need to create linkages between their own compartmentalized funding categories. In order to do this, funders should sit down with their grantees from the political, social, and structural areas to get their feedback on what funding practices facilitate and which impede the kind of collaboration needed for an NEA.

Practitioners.

Reflect
Practitioners, both governmental and non-governmental need to examine their theory of practice (if they can even articulate one). This is a necessary step in order to see where collaboration truly fits into their theory of what they do.

Map
Practitioners need to know where they fit on the Political-Social-Structural spectrum in regard to their work on specific conflicts. Knowing where you fit is a first step to knowing whom to reach out to.

Plan
A first, cautious step toward the implementation of an NEA is to put together small but diverse groups of actors working on a common conflict to communicate and share information.

Organize
As mentioned above, groups of organizations in a common field can begin to organize themselves to make it easier to collaborate with organizations from other fields.

Academics
There are many fruitful areas for research and knowledge creation in the field of peacebuilding. Three such possibilities include:

Peace Processes
There has been substantial experience in the last ten years in the area of political peacebuilding processes. A review of such efforts with a lens for understanding how political, social and structural factors helped account for the success or failure of these efforts would help define the needs and mechanisms for cross-sectoral collaboration.

Evaluation of cross-sectoral partnerships
There has been a lot of experimentation in the field between conflict resolution and development organizations, coordination between formal and informal actors in the political peacebuilding track, etc. and we need better review of the lessons learned and best practices.

Social Capital
There is not an adequate theory for how the political, social, and structural peacebuilding tracks can work together to build a sustainable peace. Rebuilding Social Capital in zones in conflict is an interesting candidate for providing a more holistic approach to peacebuilding.

Notes
1 I was introduced to a version of this framework by Dr. Louise Diamond.
2 I was introduced to this term by Kevin
   Clements, currently the Secretary General of
   International Alert, who graciously allowed
   me to borrow this term and to take liberties in
   defining it.

Annex 3

Background Paper prepared for Working Group 12, organized by Cordaid and Pax Christi (the Netherlands) and International Alert (UK), for the International Conference Towards Better Peace Building Practice, October 24-26, 2001, Soesterberg, the Netherlands.

Gender and Peacebuilding

'Equal access and full participation of women in power structures and their full involvement in all efforts for the prevention and resolution of conflict are essential for the maintenance of peace and security.'
Beijing Platform for Action 95 UN

Gender and Conflict

Gender is a term used to draw attention to the social roles and interactions between women and men, rather than to their biological differences. Gender relations are social relations which include the ways in which men and women relate to each other beyond that of personal interaction. They include the ways in which the social categories of male and female interact in every sphere of social activity, such as those which determine access to resources, power, and participation in cultural and religious activities. Although the details vary from society to society, and change over time, gender relations always include an element of inequality between men and women and are strongly influenced by ideology. As gender is embedded in relations or power/powerlessness it is important that when understanding violent conflict it is viewed from a gender perspective

This means that:
- women and men as social actors each experience violent conflicts differently, both as victims and as perpetrators;
- women and men have differential access to resources (including power and decision making) during violent conflict;
- in peacebuilding strategies or reduction of violence, women and men have different roles, relations and identities and;
- women and men have different needs and interests in violent conflicts and in peacebuilding strategies. (Moser, 2001).

In today's conflicts, 85 per cent of victims are civilians of which the majority are women. Women in unstable, disruptive conflict and post-conflict situations are at risk from multiple forms of violence and share a set of common vulnerabilities; they are killed, wounded, tortured, imprisoned, separated from their families or driven into exile. Increasingly women and girls are deliberate targets, with belligerents using traditional gender relations to inform their strategies of war. In conflicts world-wide, rape, sexual assault, military sexual slavery, enforced prostitution and forced pregnancy are being used as deliberate military tactics. Studies of forced migration confirm that 80 per cent of refugees and IDPs are women and children and the indefinite and long term nature of forced migration creates unique problems for women who are forced to beg for food, live in refugee camps or to earn a living in unfamiliar environments.

The burden of responsibility, in conflict and post-conflict conditions, is highest on women in caring for survivors where development is already severely impeded and where families and communities have been fractured and destroyed. Women suffer economic dislocation, an intense sense of insecurity, the unravelling of traditional social and cultural structures of support and an increased risk of domestic violence, particularly in post-conflict situations.

However, despite these overwhelming difficulties women are not just victims. In order to move away from this one-dimensional image we need to explore and understand the complex roles and perspectives that women experience during conflict situations. Their participation in fighting, their importance as caretakers and providers for the community and the often extraordinary role they play in peacebuilding, peacemaking and reconstruction needs to be recognized. Most approaches to conflict resolution and peacebuilding have either ignored or marginalized issues of gender and have failed to address the needs of women and the unique perspectives and experiences they have of conflict and post-conflict situations.

Women Building Peace

The conventional wisdom is that men negotiate the peace and women build it. However, it is now more and more widely accepted that both men and women must be fully included in all peace processes for peace to take root and be sustainable.

Despite the dangers they face, women from East Timor, Liberia, Sierra Leone, Rwanda, Columbia and Pakistan, to name but a few, have developed effective and courageous initiatives to reach across the conflict divide and build peace, from the community to international level.

In many cases, women are the only segment of society remaining that are able to pick up the pieces and rebuild, if the ranks of male contributors have been drastically thinned by violent death, psychological trauma and other debilitating results of prolonged violence. Women are often the center of community life, as providers for children and elders, as active church members, and as agriculturists. These roles give women a reservoir of knowledge about specific community survival strategies and needs. During times of conflict women are able to expand upon their community roles to provide critical services during wartime. In times of crisis women can often be propelled into public spaces. Among their most powerful resources are the community networks that they have built within their traditional community roles. They have access to grassroots people, community elders, church leaders and even combatants. They are thus able to bring these different sectors and factions together, creating coalitions for peace and discussions about conflict issues in such public forums as seminars, workshops, community meetings and advocacy campaigns.

In light of the role women in peace keeping initiatives it is important to understand that perpetrators of violence are manifest at different levels of conflict. Hoping to make peacebuilding effective it is necessary to identify the different levels of violence c.q. actions of perpetrators, because each level requires its own approach to peacebuilding. For example, if a woman in a village lost her daughter due to an individual act by a frustrated soldier serving for years in an endless war, the women in the village will focus their strategy of peacebuilding directly to the local soldiers/commanders. And this could be very effective. But if she lost her daughter due to aerial bombardments by the formal military enemy, the influence of the local women doesn't reach far enough. They need to work together in their action with other organizations who could use their influence more effectively towards the national perpetrator.

Women often become involved in alternative forms of political action and/or peacebuilding precisely because they do not have access to socially traditional or mainstream channels of action. Women often use new and innovative methods to work towards peace in their communities. In many societies, women use their knowledge of indigenous cultural practices to devise new strategies for peacebuilding, voice their opinions, and effect positive change. Because these are often socially acceptable practices that have roots deep within the culture, women are able to successfully adapt them to present day socio-cultural needs without being seen as a threat to local authorities.

Women's experiences of conflict can contribute to the development of an alternative vision of peace and security. Their socialization can lead them to prioritize issues differently than men in positions of power, with their concerns grounded in issues of social justice, human rights and human needs. In Northern Ireland, South Africa and Guatemala the inclusion of women during the peace process expanded the agenda to include issues of basic human security as well as those of national or military security. Despite their vital experiences, expertise and knowledge, women consistently remain a minority of participants in peacebuilding projects, negotiations and policies and a gendered analysis towards peacebuilding strategies, which could potentially strengthen peacebuilding efforts is rarely given any priority or attention. This is despite the many United Nations and European Commission resolutions which for more than a decade, have criticized such marginalization and called for gender issues and women's needs to be given more serious attention in all policies relating to conflict and peace.

The Role of the International Community

The last few years have been an historic period for women's movements seeking concrete action by the international community in addressing the injustices women face during conflict. Putting the issue of women, peace and security squarely onto the international agenda has required a comprehensive approach and the use of different strategies and many initiatives at local, regional and international levels.

With 189 state signatories, the 1995 *Beijing Platform for Action* (BPFA) was the first internationally-endorsed document to highlight the plight of women in situations of armed conflict and offer recommendations for action to ensure their protection and participation in all decision-making processes. It specifically upholds and builds upon a variety of international instruments, such as the *Convention on the Elimination of All Forms of Discrimination Against Women* adopted by the UN General Assembly and Economic and Social Council. However, the 2000 Beijing+5 review of the BPFA revealed that few states have acted to implement the obligations they undertook and that despite the escalation of violence in many parts of the world, little is being done by governments and multilateral organizations to stem the deliberate victimization of women in war, attend to women's security needs or to include women's voices in peace negotiations.

In November 2000 the European Parliament adopted a **Resolution on the Gender Aspects of Conflict Resolution and Peace Building.** Drawing on various declarations, conventions and resolutions, the resolution considers the status of women in the context of armed conflict and makes several recommendations aimed at transforming the situation of women to one based on inclusion and recognition of the rights they hold and the contributions they continually make to peace processes globally

In October 2000 the United Nations adopted the historic **Resolution 1325 on Women Peace and Security.** For the first time the United Nations Security Council called for the participation of women in decision-making and peace processes; gender perspectives of women in decision making and peace processes; gender perspectives and training in peacekeeping; the protection of women; and gender mainstreaming in UN reporting systems and programmatic implementation mechanisms. Needless to say if implemented, these measures would place women firmly and equally at the center of peace and security matters. For NGOs and women's organizations working for the resolution, the rationale for women's involvement in peace and security matters was overwhelming. They have witnessed the burdens that women take on during crises without getting additional social support and have helped women in war zones create their own structures to cope with issues of survival. In situations like Northern Ireland, Catholic and Protestant women came together around issues of women's equal rights to social services, health, employment and education. Elsewhere in Bosnia and across the Balkans they have joined together to deal with the trauma of war - the violence, rape and abuse. These issues and activities have proven to be an effective entry point in crossing the conflict divide and uniting for peace.

However, despite some positive progress around issues of peace, security, prevention and reconstruction, women's voice are still largely ignored in the mainstream policy debate and the work done at the grassroots is not fully recognized or appreciated by major institutions and policy makers.

It is a multifaceted challenge. On the one hand in conflict zones, women peacemakers are often working in an environment which is hostile to their efforts. They are ignored and sidelined. The pressure from the public and private family domain for them to stay 'at home' is too strong. They receive little or no support or resources from the international community. As a result their efforts remain invisible as with no clear or documented evidence, it is difficult to prove their positive contributions.

On the other hand, women themselves have not always taken up the challenge to prove themselves effectively. While there is much talk of women from conflicting sides uniting around issues of mutual survival and rights, and overcoming the distrust based on identity or religious and ethnic differences, in reality the lack of trust often hampers their efforts. In some instances women lack the necessary skills to engage effectively in peace processes. Elsewhere they have concentrated too much on local initiatives and thus been left out of the national and official peace plans. In many instances women who have been active in times of crises have stepped aside when peace returns.

The momentum and level of interest generated by Resolution 1325 created a unique opportunity to place women firmly at the center of the contemporary international peace and security discourse. But unless the moment is seized, the opportunity will pass. It is thus imperative to take a closer look at how women contribute to peace processes. Analysis of their efforts, documentation of 'know-how' and lessons learnt are needed. It is important to begin to record women's peace works in a manner that can be used as evidence of women's contributions for policy makers, the media and others and it is also imperative that women activists themselves are able analyze the experiences to date, identify weaknesses, highlight successes, learn from each other and ultimately strengthen their approach.

Conclusion: From Empowerment of Women, to Mainstreaming Gender?

Since the Beijing Conference in 1995 'women and conflict' and 'women and peace' have been put on the international agenda. Anno 2001 it is now time to shift the focus from 'women and conflict' to 'gender and conflict'. Over the last six years, women's organizations in different conflict regions have been established and more and more women and peace coalitions across countries have been initiated. Research, campaigns, conferences and articles on the role of women in conflict have increased. There is also more attention for the role of women in conflict and the unequal control over scare resources in violent conflict-situations. For example, the WFP developed a gendered approach to reach the target group in famine struck Sudan by making use of effective channels dominated by women or men to reach the whole target group.

From Women empowerment to engendering
Looking at peacebuilding initiatives, one might conclude that the engendering of peacebuilding has not reached a satisfactory level. Though in some cases women are attending formal negotiations, in general they are still 'just attached to the negotiating table'. It became clear that women were not yet used to participate in formal decision processes. They didn't have the strategies, the diplomatic and lobbying skills to present themselves formally in the peacebuilding channels, while their perspective on the conflict and the peace approach was also needed. Therefore women started to empower themselves first. A barrier that still remains is the failure of dominant political actors and institutions to mainstream gender into the peace process

Consequently the question arises, whether it is still necessary to focus mainly on the empowerment of women in peacebuilding activities. Though empowerment of invisible actors, like women, youths, and the elderly is important to raise them to a specific level of influence. In these cases isolation could be useful but as soon as the state of empowerment has been reached co-operation should be stimulated. Should the focus now be shifted from women's empowerment, to a more gendered approach? Other (in)formal connecting actors need to be educated to stimulate the equal participation of men and women in decision- making processes about peace and development.

Some documentation

Alarakhia, S., *Engendering the Peace Process in West Africa*. The Mano River Women's Peace Network; Femmes Africa Solidarité, Geneva, 2000

George, C., *Engendering The Peace Process in Burundi*. Femmes Africa Solidarité, Geneva, 2000

Cockburn, C., *The Space Between Us, Negotiating Gender and National Identities in Conflict*. Zed Books, 2001

Cockburn, C., *Gender and Democracy in the Aftermath of War*. University of Humanistics, Utrecht, The Netherlands, 2000

Moser, C. Clark, F. (eds.), *Victims Perpetrators or Actors, Gender, Armed Conflict and Political Violence*. Zed Books, 2001

Pankhurst, D., *Mainstreaming Gender in Peacebuilding: A Framework for Action*. International Alert, London, UK, 2000

Reimann, C., *Why gender does not matter! Thoughts from a Theoretical Perspective*. Peace Studies Papers working paper, University of Bradford, UK, 2001

Sorensen, B., *Women and Post-Conflict Reconstruction: Issues and Sources*. War Torn Societies Project, Occasional Paper No.2, 1998 - taken from the Internet http://www.unrisd.org/wsp/op3/op3.htm

Annex 4

Report of Working Group 14 organized by International Alert and Saferworld for the International Conference Towards Better Peace Building Practice, October 24-26, 2001, Soesterberg, the Netherlands.

Security and Peacebuilding

Lack of governance of the security sector (armed forces, police, intelligence services, etc.) is often a source of conflict and a key obstacle to peacebuilding. Of the 44 countries in conflict in the world, many have security forces that are symbolic of societal cleavages (either ethnic or political) that are at the heart of violence, and are frequently associated with repressive acts against civilians and violations of human rights. The transformation of the security sector is critical to the success of peace agreements and the fostering of structural stability so that societies can live in a safe and secure environment.

In the past, external support directed towards the security sector of conflict-affected countries was provided for strategic reasons to pursue national interests or withheld because of the risk that it could have counterproductive results. However, in recent years there has been increasing recognition by the donor community that in the absence of security, key development objectives and structural stability will not be achieved. Although politically sensitive, the reform of the security sector is now seen as a key intervention to promoting sustainable peace and development.

The security sector is taken to mean all those organizations, which have authority to use, or order the use of force, or threat of force, to protect the state and its citizens, as well as those civil structures that are responsible for their management and oversight. This can be seen as forming three pillars of the Security Sector:
- Groups with a mandate to wield the instruments of violence - military, paramilitaries and police forces;
- Institutions with a role in managing and monitoring the security sector - civilian ministries, parliaments and non-governmental organizations; and
- Bodies responsible for guaranteeing the rule of law - the judiciary, the penal system, human-rights ombudsmen and, where these bodies are particularly weak, the international community.[1]

The overall aim 'Security Sector Reform' is the transformation of security institutions so that they play an effective, legitimate and democratically accountable role in providing external and internal security for their citizens.

It includes on the one hand the professionalization of security forces, but equally so on the other the strengthening of civil institutions to provide proper public management and oversight of the security sector.

A policy framework for security sector reform has been established over the last few years, through discussions within the OECD DAC and the issuing of documents by a number of donor governments, notably the UK and Germany. Security sector reform is now firmly on donor's agendas. However there has been little experience of comprehensive security sector reform and there is some disparity between the realities on the ground and the policy framework being used by donors. Few evaluations have been carried out into the effectiveness of security sector reform activities, and little has been done to draw out the lessons learned from the interventions that have taken place.

Purpose
The security and peacebuilding working groups will seek to draw out lessons learned from field experiences of security sector reform, as a first stage in developing a 'better practice' framework', with a view to improving peacebuilding practice and enlarging the impact of effective security sector reform work.

Round 1 **Police reform and community policing**

Background
A key security sector reform priority is the need to re-orient police forces from regime security to the protection of local communities. Many developing, transitional and post-conflict countries have inherited a paramilitary model of policing with a predominantly reactive, authoritarian approach which has done little to secure the trust and co-operation of community and has failed to control crime. The challenge of police reform is seen primarily as the development of state and non-state policing systems, including crime prevention which focus on community needs and community involvement. This approach demands a professional police service working alongside civil society organizations and non-state systems which are focused on crime prevention and committed to partnership with the police.

The objective of the working group was to identify lessons from recent and ongoing experiences of police reform. With this aim in mind the working group was divided into two sessions:

The first session aimed at illustrating recent experiences of police reform in two separate cases: Malawi and Northern Ireland.

The second session focused on drawing out lessons from the case studies through discussion around a number of areas which had been put forward by

International Alert and Saferworld as a possible framework for better practice. The session therefore provided an opportunity not only to identify lessons from field experiences but also to reflect on the form a better practice framework might take.

Session 1   Case Studies

Case Study 1 - Malawi

An overview of the Malawi Community Policing Program
Willie Chingaru, Malawi Police Service

Following a change of government and a process of democratization in Malawi, Community Based Policing has been adopted by the Government as the style of policing to be practiced by all members of the Malawi Police Service. A Democratic (Community-based) Policing Model appropriate for Malawi has been developed and adopted service-wide. A comprehensive community-based policing strategy has been implemented supported by a Policy Framework and 'Guidelines', all as a result of community consultation and participation. The community-based policing strategy involves:

- The creation and ratification by government of a National Community Policing Services Branch at Police headquarters.
- The emergence of a Model Community Policing Station as a developing 'center of excellence' which has received national and international recognition.
- Publication/distribution of community policing guidelines, posters, and leaflets based on community participation/consultation workshops.
- Development of a plan for the phased provision of essential community policing equipment and materials for Community Policing Forums.
- Integration of Community Policing Policy and Guidelines into MPS recruitment, management and specialist staff training.
- Progress Victim Support and Domestic Violence Awareness Programme with workshop support and publications (part of MASSAJ planning).
- Support for civic education training and media materials and information sharing through partnership with NGOs

Technical co-operation support to the Malawi Police Service and reform process through the Malawi Police Organisational Development Project (MALPOD) - *Graham Mathias, MALPOD and David Cushing, Policing Advisor, DFID Malawi*

MALPOD provides technical support to the Malawi Police Service and is funded by the UK Department of International Development. The purpose of the project is to strengthen the management, operational and human resources capacity of the Malawi Police Service (MPS). The project has 5 components:

- A Strategic Development component introducing strategic management at all levels of the MPS.
- A Human Resource Development component, which provides technical assistance and training expertise and equipment for the implementation of the MPS Human Resource Strategy.
- An Information Systems and Technology Strengthening component (ISTS).
- A Buildings Renovation component.
- An Operational Policing component which concentrates on Crime Management and professionalizing policing services.
- A Community-based Policing component, which focuses upon continued implementation of the MPS Community Policing strategy.

The success of MALPOD in building capacity and component sustainability in the MPS and in particular the transformation of the Malawi Police from a 'Force' to a 'Service' through the implementation of a Democratic (Community-based) Policing Model has led to recognition by the respective Governments to encourage a parallel program of change across formal, informal and customary law and access to justice institutions. All future support for the MPS will be within the framework of this wider sector program (MASSAJ). Key stakeholders include the GoM Ministers, community and business groups, other sectors of the wider criminal justice system and NGO's involved in human rights.

Police Reform and Community Policing - The role of civil society
Undule Mwakasungula from the Policing and Firearms Project of the Malawi Centre for Human Rights

Experience in different countries has shown that law enforcement cannot be effective without civil society and community co-operation. In Malawi it was clear that local communities and civil society needed to participate in reforming the Police Service in order to address all the security problems. In 1999 a pilot project was designed that focused on promoting community safety in poor areas and generally reducing illegal firearms by strengthening the Community Policing Fora (CPFs) in local communities and reforming the Police Service to respect international human rights norms and the rule of law.

Summary of main achievements:

- Increased knowledge of the scope of the problem of armed crime and sources of firearms in Malawi through analyzing police statistics and monitoring the media on serious and violent crime.
- Enhanced public awareness of the dangers of illicit firearms and the need for community policing by broadcasting regular radio programs on relevant topics, e.g. "Firearms and violence - What can we do?" and "Community Policing - How they can help us?"
- Improved the police/media relationship and raising public awareness by organizing a national seminar for senior police officers and journalists who write on issue of violent crime and community co-operation to combat it.
- Produced materials, e.g. posters and community safety booklets, to raise public awareness and to improve the Malawi Police's intelligence of illegal firearms. These materials were based on similar work done in South Africa.
- Produced a training and promotion video tape called "Protecting our lives", that highlights the current activities and challenges of the Malawi Police and civilian members of the new CPFs in dealing with firearms proliferation and violent crime.
- Initiated contact with new partners (churches, teachers, journalists, lawyers, the business community etc.) to promote public awareness and to cultivate support for professional policing projects.
- Formulated a proposal for legal reform of Malawi's legislation to better address issues around combating violent crime and the transfer of arms.
- Strengthened the capacity of CPFs in priority communities affected by armed violence by providing bicycles, torches and whistles.
- Assisted in establishing a training program for community-based police/civil society groups, that focuses on creating a genuine partnership between communities and local police.

Lessons Learned from the Community Policing Reform Process
Graham Mathias, MALPOD

- Value of consultation and involvement with the public and involvement of partners who are able to build trust and confidence between the Police and their communities - to empower communities.
- Importance of the collection of relevant data and crime management information. This has been demonstrated by the need for more specific information relating to firearms to aid the MALPOD/NISAT collaborative strategy.
- Importance of investment in financial and operational resources and capital infrastructure.
- Value of Mobilizing local communities to jointly assess the most appropriate use of police resources and crime prevention strategies to reduce crimes and local communities' 'fear of crime' and improve confidence in the delivery of police services.

Case study 2 - Northern Ireland

Michael von Tangen Page, International Alert

In order to draw lessons from police reform in Northern Ireland it is essential to understand the context of the conflict and the role of policing within that conflict. The Northern Ireland conflict can be described broadly as a sectarian conflict between the two major communities in the Irish province which remained part of the United Kingdom following the partition of Ireland in the 1920s, the minority Catholic and the majority Protestant community. It is not however a religious conflict in the sense that the fighting is about theological principals, rather over the years religion has become an ethnic delineator.

Following partition, Northern Ireland vigorously 'Protestantised' the infrastructure of the state in the face of what it saw as the terrorist threat from the south. While there ere occasional insurgencies carried out by the Irish Republican Army (IRA)- a splinter group who had refused to accept the partition of Ireland it was not until the late 1960s that the situation deteriorated significantly. In the late 1960s Catholic civil rights activists started campaigning against he discrimination that they had suffered over the previous 50 years. In the civil strife that followed the British army were sent in to aid the civil power- the IRA re-emerged and began attacking the police and the army. There then started a thirty year low intensity three way conflict between the security forces (including the police forces), Irish republican paramilitary groups and loyalist paramilitary groups.

The local police force which had always been largely Protestant became more Protestant dominated- partly as Catholics were unwilling to join and partly because it was very dangerous for them to do so. By the early 1990s the police force was 91 percent Protestant. In 1977 the decision was made that the police should become the leading force in the conflict in Ireland with the army taking the role of providing support where it was seen as necessary. At the same stage the loyalist paramilitaries were also becoming a problem and a three-way conflict developed with the RUC attempting to combat loyalist and republican activities.

In the early 1990s it became clear to all the major actors in the conflict that a military solution was not possible. Following a four way dialogue between the British and Irish governments along with loyalist and republican paramilitaries and a ceasefire, in April 1998 an agreement emerged that had the support of both communities. The agreement, known as the Belfast or Good Friday Agreement attempted to deal with a wide range of conflict causes- the government of Northern Ireland was to be administered by a coalition made up of both Catholic and Protestant politicians. Importantly a commission was to be established in order to assess the future of the RUC in the new context.

Response- The Patton Commission
An international commission was established by the British government
under the chairmanship of the prominent British Catholic politician
Christopher Patton who had been a Minister of State in the Northern Ireland
office during the 1980s. This exhaustive process of consultation took a year.
The submissions demonstrated the extent to which Northern Irish society is
polarized and the very difficult tight rope along which the commission had to
walk. The eventual report recommended the following:
- The end of the Full time Police Reserve thus reducing the number of police.
- Cutting the Special Branch by 50 percent.
- Changing the emblem of the RUC and name to PSNI- but retention of the
  uniform to symbolize both continuity and change.
- Changing its composition to reflect the wider community of about 50/50
  representation over a period of phased redundancy and recruitment.
- That people from paramilitary organizations may not join the new police
  service.
- That a new police authority is established that has a wider range of
  members and that local police community partnerships are established in
  each council area of Northern Ireland to encourage local accountability.
- That a police ombudsman be appointed.

Problems
This report was widely criticized by both unionists and nationalists as it failed
to satisfy either side- the force was not to be disbanded as republicans had
demanded- however, it was going to be significantly changed so unionists
were not at all happy either. The government implemented the bulk of the
Commissions recommendations into a new police act and the force will be
officially reconstituted as the Police Service of Northern Ireland. However,
there were a few changes introduced which were designed to keep the police
happy. Firstly extremely generous early redundancy packages were offered to
serving officers. Secondly in recognition of the 302 officers killed since 1969
the entire force was awarded the George Cross for bravery. In recognition of
the sensitivities of the new situation new recruits were not to be trained in the
use of plastic bullets (baton rounds) in riot control. However, this has not been
enough for Sinn Fein the political party allied to the IRA- it has argued that the
RUC is still essentially the same organization and has therefore refused to
endorse Catholics joining the force. Republicans also claimed that while
Catholics were now joining the force republicans were not and thus it was still
not fully representative. The Catholic church has also thus far refused to
endorse the idea of Catholics joining the force. The more moderate SDLP
however after some vacillation has decided to support the entry of Catholics
into the police and join the police board.

Lessons Learned
- There has to be something in the reform for the police (recognition of past work, financial compensation to officers who leave etc.)
- If possible one has to maintain some form of continuity.
- It is very difficult even if identity groups are clear to ensure that all conflict parties feel represented.
- The process of consultation with civil society is essential but can prove divisive in identity conflicts.

Malawi and Northern Ireland - reflections on the context

Policing in Northern Ireland has been bound up with the context of the conflict and has in essence been an exercise in national sovereignty and therefore has been highly politicized. Unlike Malawi, where reform was precipitated by a process of democratization, in Northern Ireland reform has taken place within the context, and has been a central component, of an ongoing peace process where the police are key stakeholders.

Consultation with civil society has been a component of both the reform process in Malawi and of that in Northern Ireland. In Northern Ireland however this consultation has taken place in the context of a civil society divided along sectarian lines where the process of consultation has the potential to be both divisive and dangerous.

Similarities between the two cases are however evident in the fact that in both cases the process of change has required an acceptance and demonstration of alternative forms of policing and the need to identify key change agents in this process.

Round 2 *Civilian/Democratic Oversight of the Security Sector*

Background
An important part of conflict transformation and Security Sector Reform is increasing civilian democratic oversight of the security sector. What are the key perquisites for success? What are the components of effective democratic oversight? How does one overcome the barriers for oversight? What are the ways in which donors can encourage civilian oversight and transparency?

The first session introduced the topic before going on to examine the practical experience of introducing civilian oversight in Guatemala and the former Soviet Union.

The second session focused on the experience of the Royal Netherlands Ministry of Foreign Affairs in supporting oversight from the perspective of the donor.

Session 1   Introduction and Case Studies

Introduction - Civilian Democratic Oversight
Luc van de Goor, Netherlands Institute of International Relations 'Clingendael'

During the last decade good governance in the security sector has increasingly become a concern of the international community. This marks a considerable shift from the Cold War era when democratic principles were of little, if any, interest to the donors of security sector assistance.

Why the New Emphasis on Security Sector Reform? The desirability of developing democratic, civilian-controlled security sectors that operate according to sound public sector management principles has become increasingly evident both within the countries where there is a need for reform and within the international community. There are at least three main reasons for this; the emergence of a new concept of security during the 1990s; the linkage between good governance in the security sector and equitable, poverty-reducing, environmentally sustainable development; and the linkage between good governance in the security sector and violent conflict.

Conceptualizing Security Sector Reform. When dealing with security sector reform it is important to pay additional attention to the actors involved: These include groups with or without a mandate to wield instruments of violence; institutions with a role in managing and monitoring the security sector; bodies responsible for guaranteeing the rule of law; and bodies responsible for foreign affairs.

Security Sector Reform and the Role of External Actors. The need for security sector reform in weak states often requires the involvement of external actors. A number of lessons have been learnt when it comes to external involvement in local processes of governance. These include; the commitment and active participation of the national stakeholder; reform should reflect a nation's history, domestic and international context, and its goals.

Case Study 1 - Guatemala

Ana Glenda Tager Rosado, FLACSO

Overview. Security sector reform (SSR) in Guatemala has to be understood in the context of 36 years of armed conflict. The process began after the peace agreement of 1996. Factors that need to be born in mind are that both civil society and the state were very weak after the conflict.

The FLACSO approach in Guatemala to SSR sought a consensus on security between the different sectors of Guatemalan society. This first required the identification of the principal security actors. After the actors had been identified an evaluation was conducted to create a number of working groups which would then develop a democratic security sector framework covering its own area e.g. intelligence. Each group was multi-sectoral in order to reflect the range of security actors in Guatemala. The groups then made their own agendas and selected entry points for SSR the most important of which was democratic control. Two separate groups were formed one that dealt with the reform of the intelligence services and the other which dealt with the institutional (oversight) sector.

Approach of Working Groups: The working groups then entered into a number of phases: 1. Action Research: this was the most important phase as they resulted in a number of working documents which were used throughout the rest of the process. These reports were consensual in content. 2. Capacity Building: this phase involved educating civilians on issues related to security policy in order to widen the debate about security in Guatemala.3. Public events: There were also a number of events that were designed to help this project largely in the form of conferences.

Methodology: The issues raised were dealt with internally through lobbying the security sector rather than going through the mass media. The working documents produced by the groups were used precisely for this purpose. This was especially important on lobbying around the issue of creating a legal framework for the intelligence services in Guatemala. It is hoped that this approach will now be widened to include the security forces and work with the Defence and Interior committees of the Congress. It is also hoped that another project will focus on the issue of civil security and the absence of clear policy guidelines and engagement from the NGO sector.

Lessons learned: The most important aspect of the FLACSO project was that while internationally funded it was a local project with an independent agenda developed specifically for the Guatemalan situation.

Case Study 2 - former Soviet Union (fSU)

Anna Matvejeva- Independent Consultant

Overview. This case study focuses on issues related to security sector reform (SSR) that run through a number of fSU countries but examples mainly drawn from Russia and Caucasus.

The factors affecting evaluation of SSR that have often been overlooked by the donor and domestic actors following the break-up of Soviet systems over the last decade include:

1. Overwhelming political and international aid attention was focused on the weapons of mass destruction.
2. Military forces acquired different political identities and roles in post-soviet systems. Witness the emergence of a military authority when these forces had previously been firmly under the authority of the party and soviet political system.
3. Outbreaks of conflict and renewal of conflict.

The above issues have meant that the development of civilian oversight over security sector can/has been viewed as attempts to weaken security forces rather than improve them.

It is important to bear in mind the different ways security forces are perceived. For example where the military is viewed as somehow defeated, its prestige declines relative to other security forces, often in relation to the police forces, whereas "successful" military forces retain levels of prestige.

Lessons Learned: Achievements of civilian oversight include the growth of investigative journalism and Civil Society Organizations while the issues so far overlooked in the debate include corruption and alternative security arrangements.

Session 2   Donor Perspectives

Drawing out lessons learned from a donor perspective.
Caroline Poldermans, The Netherlands Ministry of Foreign Affairs (MoFA)

Donor Interest in SSR: SSR is essentially about "good governance". However, whilst engaged in some individual SSR efforts (e.g. South African police reform, Rwandan judiciary and criminal court) the Dutch MoFA has also identified a need for a more comprehensive and co-ordinated approach - at present though this work has not been brought under a wider SSR program/agenda.

Role of the international community:In other sectors (e.g. health, education) there is dialogue between national governments and the international community, but for SSR the World Bank, UN etc will probably distance themselves as it is regarded as too political an issue. Partly as a result donors have their own agendas

Questions for donors: When should one engage in SSR initiatives? If viewed, as peacebuilding and conflict prevention then it should logically take place before the outbreak of violent conflict, but usually this time is not conducive to SSR initiatives. Therefore, in general the initiatives occur in post-conflict situations. The difficulty donors therefore face is that that when SSR is most needed it is also the most difficult time to actually conduct.

Round 3 **Stemming the proliferation of small arms**

Background
This session concentrated on looking at the impact of Small Arms and Light Weapons (SALW) on conflicts and the ways in which donors can try and stem the flow of SALWs into conflict zones. There were two principal areas of discussion the first concentrated on a weapons destruction program in Albania and the lessons learned from this experience while the second looked at donor engagement on the issue.

Session 1 *Case Study- Albania*

Sami Faltas, BICC

Albania was isolated from the rest of Europe during the Cold War. In 1997 widespread unrest swept the country although civil war was narrowly avoided. During the violence large caches of weapons were looted. In the north of Albania there is significant political unrest. In the south of Albania there is the problem with organized crime. The center of the country is relatively more stable than other regions, so it was chosen as a pilot zone. The government together with UNDP set up the weapons collection pilot scheme. Instead of rewarding individuals communities would be rewarded instead - collective incentives. They carried out a survey of what people needed - the most clearly identified need was for roads.

Results and Criticisms: Some 6,000 weapons were collected together with 130 tonnes of ammunition. There were a number of favorable preconditions. Firstly, people were more or less ready to disarm. Secondly, they had already sold what they could. There were a number of criticisms about the program. Firstly, there were delays in the delivery of development initiatives. Secondly, although the community had been actively involved in the design phase, they were largely excluded from the implementation phase. The approach in Gramsh was good - it empowered local communities. However, the preconditions there would make it hard to replicate in other areas.

Small Arms and peacebuilding: Small arms and light weapon (SALW) are not a root cause of conflict but they increase the scale of conflict. This often means that SALW initiatives are a good entry point in the peace agreement phase for peacebuilding efforts. People don't always act on urges for violence but the presence of SALW gives greater opportunity for violence to break out. The peacebuilding agenda needs to embrace this concept - violence and insecurity versus war and peace. Efforts to control or combat violence and insecurity should be part and parcel of peacebuilding efforts. You are strengthening authorities which gives more power to the state which raises questions of legitimization of state authorities and delegitimization of other actors. This may undermine efforts at conflict resolution.

Session 2 Donor Perspective

Dr Bjorn Holmberg, Swedish International Development Agency (SIDA)

Sweden has promoted the conditions for dialogue and conflict de-escalation; the promotion of security through demilitarization, DD&R (disarmament, demobilization and reintegration), weapons control and SSR; and structural conflict prevention through addressing the root causes of violence.

Activities: In Central America SIDA has addressed the problem of weak or non-existent weapons legislation, the lethal mix of a culture of violence, poverty, and three million small arms. This has been largely through promoting knowledge among national parliamentarians. DD&R has largely been promoted through the support of two institutions work in this area (the Swedish Defence College & Lester Pearson Canadian Peace Keeping Training). The object of this has been to create a global pool of trainers and skilled practitioners from all sectors of society who have skills in this area. SIDA feels that it is vital to have a DD&R input into peace processes.

Lessons learned: In dealing with the problem of SALW SIDA has learned the following lessons: Neutral NGOs have a significant benefit in working in this area; NGO's can also work on an informal basis which is often more effective; You also need the involvement of international governmental organizations (OAS/UN etc.)

Key findings

1. Security is essential to development - people must be safe and feel safe.
2. This means that the threat of armed violence must be reduced.
3. When people see better ways of achieving security, justice and progress they are less inclined to engage in armed violence.
4. If law-breakers face prosecution and social disapproval people will be discouraged from engaging in armed violence.
5. If the authorities are to control the possession, movement and use of weapons they need power, legitimacy and resources to carry out these functions.
6. The authorities will achieve legitimacy if they are effective, transparent and accountable, and respect and protect the citizens' rights and liberties.
7. Non-governmental organizations must monitor, criticize wherever appropriate, and support whenever possible.
8. Civil society must also ensure that attempts to enhance security address the perceived needs of the population and involve the local community.
9. Civil society should lead efforts to change minds and attitudes towards guns and violence.
10. Donors should work both with governments, helping them to reform their security forces, and civil society, encouraging it to play a critical and supportive role in the prevention of violence - therefore we need both capacity building of governments and civil society.
11. Different contexts may require radically different approaches. There needs to be coherence between efforts to enhance security by various actors in various regions

Documentation

Security sector reform

Ball, Nicole. *'Reforming the Security Sector: Policy Options for the British Government'*, a Discussion Paper, Saferworld, (1998)

Chalmers, Malcolm. *'Security Sector Reform in Developing Countries: an EU Perspective'*, Saferworld, London, (January 2000)

Hendrickson, Dylan. *'A Review of the Security Sector Reform'*, The Conflict, Security and Development Group funded by DFID. Centre for Defence Studies at King's College, London, (September 1999)

OECD, *'Security Issues and Development Co-operation: A Conceptual Framework for Enhancing Policy Coherence'*, DCD(2000)4/REV2

Wulf, Herbert (Director, BICC/Bonn International Centre for Conversion). *'Security-Sector Reform in Developing Countries/An Analysis of the International Debate and Potentials for Implementing Reforms with Recommendations for Technical Cooperation'*, GTZ Deutsche Gesellschaft für Technische Zusammenarbeit GTZ GmbH Division 43 Health, Education, Nutrition and Emergency Unit, (2000)

Police reform and community policing

Independent Commission on Policing for Northern Ireland, *'A New Beginning: Policing in Northern Ireland'*, (September 1999)

Neilds, Rachel. *'Policing the Peace: International Support for Police Reform in War-torn Societies'*, Conflict, Security and Development Group

funded by DfID at the Centre for Defence Studies/ King's College, London, (2001)

Safer Communities, *A Handbook on Community Policing*, Public Affairs Committee (Malawi) and the Centre for Human Rights and Rehabilitation (Malawi).

Civilian/Democratic Oversight of the Military

FCO *'A Need to Know-The Struggle for Democratic Civilian Oversight of the Security Sector in Commonwealth Countries'*, Foreign and Commonwealth Office, The Ford Foundation and Commonwealth Parliamentary Association, (2001)

Stemming the Proliferation of Small Arms

McLean, Andy. *'Tackling small arms in the Great Lakes region and the Horn of Africa - Strengthening the capacity of sub-regional organisations'.* Saferworld, 2000.

Lilly, Damian. International Alert/Saferworld *'Civil Society Perspective on Security Sector Reform'* Unpublished Background Briefing presented at Conflict Prevention and Reconstruction (CPR) meeting, Oxford (May 2000)

Lora Lumpe (ed), NISAT. *'Running Guns - The Global Black Market in Small Arms'*, Zed Books, (2000).

'Small Arms Survey 2001 - Profiling the Problem', Oxford University Press (2001).

For further information please contact:

Sarah Bayne, Saferworld (sbayne@saferworld.co.uk; tel +44 207 881 9290)

Damian Lilly, International Alert (dlilly@international-alert.org; tel +44 207 793 8383)

Notes

1   Hendrickson, Dylan. 'A Review of the Security Sector Reform', The Conflict, Security and Development Group funded by DFID. Centre for Defence Studies at King's College, London, (September 1999) p 29.

Annex 5

Background Paper prepared for Working Group 15 and Panel Debate organized by Cordaid and Justitia et Pax (the Netherlands), for the International Conference Towards Better Peace Building Practice, October 24-26, 2001, Soesterberg, the Netherlands.

Religion: Source of both Peace and Conflict?

Religion or belief is central to the daily lives of millions of people around the globe. Throughout history women and men have worshipped a deity, and in some cases more than one, as an expression of the wonder and mystery of life. Through the relationship with God or the Ultimate Reality, religion or belief offers people a reference system for the meaning of life, stimulates and shapes their sense of identity and promotes harmony, care for fellow human beings and the environment. Religion or belief is therefore strongly connected with personal identity formation and group belonging. From a broader perspective, religion, together with ethnicity, language, class and a common history, is a main element in building the collective identity of a people. Religion helps define and distinguish the 'in' group from the 'out' group, the 'we' from the 'you': it is both inclusive and exclusive.

This touches upon the ambivalent consequences of religion or belief. Regretfully, besides its inspiration of fraternal feelings and humanitarian values, religion or belief may be conducive to racial hatred or ideological conflicts. In other words, in principle, religion is not the problem but the ways in which religion is practiced and used - or rather abused. This 'religious violence' seems to be equally connected to human life. Through the relationship between religion and nationality, ethnicity, social and cultural status and even political aspiration, religious issues have perhaps been the most common denominator in armed conflict and strife between and within nations. No period in history and no part of the world has escaped. The recent dramatic attacks on World Trade Centre and Pentagon in the USA are yet another, though extremely cruel, example of the hatred and violence that can grow out of the interconnectedness of religion and politics. It may have come as a surprise to those who saw religion as an outdated concept in the 'modern secularized world', but ethno-religious and inter-religious conflicts as well as the instrumentalized, political use of religion are causing growing concern in many parts of the world.

This being said, it is clear that the role of religion in respect to peacebuilding and conflict prevention is equally ambiguous. Religious institutions such as churches and mosques are frequently to be found at the heart of conflict prevention and peacebuilding activities. However, there are also examples of religious institutions failing to promote peace and even fanning the flames of conflict.

While conflict in itself is not necessarily antipathetic towards the development of a just world - and can well lead to positive change — conflict becomes intolerable when it is expressed through violence, either physical or psychological. The difficulty with religion is that its positive, resourceful side is inextricably linked to its more restrictive, negative side. If religion enhances a creative side in human beings this is, basically, because it is able to provide an ultimate meaning of life, a founding truth. It is for this reason that it becomes difficult for believers to tolerate other faiths that proclaim contrasting claims to truth. Furthermore, the mere existence of competing faiths opens up, at least potentially, the possibility of doubting religious claims to truth. This jeopardizes the resourceful character of religion. Thus, to an extent, religious *freedom* conspires against *belief* and its psychologically positive consequences. Therefore, it is essential that religious conflict is kept within the boundaries of symbolic confrontation. It could be argued that verbal and ritual condemnation should be allowed for but no institutional or physical attacks, as these would objectively limit the liberty and rights of others.

In the workshops and the plenary debate the following questions will be dealt with:
- What causes religious institutions or communities to be a factor in armed conflict?
- What causes religious institutions or communities to be a factor towards peace?
- What lessons can be learned from peace initiatives originating from faith-based communities?
- What is the extra value of religion in this sense?
- How can these initiatives be stimulated by international advocacy?

A Factor Contributing to Violent Conflict

When a religious movement is small it usually lacks the power to influence the political arena, except when it is linked to important political groups. Minority religions are often the victims of intolerance and violence. But when a religious movement gathers more followers it will become more influential and powerful insofar as ethnicity and religion are bound together through the inculturation of the religion.

This power can be employed for war or for peace. When religion becomes implicated in ethnicity and allies itself with political and economic power, it will become violent. It will take on features of the ethnicity, creating feelings of identity and closeness and leading to the rejection of the unknown. Moreover, it will share the characteristics of political power in which violence, claiming its monopoly, is the philosophy of life.

Many of the conflicts which have resulted in so much bloodshed and enmity throughout the world have complex social, political, economic and cultural causes. The disturbing fact is that these conflicts often tend to be simplified to a confrontation between religious groups, values and virtues. For the sake of *world* peace, subtle distinctions should be made. Below follows some (often inter-related) distinctions, intended to initiate workshop discussion. Firstly, there is religious tension caused by the politicization of religion. Secondly, religious tension arising out of latent suspicion covertly cherished by each religious community towards one another. Finally, there is religious tension arising out of a mixture between politics and religion. Analyzing the situation in this way we may better figure out ways towards reconciliation and co-operation amongst religions.

The politicization of religion: due to its power of amplification, religious emotion and bonds have been used to support or to overthrow certain power structures. This has enabled religious animosity to grow into hatred and develop its own momentum. Religious conflict then becomes part of a larger political conflict. It makes no real difference whether the conflict is intra-religious (such as between Catholicism and Protestantism, or between Sunni and Shi'ite Muslim groups) or inter-religious (such as between Islam and Christianity). However, the real outsiders, especially when forming a minority group, are often a much easier target than their fellow majority religionists. They make an easy scapegoat for political, social or economical problems and their persecution may provide an outlet for frustration and social unrest, without the government having to tackle the real problems.
For poor and marginalized people, religion itself and also social projects set-up by religious communities, may be the source of survival, resistance and empowerment. In some cases this leads to violations of their freedom of religion and other human rights (e.g. the massive violations against the Maya people in Guatemala during the civil war period).
But in all cases the conflicts leave deep scars in and between religious communities. The existence of hard-line groups on both sides that sometimes resort to violence adds to an atmosphere of apprehension. This can lead to an unfortunate tendency to religious segregation.

Antagonism between religions: why does religion lend itself to easily to being provoked into violence? As noted above, one of the causes of conflict is inherent to religion's provision of 'the' ultimate meaning of life and a founding truth. For believers it is often difficult to tolerate other faiths that offer contrasting claims to truth; from symbolic confrontation this sometimes leads to violence, especially when the 'others' are regarded as apostates from the 'true' religion.

This may result in a powerful hidden enmity, e.g. between Islam and Christianity with an ever-haunting fear of Islamization versus Christianization. Mutual suspicion is a hidden time bomb that can be easily triggered. If conflict breaks out, regardless of the cause, it can easily feed on these suspicions. Mutual trust turns out to be less stable than was hoped. Besides feeling themselves easy targets for the common social frustrations of the masses, some Christian communities feel themselves threatened by the *worldwide resurgence and power of Islam*, especially the fundamentalist Islamic and radical movement. In its turn, non-Christian communities sometimes hold a fear of Christianization. This is perceived as, firstly, 'the basic intention of Christianity to convert people', as an active, aggressive and triumphalist religion (as in the colonial past but also lately by certain Evangelical groups). Secondly, in defending local cultures, Christianity is seen as trying to limit the influence of other cultures while creating a missionary field for its own. Thirdly and currently of particular importance, *Christianization* is also identified with notions such as *modernization, westernization, global economic dominance and secularization*, practically identical with everything that is perceived as opposed to traditional religions and cultures.

The mixture of religion and politics: Religious communities often play an important role in society with their own education system, intellectual associations, social-developmental initiatives and charitable institutions etc. This decisive role may result in a symbiotic unity between religion and politics. Its positive side is the politicization of the consciousness of the religious community. Many turn to their religion as an inspirational source of rejuvenation. The negative side is that religions become dividing forces within society. Political aspirations and social movements are split according to religious lines; their tensions immediately become religious confrontations. Secondly, this situation deprives society of the possibility of inter-religious mediatory groups.

A Factor Contributing to Peace

The commandment to live in peace and harmony lies at the heart of all religions. Thus religious communities (be they institutionalized or grassroots) have a moral obligation to support peacebuilding initiatives.
In order to tackle these conflict-promoting factors, members of religious communities can pursue inter- and intra-religious dialogue and action. In doing so they show that respect for and co-operation with each other is possible, hereby overcoming stereotyping and animosity. They show respect for each other's right to religious freedom. They are well-placed to alert local leaders and people to the dangers inherent in the politicization of religion, and, through the exchange of information and joint research, they can help unmask the motives and agents of 'religious' violence and attract attention to the victims.

However, for religious groups and individuals to become involved in peacebuilding initiatives it is of the utmost importance that they critically reflect on their own role and behavior in the dynamic of the conflict, especially when their religion is a factor in the conflict. They should try to recognize faults and weaknesses within their own religion and become aware that religion can be turned into an ideology in order to justify any objective. Seeing the asymmetrical gap between divine intention and human political scheme, prophetism has the courage to judge it as simple human self-deception instead of divine concern. Only when they analyze and accept their responsibility can they be a reliable partner for peace.

On many occasions religious leaders and groups have indeed played a role in preventing and transforming violent conflict because of the moral authority that they carry in many communities. If they are not part of the elite but find themselves at a critical, 'neutral' distance from the political elite they are well-positioned to undertake mediating roles between conflicting parties. They may mediate between guerrilla and government, between local groups and local or central government and between kidnappers and government and/or army. In such cases their independent position commands respect from both sides. Moreover, they often give victims a voice by monitoring and denouncing misuse of power and outright human rights violations. Throughout the globe you will find human rights / justice and peace groups, backed by their religious institutions, doing such work, often endangering their own lives.

There's been much talk lately of the need for *reconciliation* in order to establish real, long- term solutions. Religions are well equipped to articulate the essential ethic of reconciliation. But generally there is a considerable gap between articulation and the translation of the ideas into practice, while at the same time, today's world has a far greater need of reconciliation than at any other time in the past [Assefa 1999]. Contemporary conflicts are mainly civil wars and the belligerent parties often share the same geographical area and even community, there might be strong economic interdependence between them, they usually have a wide variety of social ties, including inter-marriages. One has to move towards processes where not only the underlying issues to the conflicts are resolved to everyone's satisfaction but also the antagonistic attitudes and relationships between the adversaries are transformed from negative to positive.

While there has been much *talk* of reconciliation, elite leaders often invoke the spirit of reconciliation when in fact they mean that they want things to get back to business-as-usual as quickly as possible. But reconciliation is no short-term process and it cannot be imposed from above, especially when the culprits come from 'above' and are not prepared to acknowledge their responsibility and guilt. People at grassroots, especially in regions that have suffered most from conflicts, therefore, tend to distrust the word 'reconciliation' as they feel it doesn't do justice to their suffering. And there cannot be reconciliation without justice. Assefa therefore argues that: 'The central question in reconciliation is not whether justice is done, but rather how one goes about doing it in ways that can also promote future harmonious and positive relationships between parties that have to live with each other whether they like it or not.' There is a need for restorative rather than retributive justice.

There is a growing realization that religious people and groups have an important role to play in reconciliation processes. In many such processes around the world they are engaged in providing relief to those who have suffered, helping uncover the truth, facilitating healing processes to mend the deep emotional wounds (not only of the victims but also of offenders), and participating in truth and reconciliation commissions. An appraisal of these initiatives and sharing the lessons learned is highly valuable for progress in establishing a peaceful future.

Documentation

Assefa, Hizkias, 'The meaning of reconciliation', in: European Centre for Conflict Prevention, *People building Peace. 35 Inspiring stories from around the world*, Utrecht 1999.

Johnson, Hilde F. *Freedom of religion or belief in the OSCE-region: Challenges to law and practice*, keynote address OSCE Seminar, The Hague, 26 June 2001

Miguez, in: J.M.M. Naber (ed), *Freedom of religion: a precious human right*, Van Gorcum, Assen 2000

Naber, Jonneke, 'Introduction', in: J.M.M. Naber (ed.), *Freedom of religion: a precious human right*, Van Gorcum, Assen 2000

Rachmat, Agus M., *Interreligious Conflict and Reconciliation in Indonesia*, written for workshop 'Religion, conflict and reconciliation' at Vrije Universiteit Amsterdam, www.pax-christi.nl .

van Workum, Johan, 'Religion - the strongest power', in: European Centre for Conflict Prevention, *People building peace. 35 Inspiring stories from around the world*, Utrecht 1999.

For more information please contact: Jonneke Naber, Justitia et Pax, j.naber@jupax.antenna.nl

Annex 6

Report from working group II organized by Swiss Peace Foundation/Centre for Peacebuilding (Switzerland) and European Centre for Conflict Prevention (the Netherlands) for the International Conference Towards Better Peace Building Practice, October 24-26, 2001, Soesterberg, the Netherlands.

Lessons Learned on Networking

On National and International Levels and Interactions of NGOs with Governments

Coherence and integrated approach are terms which seem to appear in almost every policy paper and communiqué written by, amongst others, the UN, G8 or EU, and the NGO community. This is because more and more people and organizations - and not only governmental, but also non-governmental organizations - have become involved in conflict-prevention or peacebuilding activities. At the same time, the field remains fairly dispersed. In order to avoid duplication of activities, or to identify gaps in the field, the necessity of improving information sharing and co-operation in the area of conflict resolution and peacebuilding becomes increasingly evident. The obvious instrument for this is networking.

This fact was recognized already in 1997 at a large international NGO conference on conflict prevention in the Netherlands. As a follow-up to the conference, the European Platform for Conflict Prevention and Transformation was created 'to facilitate the exchange of information and experience among participating organizations, as well as to stimulate co-operation and synergy.' Over the last few years, national platforms has been established in for example Finland (Citizen's Security Council, KATU), Germany (German Platform for the Peaceful Management of Conflicts), Canada (Canadian Peacebuilding Coordinating Committee) or Ireland (Irish Peace and Reconciliation Platform). The future may see new forms of networks, bridging the gap between the state and non-state actors, facilitating dialogue and co-operation between the two.

Most of the platforms or networks shared more or less the same objectives, which are:

- Stimulating networking, nationally and internationally;
- Facilitating information exchange / clearinghouse function;
- Encouraging co-operation;
- Initiating awareness raising activities (educational, media and advocacy projects);
- Initiating lobby activities;
- Enhancing capacity and expertise;
- Stimulating the exchange of lessons learned and best practices.

Report from working group 11

Due to the large number of participants, Working Group 11 met twice. Each meeting was divided into two sessions. The first session dealt with lessons learned and experiences drawn by national and regional platforms and networks such as the European and Finnish (KATU) platforms and the African network WANEP (West African Network for Peacebuilding). All gave short presentations on tasks, functions and structure. The second session focused on the interference or interaction between governments and NGOs. This is a general summary of both meetings and sessions.

Session 1: Lessons on national and regional platforms / networks
Facilitation: Thania Paffenholz, Centre for Peace Building-Swiss Peace Foundation (CPB), Switzerland
- Introducing the issue, including some lessons from the European Platform, by Paul van Tongeren, Executive Director of the European Centre for Conflict Prevention (ECCP), The Netherlands;
- Lessons from the Finnish Citizen's Security Council, KATU, by Anne Palm, Secretary-General of KATU;
- Lessons from the West African Network for Peacebuilding, WANEP, by Emmanuel Bombande;
- Debate.

General findings / lessons are:
- A differentiation should be made between networking on a global, regional and national level;
- A differentiation should be made between networking in the North and in the South;
- The field is still quite young, scattered and therefore weak;
- What conflict prevention and peacebuilding are about has to be made known to a much wider audience. We have 'to go public'. For this a campaign is necessary (nationally and 'supported' internationally);
- There is a need for a 'Network of Networks'; more work has to be done to

look at how this should be done. This is especially true for networking between northern and southern networks. The European Centre will organize a special meeting on this subject.

The field is weak:
There are still relatively few large conflict resolution / peacebuilding organizations. Many of these organizations have no, or minimal, staff. Many organizations have only volunteers. World-wide, there are approximately 20 organizations working in this field which have more than ten people on their staff. Therefore it is crucial to join forces.

There is some movement towards more networking but it is a slow and difficult process. Experience in Germany, for example, shows that it can take some years before networks begin to formalize.

Advantages of networking are:
- Scarcity of resources, both financial and human, makes it necessary to seek complementary partnerships.
- Consequently, an exchange of information and experience is needed.
- This helps avoid the duplication of activities.
- Exchanging experiences helps us to learn from each other's successes and failures, which saves time and money.
- Networking is particularly effective in the field of lobby and advocacy where joining forces (coalition building) helps to strengthen the position of the field as such. The voice of a coalition of NGOs is harder to ignore than the voice of one.
- The outreach of participating organizations is greater with publications and articles, for example, able to reach a broader audience.
- A broad network, comprised of organizations from different fields (conflict resolution, humanitarian aid, development co-operation) and from different regions (for example Northern and Southern NGOs) is the best guarantee against one-sided approaches towards complex issues such as conflict prevention and peacebuilding, since all participating organizations will approach the subject from their own angle. It effectively breaks down barriers.
- Networking is a methodology in itself. It enhances changes of focus, co-operation and co-ordination between different actors in the field, who have to work together in order to be able to do justice to the complexity of the issue at stake.

Difficulties in this respect are:
- Bringing together different NGO-sectors. Since conflict prevention is a new field, it is also relatively unknown and consequently, it can be difficult to convince potential partners to join a network. One of the main problems is to overcome the reservations and barriers between various NGO-sectors

and -milieus. The main driving forces are often conflict resolution-, research- and human rights organizations. Development and humanitarian assistance NGOs tend to be more reluctant to join, not least because they fear that in the end they might lose part of "their" resources from the governmental budget to the conflict resolution "newcomers". These reservations and barriers are also related to large cultural, organizational and traditional differences between the various organizations. For example: peace groups often exist by the grace of some enthusiastic volunteers, and development- and humanitarian organizations are often quite well staffed.

- Financing a secretariat. The strength or weakness of a network seems to depend on the existence or absence of an active secretariat. The financing of a secretariat proves to be very difficult. Most of the networks are quite loose and do not have paid membership. External funding is hard to find because the typical service tasks of a secretariat are not very well suited to project funding, and donors are not very keen on providing core funding.
- Balancing complementarity and competition. As a secretariat, it is difficult to balance the interests of different participants within the network and quite feelings of jealousy can develop quite easily. Related to this, the question of ownership of the network was raised. Relevant questions in this respect are:
- Who defines our tasks?
- What criteria do we use?
- Again, this is related to the question of how a network's activities should be limited. Since this field is young and developing, a lot still has to be done. How do you prioritize? And who defines these priorities?
- Developing a public voice. The different mandates, internal procedures, and political profiles of the participating organizations make it difficult and sometimes impossible to identify consensus positions on specific issues, such as EU policies, and to speak with one voice.
- At the same time, the last point touches the issue of losing profile. When a network does manage to act as one entity, organizations acting within that network cannot profile themselves that much as they would like to (for reasons of fundraising, for example).
- Related to the former two points, is the problem of finding a balance between inclusiveness and becoming to broad as a network. If every organization can join, what do we have in common?
- Networking costs time, money, and energy: in the end, it is not always easy to calculate if you are a net payer or receiver (not only in money, but also in information, experience and so on). Especially in international networking, the distances make networking expensive and time consuming. Networking will become 'virtual' and less based on personal contacts.

It is therefore recommended:
- To start with a small group of organizations and find a common interest.
- To start with clear ground rules for membership: agreement on and

understanding of the mandate, objectives and expectations of the participating organizations.
- That the participants of a network should define the role of the network (and not the other way around).
- To clarify the distinction between this network and networks of other fields, such as the humanitarian aid, and development networks.
- To further clarify the benefits of joining a network.
- To network around concrete issues. Do not network just for the sake of networking.

Some remarks on the difference between networking in the 'North' and in the 'South'
It was noted that in the South and in conflict regions, even more so than in the North, joining forces and networking is a prerequisite to effective peacebuilding.

- Networking is seen as a methodology, an approach towards peacebuilding. The complexity of a conflict makes a collective approach of a variety of actors necessary.
- Networks are needed to build capacity for collective intervention.
- Therefore, networking should go beyond information exchange.

It was recognized that co-operation between networks in the South and in the North should be increased and improved. Their roles should be complementary. However, a lesson learned is, that this is not always the case. Growing numbers of international development and humanitarian aid organizations are have taken up conflict prevention and peacebuilding in their work. Sometimes, international NGOs 'steal' from local organizations, take over the job of local organizations, and leave the issue of 'local ownership' aside, without exactly knowing the local situation and conditions.

A model of networking:

Functions of networks

| Passive ↓ | • Information sharing
• Dialogue (forum)
• Exchange of experience
• Providing expertise | Less commitment needed, loose network |
| Pro-active | • Advocacy
• Lobbying and campaigning
• Co-ordination between member groups
• Collective interventions | ↓
Much commitment needed, more formalized structure |

Session II: National infrastructures for conflict prevention and peacebuilding: lessons learned from the interaction between governmental and non-governmental actors

Aim:

generate lessons from the institutionalization of co-operation between governmental and non-governmental organizations in order to develop coherent peacebuilding policies.

Many countries have experienced an institutionalization of conflict prevention and peacebuilding within governmental and non-governmental organizations during recent years. The institutionalization and professionalization of peacebuilding activities and strategies is, however, only a first step in the direction of more coherent and effective peacebuilding policies. The dialogue between national governmental and non-governmental actors is crucial in this regard. Different countries have established more or less institutionalized co-operation mechanisms such as national centers, platforms or forums bringing together the different actors engaged in the field.

Facilitation: Paul van Tongeren, European Centre for Conflict Prevention (ECCP), The Netherlands

- Introducing the issue, by Thania Paffenholz, Centre for Peace Building-Swiss Peace Foundation (CPB), Switzerland
- Presentation of CPB / KOFF, Switzerland
- Presentation of FriEnt, Germany
- Contribution by Ragnar Ängeby, Head Conflict Prevention Secretariat of the Policy Planning Group in the Swedish Ministry of Foreign Affairs
- Debate

During this second session, two different models of institutionalized dialogue between the government and the NGO community were presented: KOFF in Switzerland and FriEnt in Germany). Since these two examples are relatively new (established in respectively April and September this 2001), most of this session was devoted to informing the participants about how this dialogue had been established and institutionalized. The lessons learned therefore didn't concern the dialogue itself, but more the process of bringing it about.

Some conclusions / lessons:
- The situation differs across countries. In western/northern countries, such as in Sweden or Finland, co-operation between NGOs and governments is a relatively normal phenomenon. However, while Sweden may be an example of a EU country favoring co-operation between NGOs and government, many other EU member states do not put this very high on their agenda. In conflict regions, NGOs are very often seen as in opposition to the government. 'Networking with the government may be the last thing you want to do'.
- Institutional hosting of the network is important. In Switzerland the participants decided to host KOFF at the Swiss Peace Foundation, which is neither a governmental institution, nor a NGO, but a research institute;
- The lack of resources requires prioritization of tasks executed by networks.
- It is difficult to occupy the 'in between' role; both sides have different expectations of what KOFF should offer.
- Institutionalization has to be balanced with flexibility.
- NGOs have to find a balance between interaction and independence.
- Therefore, it is important to create common objectives between NGOs and government, in order to reduce the risk of competition. The dialogue should be focussed on common issues.
- It is important to take into account the different cultures and procedures of government and NGOs, and of NGOs and different parts of the government.
- It is therefore necessary to agree on the terminology used by different actors.
- Both partners benefit a lot from the contacts with other (international) networks.
- It is important to communicate 'best practices' and 'success stories' to both government and NGOs.
- A learning process and confidence-building process is needed for both sides.

Annex 7

Background Paper prepared for Working Group 16, Swiss Peace Foundation and FAST (Switzerland) for the International Conference Towards Better Peace Building Practice, October 24-26, 2001, Soesterberg, the Netherlands.

Conditions, Feasibility and Major Lessons
Early Warning and Conflict Prevention

The Swiss Peace Foundation (SPF) launched a political early warning project called FAST (Früh-Analyse von Spannungen und Tatsachenermittlung) in 1998.[1] The driving force behind the FAST project, funded by the Swiss Agency for Development and Cooperation (SDC, Department of Foreign Affairs), was the destructive experience of violent conflicts (mainly in Rwanda) that led to immense human suffering but also to loss of investment as well as enormous and costly post-conflict emergency requirements. In Switzerland, the SDC realized that without being aware of potential crisis situations in countries it supported through development co-operation, it could loose its investment and jeopardize its staff. Thus it aimed at integrating early warning and conflict prevention analysis in its own assessment capacities, mandating the SPF to develop an external early warning system as a control mechanism and decision-support tool.

In light of the above, the objective of FAST is early recognition of impending or potential crisis situations in order to act early and prevent violent conflict. More specifically, FAST aims at enhancing political decision makers' ability to identify critical developments in a timely manner so that coherent political strategies can be formulated to either prevent or limit the destructive effects of violent conflicts or identify windows of opportunity for peacebuilding. Only by involving policy makers in the process of formulating policy options and case scenarios can we fine-tune early warning by adapting to client needs, build trust in the analysis and recommendations, influence overall policy planning, and also function as a pressure mechanism (Schmeidl and Adelman, 1998). Close interaction with decision-makers through meetings and consultations may ultimately minimize what frequently has been called the warning-response gap.

Still, it is important to separate analysis from the decision-making process in order to prepare policy options that are as objective as possible (Gurr, 1996; Adelman, 1998). Thus, as FAST is hosted by a non-governmental organization, it enjoys a level of political independence which in-house early warning mechanisms generally lack. In addition, FAST does not focus on advocating specific policy options but simply provides independent analysis, case scenarios, and policy options. With this emphasis, FAST keeps in line with the general functions of early warning (among others see Schmeidl, 2001):

- Collection of information
- Analysis of information (attaching meaning, setting into context)
- Formulation of case scenarios
- Formulation of response options
- Communicating findings to decision-makers.

Unique Features of FAST

In order to establish a solid foundation, FAST aims to answer basic early-warning questions: who to warn, when, of what, and how. As FAST is funded and mandated by the SDC, the often difficult question of to whom the warning should be targeted was easily answered.[2] Since the SDC deals mainly with development co-operation linked to long-term structural prevention, FAST focuses on both short- and long-term perspectives; short-term in order to complement the SDC time-frame and long-term to allow for policy options that balance short-term objectives with long-term strategies. Thus, answering the question of when to warn, FAST monitors both potential short-term (three to six months) and long-term crises as well as structural and operational strategies for conflict prevention.

While it is important to be clear about the nature of early warnings, most decision-makers are generally assigned to prevent and respond to complex multidimensional humanitarian disasters without trying to force them into specific categories. As the SDC is concerned about a certain level of stability in target countries in order to successfully implement its projects, FAST focuses on armed conflict in general, i.e., intra- and inter-state war, ethno-rebellion, genocide, etc.[3] Such a focus acknowledges that conflict is not necessarily negative in itself or something that must be prevented. Moreover it is possible, that especially development assistance can lead to social conflicts that reflect change and development. This is positive, and even necessary, as long as institutions are in place to allow channeling and eventually transforming such conflict in a peaceful and non-destructive way. Only when a country's government and political and legal institutions prove unable to cope with conflict so that violence escalates in a destructive manner should a warning be issued and preventive action considered. In summary, "it is not disharmony per se that needs remedy; it is rather its resolution through armed force and other forms of coercion that calls for prevention" (Lund, 1996, p.383).

The "how" of early warning is often more complicated (see methodology discussion). Believing in a comprehensive approach and the benefit of using multiple methods, FAST combines qualitative and quantitative elements in its methodology. This enables FAST to work comparatively and take advantage of the benefits of either method by seeing general structures (the forest and not just the trees) while being sensitive to country-specific elements (seeing individual trees, understanding their unique features).

This formulation of client- and mandate-specific policy options[4] is what links FAST methodology to an integrated response development. Instead of working from a generic toolbox, FAST makes recommendations with a general strategy, taking the action framework of its clientele (here SDC) into account. While other aspects of the FAST approach remain more or less standard, it is policy options that are specifically adapted and fine-tuned for new clients. This can best be described with the analogy of planning food for a dinner party. We not only need to know how many people are coming but who is coming (i.e., dietary restrictions for vegetarians or people of a particular cultural/religious background), the time of the day (e.g., whether or not to serve alcoholic beverages), and the season (such as refraining from serving a heavy turkey dinner on a hot summer day), etc. Without such knowledge, we may prepare the perfect dinner for the wrong set of people. In policy language, such a process may be defined as an analysis of stake holders (on the response side) and surrounding political environments influencing the likelihood of action and response potential.

As Figure 1 on the next page demonstrates, there are two FAST core products for each country monitored: FAST country risk profiles and FAST updates.

FAST Country Risk Profiles
The annual FAST country risk profile presents an in-depth base-line assessment of the situation in target countries. It discusses root, proximate, and intervening factors that may lead to armed conflict, hamper conflict mitigation, or provide a window of opportunity for de-escalation and peacebuilding efforts (see Clark, 1989; Gurr, 1996; Rupesinghe and Anderlini, 1996; Schmeidl and Jenkins, 1998). The latter set of indicators is divided by the importance of increasing or decreasing conflict escalation (see Figure 2 for a more detailed explanation of these factors).

FAST Products and Methodology: An Overview

The mix of methods applied within the FAST-framework and the corresponding products are shown in Figure 1:

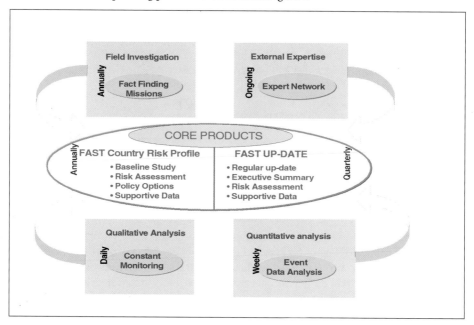

Figure 1: Methodological Overview

Identification of intervening factors is often the first step to policy options, as these factors focus on conflict-mitigating or -inhibiting factors.

As FAST target countries are not all in pre-conflict situations, intervening factors take on a different role, depending on the conflict cycle. In pre-conflict/post-conflict countries, intervening factors determine the likelihood of (renewed) armed conflict escalation, while in in-conflict situations, intervening factors track indicators that either increase or decrease the likelihood for armed conflict or peacebuilding. In all cases, however, intervening factors are not simply negative events or developments that can lead to violent conflict, but also windows of opportunity for positive developments (signals of hope).

Core indicators derived from the background analysis are depicted in the analytical framework (see above) and are used to guide daily monitoring and continuous updates. In order to keep the FAST analysis flexible, the

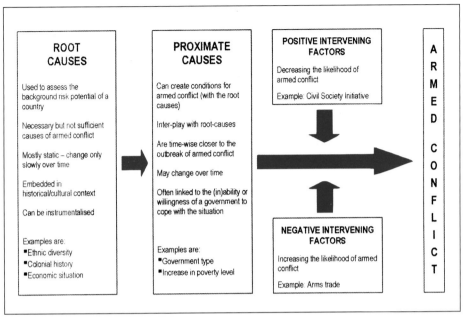

Figure 2: Backbone of FAST Analysis: The Analytical Framework

frameworks are updated if novel important factors appear. This is mostly done for intervening factors, some for proximate causes but not for the more static root causes. FAST establishes more than one analytical framework for countries with multiple-conflict potential (e.g., domestic and international, or multiple domestic conflicts). This is done as the underlying analytical explanations most likely differ, even if the rough categories remain the same.

A crucial feature of the annual assessment is formulation of case scenarios and detailed policy options identifying an overall strategy, steps toward implementation (including obstacles to be overcome), and specific tools/programs. In addition, key actors are profiled[5] and a set of additional background (supportive) information is provided (see below). As the purpose of this paper stresses FAST methodology, it will not go into more detail about these aspects of the FAST overall early warning system.

One of FAST's strengths is the uniform structure of all products, allowing for an easy cross-country comparison and information retrieval.[6] The annual country risk profiles are structured as follows:

- Executive summary (one page)
- Risk assessment with

- Supportive information (analytical framework, map).
- Analysis including the following sections: root causes, proximate causes, intervening factors, analysis of major actors, outlook - future scenarios.
- Policy options including the following sections: General strategy, obstacles to achieve such strategy, steps to implement the strategy, tools/programs linked to this strategy.
- Appendix with chronology of events, descriptive actors list, tension barometers, (graphical depiction of conflictive and co-operative interactions in the countries), strategic information on political, economic/ecological, socio-demographic, and military aspects of a country, references).

FAST Updates
In order to keep clients in touch with developments in the countries monitored, FAST provides quarterly updates of the situation on the ground. This frequent analysis is necessary in order to stay in touch with current developments and to avoid missing important events. As Gupta (1997, p. 375) fittingly said "It is extremely difficult to forecast, especially the future, but if you forecast, forecast often."
FAST updates use the analytical framework as their basis and mainly focus on factors that either increase or decrease the likelihood of armed conflict in the short run. Intentionally kept short, FAST updates do not exceed three pages of text and provide only essential supportive information in the form of a short chronology of main events and tension barometers. Thus, FAST updates are meant to "keep abreast" of the situation, taking into account the time constraints faced by policy makers. Similar to the country risk profiles, updates also feature a common structure:

Analytical framework (put here first to remind the reader of the analysis's underlying elements).
Risk assessment mainly along intervening factors (2-3 pages).
Supportive information in the form of a brief chronology of main events covering the past three months (1-2 pages), and selective tension barometers (1-2 pages).

The lean structure of FAST updates allows even the busiest policy maker to stay informed about the target countries. As SDC still considers FAST to be a proprietary product, FAST currently posts only a one-page executive summary for each country of the three regions monitored onto the web at present (http://www.swisspeace.ch).

FAST Methodology: A More Detailed Discussion

As Figure 2 shows, FAST core products are based on a combination of quantitative and qualitative methods. This choice of methods as well as a decision on how to balance the methodologies used emerged from challenges posed to early-warning analysts. In order to illustrate how FAST tried to tackle these challenges - and continues to do so - they are briefly outlined below:

What to warn about (type of conflict): As stated above, it is important to be clear about the nature of an early warning, as it affects model specification, indicator selection, timing of warning, and preparation of response options (the latter may be linked to the mandate of the organization expected to respond). Thus while in an academic setting, one must distinguish between various types of conflicts (inter- or intra-state, ethnic, religious, genocide), in real life, when attempting to give an early warning, it may not necessarily be clear from the beginning which type of conflict is likely to emerge. In addition, one could further argue that even if we can select core indicators explaining specific conflict constellations, they may nevertheless differ, depending on specific settings (countries, regions).

What to warn about (intensity of conflict): For the sake of early warning, peace and conflict must be considered a continuum and not a dichotomy (especially as early warning functions throughout the stages of conflict). Furthermore, it is important to focus on latent and simmering conflicts as pre-cursors of greater violence in the monitoring exercise. This means there are gradual developments in either direction, and one can identify both early warning signals of an impending crisis or signals of hope that show windows of opportunity for strengthening peace efforts. The question that remains here is how to establish a threshold value on when to issue a warning if a simmering conflict escalates. Yet finding threshold values on when to warn of conflict (or destructive armed conflict in particular) is one of the most difficult tasks of any early warning model. This is most likely appreciated by students of armed conflict trying to distinguish between low, medium, and high-intensity conflicts.

Predicting vs. anticipating conflict: Quantitative analysis has largely been used for predictions, using deductive principles. However, quantitative and systematic modelers admit that the main purpose of their research is to rank countries by "risk" potential, because static models are unfit to make proper forecasts (see Gurr and Moore, 1997; Schmeidl and Jenkins, 1998). Furthermore, while there are important core indicators that can be used to establish the risk for certain countries, anticipating the outbreak of violent conflict must more likely be based on prevailing context-specific indicators.

Stake-holder Analysis: It is crucial to focus on actors and know the stakeholders in the process that may lead to armed conflict. Here it is equally important to know their attitude(s) on the conflict / peace process as well as their resources to accomplish their goals. For the purpose of early warning and conflict prevention, one needs to be especially familiar with spoilers that lack interest in peaceful conflict resolution as well as potential actors willing to work for conflict prevention and peacebuilding (Krummenacher, 2001; Rubin, 2001; Stedman, 1997, 1998).

In light of these challenges, FAST currently focuses heavily on context-specific qualitative assessments using quantitative analysis (event-data) merely as a supportive element. The next sections describe the approach in more detail.

Qualitative Analysis

As stated above, qualitative analysis is necessary for maintaining a context-specific understanding of countries monitored and for anticipating even minor changes that can be initiated by local, regional, and international actors. The qualitative understanding of the FAST analysts is enhanced by the following set of supportive tools:

Constant Monitoring of Events and Developments
Aside from tracking relevant literature and secondary sources for analytical purposes, it is essential to stay abreast of developments in target countries through daily monitoring of events and developments based upon information from various news agencies or gained from the "local information network" (detailed description follows). Early warning, and thus monitoring of countries, needs to be a constant and on-going process. Crises can emerge seemingly out of nowhere, which means that ad-hoc analyses may miss crucial developments at a conflict's early stages. Jongman (2000), for example, showed that five of the PIOOM[7] classified as low-intensity conflicts escalated into high-intensity-conflicts within the past year: Chechnya, East-Timor, Kashmir, Kosovo, and the war between Ethiopia and Eritrea. Notably the coup d'etat in Fiji during May 2000 was not predicted by the world community, as nobody paid very close attention to this small island.

Local Information Network
In areas poorly covered by international news media, FAST uses local information networks where indigenous analysts track and report relevant information on a specific set of indicators that feeds into graphs called tension barometers (this aspect is discussed in more detail in the quantitative section). However, the local networks also provide a different way of interpreting events and thus also function as external advisors or experts to the FAST team of analysts.

Expert Network
Frequent exchange with external experts (from both the target region and other internationally renowned individuals) is a crucial part for the FAST analysis in order to discuss information received, analytical insight, case scenarios, and response options. This leads to synergy between local

understanding and outside expertise and results into a very nuanced analysis. The practice of balancing internal assessment with outside opinions helps FAST counter the problem of "mental blindness" that traps many analysts and is considered a major obstacle of early warning. The phenomenon is usually considered as a cognitive structure that impairs our perception and judgement. In some cases this can be seen as wishful thinking or a hope for the best that averts the "worst possible case" scenario (e.g., not wanting to see genocide in Rwanda). Aside from psychological reasons or even fears, "mental blindness" can also be caused by political considerations or fear of failure. "Because policy choices in a crisis are often so difficult to make, individuals (as well as small policymaking groups and organizations) may discredit information that calls into question existing expectations, preferences, or policies" (George and Holl, 2000, p.24).

Fact-Finding Missions

In order to obtain hands-on-knowledge, assess the situation on the ground, and make contact with local analysts, FAST analysts travel once a year to the region they cover. These fact-finding missions are of particular importance in countries with difficult outside access by international news media (e.g., Kashmir in Pakistan, Northeast India) and countries with a potentially one-sided view by Western news media (e.g., Afghanistan). In addition, visits to our clients' local projects allow for a better formulation of targeted response options.

Quantitative Analysis: Event-Data

Analysis

While continuing to develop the quantitative element within its methodology, FAST currently mainly uses event data counts to supplement its qualitative analysis. Use of automated event data analysis has significant implications for early warning due to its consistency, transparency, speed, and interactivity. Automated event analysis promotes timely evaluation of information that is extremely important for early warning purposes.
The basic logic of event-data analysis[8] is that all relevant events are coded by identifying the initiator and recipient of action, the action itself, and the time and scope of action. Each action corresponds to a specific event-type (indicator), and in this is assigned a numeric value. By aggregating all relevant events on a weekly or monthly basis, we get an accurate picture of overall conflict potential or stability in a given country. The advantages of event-data analyses (especially for early warning) are as follows:

- Event data allows speedy tracking of specific violent or co-operative incidences over time and supports qualitative assessments.

- A multitude of information is broken down into its component parts and depicted in easy-to-read graphs, demonstrating aspects of conflict and co-operation within and between countries.

- Event data counts and respective graphs provide checks -and balances against a desensitization toward violence and/or media hypes.

- "Event-data analysis challenges the analyst's perception so that he or she might become aware of his or her own 'blind spots', biases, and assumptions" (Siegfried, 2001, p.110). This is another way to counter the problem of "mental blindness" discussed earlier.

- Event data graphs permit comparison among countries.

- Event data analysis, if further developed, enables forecasting conflict trends.

Currently, event data is provided for FAST by an automated coding method developed by Virtual Research Associates (VRA[r]), a Harvard-based group of academic analysts (see Bond, Bond, Silva, and Oh, 1999 for a more detailed description).[9] There is a multiple set of individual events depicting conflict and co-operative behavior within and between countries. These events feed into tension barometers as raw data but also as composite measures (some merely a compilation of indicators while others are based on more complicated analyses). Non-standardized graphs show fluctuations depending on the current numerical value of events coded as well as the number of events within a given time-period. In order to allow for cross-country comparison, standardized graphs rely on the current numerical value of a given set of events in proportion to the total number of events. As the number of graphs based on single indicators is rather large (based on WEIS [World Event Interaction Survey] but now extended into IDEA [Integrated Data for Event Analysis] categories, see Bond et al., 1999 for more detail), only the summary graphs currently used by FAST are listed here:

- Co-operation: captures various forms of accommodative or co-operative behavior between diverse domestic or international actors. Such behavior can vary from verbal agreements, meetings to specify joint efforts, or operations to promote mutual benefits between domestic actors (based on Goldstein, 1992).

- Conflict: captures contentious or conflictive interactions (e.g., antagonism, contradictory action, or disagreement) between diverse domestic or international actors. The type of conflict can vary from verbal antagonism, disagreements, or contradictory action to outright physical force with various levels of intensity (based on Goldstein, 1992).

- Conflict Carrying Capacity (CCC): reflects the stability of the system or polity rather than a particular regime or administration; a CCC trend line approaching 1.0 suggests 100% (based on Jenkins and Bond, 2001).

- Forceful Action (FA): refers to the proportion of any and all uses of physical force and any associated manifest violence by any actor (based on Jenkins and Bond, 2001).

However, the automated data currently generated by VRA using Reuters (r) news service has certain draw-backs, the major one being lack of satisfactory coverage in all the world's countries due to the following reasons (for more detail, see Schmeidl and Bond, 2000):

- The VRA parser can only read English-language news wires at present.

- Event-data analysis is based on the principle of daily logging, news dispatches often tend to be based on the principle of interval reporting. The intensity of coverage may increase as a crisis occurs ("blood sells") but is weak or non-existent during more peaceful times (thus not all important events leading up to conflict escalation may be reported; see Siegfried, 2001).[10]

- International journalism is based on the principles of covering events believed to be of general interest to the rest of the world (not all countries and regions are).

- As a guiding principle, Reuters only needs to report those events with a greater connotation at the national level. Yet this eliminates possible important events at a district or provincial level that can also be of importance - especially since early warning tries to track those tensions that could escalate later.

In light of these constraints, the event-data principle of no report meaning no event does not hold true in countries or regions of lesser interest to (English-speaking) news-services. It may simply mean that no English-speaking journalist was present or that on-going events were deemed to be of no particular international interest or importance. This was to some degree the problem in Rwanda, as journalists focused on South Africa and only reported about Rwanda on the side (for more detail, see Schmeidl and Bond, 2000). It follows that the sole use of news-service coding provides clear drawbacks for early-warning requirements. Thus event-data analysis will remain a supportive element for early-warning efforts for a long time at best.

FAST had to tackle precisely these problems, as many countries it monitors are not covered sufficiently by Reuters. Central Asia, for example, is covered well by media in the Russian language, but this would require analysts (or machines) to read Russian. Similarly other language news-wires (French,

Portuguese) may be more relevant for certain parts of Africa than English ones are. Thus the English-language requirement for the current VRA parser is clearly something event-data analysis can improve upon. However, other language news sources may nevertheless adhere to the same principle of English-language news - "blood sells" - so it might be difficult to overcome this particular problem of sensational information production in general; unless one uses other input than news services.

Hence FAST chose a second option to improve upon Reuters' data feed. In collaboration with VRA, it created an alternative news-feed in the form of local information networks of field-monitors that log relevant information after the same principles as the VRA parser (to allow for compatibility of data). Currently all Central Asian countries monitored have such a network, and Pakistan has just reduced its news feed to two under-reported provinces (NWFP and Baluchistan). Networks are also being currently set up in Mozambique and Madagascar, and a proxy network for Afghanistan is being implemented from Pakistan (using refugees, other migrants, and traders as sources).

This system's experience has shown better coverage overall in numerical terms as well as diversity of events reported. For example, the local information network for Uzbekistan logged 53, 126, and 196 events for the months of March, April, and May 2001 respectively. By contrast, Reuters only logged 9, 5, and 4 events respectively, making efforts of statistical analysis obsolete.

In light of the above, while human-assisted field coding clearly allows use of local expertise (and also provides the aspect of capacity building), automatic coding improves upon the speed of digesting information and allows impartial assessment, as the machine does not make interpretations beyond indicators it has been programmed to track. A combination of both allows for optimum data-feed. Thus event-data generation based on a local information network seem an excellent solution to the early-warning information problem, one that needs to be further strengthened. However, it does not solve all analytical problems linked to forecasting conflict escalation or de-escalation processes. These are some challenges that must still be met before FAST can place greater reliance on event-data analysis for its assessments and use tension barometers to their maximum potential.

Instead of a Conclusion, Remaining Challenges

Since automated event data efforts have only recently been put into service for anything close to real-time monitoring, there is little evidence of its actual benefits for forecasting crisis escalation. As long as analysts lack appropriate methods to evaluate trends presented to them by event-data, they must rely on their qualitative judgement to make conflict assessments. Thus FAST's future goal is to improve its forecasting ability by developing quantitative methods that help (a) to verify if developments are significantly different from those in the past and (b) to propose trends for the future. While VRA has begun to work with FAST on an interim solution that involves tracking the mean of event-data inputs over time (mainly through use of Z-scores to establish threshold values), Gary King from the Center for Basic Research in the Social Sciences at Harvard University (USA) has agreed to work on a collaborative project to develop a more sophisticated approach to solve the methodological problem.

The idea is to use modern statistical methods to reveal underlying patterns instead of using the human eye to try to parse patterns from data with a low signal-to-noise ratio. Identification of these patterns is important for forecasting. Preliminary analysis has shown that this is not easy but also not impossible. One FAST analyst (Siegfried, 2001) searched for conclusive patterns of crisis escalation using the Goldstein scale for conflict and co-operation and had difficulty identifying one specific constellation. Even within the four patterns identified, great ranges existed. This illustrates the problem that still exists in forecasting armed conflict properly. In conclusion, while the future obviously won't be entirely predictable, reduction of uncertainty may prove quite valuable. In the years ahead FAST will attempt to reduce this uncertainty and improve upon its existing forecasting ability.

References

Adelman, Howard. 1998. Defining Humanitarian Early Warning. In Susanne Schmeidl and Howard Adelman (eds.) *Early Warning and Early Response*. Columbia International Affairs Online, Columbia University Press. www.ciaonet.org

Bond, Joe, Doug Bond, Jayson Silva, and Churl Oh. 1999. *The VRA Reader*. VRA Press Weston, MA.

Clark, Lance. 1989. *Early Warning of Refugee Flows*. Refugee Policy Group, Washington, DC.

George, Alexander L. and Jane E. Holl. 2000. "The Warning-Response Problem and Missed Opportunities in Preventive Diplomacy." pp.21-39 in Bruce W. Jentleson (ed.) *Opportunities Missed, Opportunities Seized: Preventive Diplomacy in the Post-Cold War World*. Rowman & Littlefield Publishers, Inc., Lanham, MD (for the Carnegie Commission on Preventing Deadly Conflict).

Goldstein, Joshua S. 1992. "A Conflict-Cooperation Scale for International Events Data. *Journal of Conflict Resolution*. 36(2): pp 369-385.

Gupta, Dipak K. 1997. "An Early Warning About Forecasts: Oracle to Academics." pp.375-397 in Schmeidl, Susanne and Howard Adelman (eds.). *Synergy in Early Warning Conference Proceedings*. York Centre for International and Security Studies, York University.

Gurr, Ted Robert.1996. "Early Warning Systems: From Surveillance to Assessment of Action." pp.123-144 in Kevin M. Cahill (ed.) *Preventive Diplomacy: Stopping Wars Before they Start*. Basic Books, N.Y..

Gurr, Ted Robert and Will H. Moore. 1997. "Ethnopolitical Rebellion: A Cross-Sectional Analysis of the 1980s with Risk Assessments for the 1990s," *American Journal of Political Science*, 41(4): pp.1079-1103.

Jenkins, J. Craig and Doug Bond. 2001. "Conflict Carrying Capacity, Political Crisis, and Reconstruction: A Framework for the Early Warning of Political System Vulnerability." *Journal of Conflict Resolution*. 45(1): pp 3-31.

Jenkins, J. Craig and Doug Bond. 2001. "Conflict Carrying Capacity, Political Crisis, and Reconstruction: A Framework for the Early Warning of Political System Vulnerability." *Journal of Conflict Resolution*. 45(1): pp. 3-31.

Jongman, Albert J. 2000. "Mapping Dimensions of Contemporary Conflicts and Human Rights Violations." *Back of the PIOOM 2000 World Conflict and Human Rights Map*. PIOOM, University of Leiden.

Krummenacher, Heinz. 2001. *Conflict Prevention and Power Politics: Central Asia as a Show Case*. Swiss Peace Foundation, Berne. Working Paper 33.

Lund, Michael S. 1996. "Early Warning and Preventive Diplomacy." Pp.379-403 in Chester Crocker and Fen Osler Hampson [eds.] *Managing Global Chaos: Sources of and Responses to International Conflict*. U.S. Institute of Peace, Washington, DC.

Rubin, Barnett R. 2001 (in press). *Unfinished Manuscript on Preventive Efforts*. The Century Foundation and the Council on Foreign Relations, New York, NY.

Rupesinghe, Kumar and Sanam Naraghi Anderlini. 1998. *Civil Wars, Civil Peace: An Introduction to Conflict Resolution*. Pluto Press, London.

Schmeidl, Susanne and Doug Bond. 2000. *"Assessing the Implications of Automation in Event Data Analysis: An Examination of the Conceptual and Empirical Differences Between Human-Assisted and Fully-Automated Coding."* Paper presented [a9]at the Annual Convention of the International Studies Association, Los Angeles, USA.

Schmeidl, Susanne and Howard Adelman (eds.) 1998. *Early Warning and Early Response*. Columbia International Affairs Online, Columbia University Press. www.ciaonet.org

Schmeidl, Susanne and J. Craig Jenkins. 1998. "The Early Warning of Humanitarian Disasters: Problems in Building an Early Warning System." *International Migration Review* 32: pp. 471-486.

Schmeidl, Susanne. 2001. "Early Warning and

Integrated Response Development."
Romanian Journal of Political Science (Special
Issue on Conflict and Reconciliation sponsored by UNDP Office, Romania). 1(2): pp. 4-
50.

Schrodt, Philip A. and Deborah Gerner. 1994.
"Validity Assessment of Machine-Coded
Event data Set for the Middle East, 1982-
1992." *American Journal of Political Science* 18:
pp. 825-64.

Siegfried, Matthias. 2001. *Patterns in the
Escalation Process of Armed Conflict.*
Unpublished M.A. Thesis. University of

Freiburg (available through FAST, Swiss
Peace Foundation).

Stedman, Stephen John. 1997. "Spoiler
Problems in Peace Processes." *International
Security* 22: pp. 5-53.

Stedman, Stephen John. 1998. "Conflict
Prevention as Strategic Interaction: The
Spoiler Problem and the Case of Rwanda," in
Peter Wallensteen (ed.) *Preventing Violent
Conflicts: Past Record and Future Challenges.*
Uppsala, Sweden: Department of Peace and
Conflict Research, Uppsala University, Report
No. 48.

Publications about FAST

Krummenacher, Heinz. 2001. *"Early Warning:
Eine Momentaufnahme in Theorie und Praxis."*
Schriftenreihe des Oesterreichisches
Studienzentrums für Frieden und
Konfliktlösung — ÖSFK (ed.) Zivile
Konfliktbearbeitung, Teilprojekt 8. Agenda
Verlag, Münster.

Krummenacher, Heinz; Günther Baechler, and
Susanne Schmeidl. 1999. "Beitrag der
Frühwarnung zur Krisenprävention -
Möglichkeiten und Grenzen in Theorie und
Praxis." pp.77-99 in Oesterreichisches
Studienzentrums für Frieden und
Konfliktlösung/ Schweizerische

Friedensstiftung (eds.) *Friedensbericht 1999:
Theories und Praxis ziviler Konfliktbearbeitung.*
Rüegger, Chur/Zurich.

Krummenacher, Heinz and Susanne Schmeidl.
1999. "Fast: An Integrated And Interactive
Early Warning System: The Example Of
Central Asia." *The Soviet and Post-Soviet
Review* 24(3): pp. 147-161.

Schmeidl, Susanne. 1999. "Fast Workshop
Report: Early Warning In Practice: The Case
of Tajikistan, Uzbekistan, and Kyrgyzstan."
The Soviet and Post-Soviet Review 24(3): pp.
161-175.

Notes

1 FAST presently focuses on the following
regions: Southern Africa, Central Asia, and
Southern Asia. Depending on customers'
needs, other countries or regions can be easily added.

2 This, however, does not suggest that FAST
cannot expand its products to other clients.
Its flexibility allows adapting the overall
methodology with ease. Furthermore, FAST
products are designed to serve diverse clients
(e.g., state authorities, non-state actors such
as NGOs or private business companies) as a
decision-making instrument or as a comparative analysis tool for existing in-house early-
warning mechanisms.

3 More specifically, FAST wants to identify critical events and developments that increase or
decrease the likelihood of armed conflict in
the near future while also looking for "windows of opportunities", i.e., events and developments that contribute to reducing violence.

4 Aside from SDC or Swiss-specific policy
options, FAST also provides a few more generally applicable recommendations, and the
SDC has begun to share FAST reports with
like-minded governments.

5 It is crucial to focus on actors and know
stakeholders in the process that may lead to
conflict. Here it is equally important to know
their attitude(s) on the conflict/peace process

as well as their resources to accomplish their goals. Furthermore, for the purpose of early warning, one needs to be familiar with spoilers who lack interest in peaceful conflict resolution as well as potential actors willing to work for conflict prevention (Rubin, 2001; Stedman, 1997, 1998).

6 In addition, each FAST regional team can decide on what country or trouble spots. It can also alter the balance between assessment and policy options area to focus its assessment, elaborating in more depth on those aspects deemed more important.

7 Projecten Interdisciplinair Onderzoek Oorzaken Mensenrechtenschendingen (Interdisciplinary Research Program on Root Causes of Human-Rights Violations) in Leiden, the Netherlands.

8 see http://www.ukans.edu/~keds/intro.html for more detail. This paper refrains from a more detailed discussion of the purpose and merit of event-data, as this has been already covered in Schmeidl and Bond (2000). More information on VRA is provided at http://vranet.com/.

9 Automated monitoring of events (social, political, and economic) has emerged over the last decade as a viable approach to early warning, spurred in large part by pioneering efforts of the Kansas Events Data System or KEDS (Schrodt and Gerner, 1994).

10 For example, the number of coded events in Kyrgyzstan jumped from 6 to 35 in 1999 when a group of Muslim rebels belonging to the "Islamic movement of Uzbekistan" intruded into Kyrgyz territory from Tajikistan. Thus, when coded events from news-wires produced a peak in the graphs, the crisis was already ongoing. More drastically, in the Horn of Africa, the border-conflict and later war seemed to have come out of nowhere - at least for event-data analysis based on Reuters. The number of codable events alone jumped from zero in April 1998 to 31 in May of 1998 when the border dispute began and from six in January 1999 to 53 in February 1999 when the border war broke out. This illustrates the assumption that news media naturally feed into early-warning analysis by focusing on crises more heavily than on peaceful developments. It can be a dangerous pitfall - the problem of late warning.

Annex 8

Listed here are the organizations and institutions who were actively involved in the program of the International Conference Towards Better Peace Building Practice, the Netherlands, October 2001. Also included are organizations and/or names of people who contributed to this publication.

Addresses and Contact Persons

ActionAid
Hamlyn House
Macdonald Road
Archway, London N19 5PG
United Kingdom
Tel +44 (27) 561 7561
Fax +44 (27) 281 0899
Email mail@actionaid.org.uk
http://www.actionaid.org

African Centre for the Constructive Resolution of Disputes (ACCORD)
Private Bag X018
Umhlanga Rocks
4320 South Africa
Tel +27 (31) 502 3908
Fax +27 (31) 502 4160
Email info@accord.org.za
http://www.accord.org.za

Africa Women Solidarity
P.O. Box 2100
1211 Geneva 2
Switzerland
Tel +41 (22) 798 0075
Fax +41 (22) 798 0076
Email faspeace@iprolink.ch
http://www.fasngo.org

Ragnar Ängeby
Ministry of Foreign Affairs
Gustav Adolfs torg 1
103 39 Stockholm
Sweden
Tel +46 (8) 405 1000
Fax +46 (8) 723 1176

Berghof Research Centre for Constructive Conflict Management
Altensteinstrasse 48a
D 14195 Berlin
Germany
Tel +49 (30) 844 1540
Fax +49 (30) 844 15499
Email info@berghof-center.org
http://www.berghof-center.org

Berghof Foundation for Conflict Studies
Sri Lanka Office
53/2, Gregory's Road
Colombo 7
Sri Lanka
Tel + 94 (1) 6697 10/11
Fax + 94 (1) 6697 12
Email ropers@sltnet.lk

Catholic Relief Service
209 West Fayette Street
Baltimore, MD 21201-3443
USA
Tel +1 (410) 625 2220
Fax +1 (410) 234 3178
http://www.catholicrelief.org

Centre for Conflict Resolution
Department of Peace Studies
University of Bradford
West Yorkshire
BD7 1DP
United Kingdom
Tel/Fax +44 (1274) 234 197
http://www.brad.ac.uk/acad/confres

Charles Stewart Mott Foundation
Mott Foundation Building
503 S. Saginaw Street, Suite 1200
Flint, Michigan 48502-1851
USA
Tel +1 (810) 238 5651
Fax +1 (810) 766 1753
Email infocenter@mott.org
http://www.mott.org

Canadian International Development Agency (CIDA)
200 Promenade du Portage
Hull, Quebec
K1A 0G4
Canada
Tel +1 (819) 997 5006
Fax +1 (819) 953 6088
Email info@acdi-cida.gc.ca
http://www.acdi-cida.gc.ca

Collaborative for Development Action
26 Walker Street Cambridge
Massachusetts 02138
USA
Tel +1 (617) 661 6310
Fax +1 (617) 661 3805
Email mail@cdainc.com
http://www.cdainc.com

Catholic Organisation for Relief and Development (CORDAID)
P.O. Box 16440
2500 BK The Hague
The Netherlands
Tel +31 (70) 313 6300
Fax +31 (70) 313 6301
Email cordaid@cordaid.nl
http://www.cordaid.nl

Department for International Development (DFID)
1 Palace Street
London SW1E 5HE
Tel +44 (207) 023 0000
Fax +44 (207) 023 0016
enquiry@dfid.org.uk
http://www.dfid.org.uk

European Centre for Conflict Prevention
P.O. Box 14069
3508 SC Utrecht
The Netherlands
Tel +31 (30) 242 7777
Fax +31 (30) 236 9268
Email info@conflict-prevention.net
http://www.conflict-prevention.net

European Centre for Common Ground
Bte 12/13
Rue Bellirad 205
1040 Brussel
Belgium
Tel +32 (2) 736 7262
Fax +32 (2) 732 3033
Email eccg@eccg.be
http://www.sfcg.org/eccg.htm

European Union
Policy Planning and Early Warning Unit
Rue de la Loi 175
B-1048
Brussels
Belgium
http://europa.eu.int

Field Diplomacy Initiative (FDI)
Leuvensestraat 7/2
3010 Leuven
Belgium
Tel/fax +32 (1648) 7654
http://fdi.ngonet.be

Forum on Early Warning and Early Response (FEWER)
Old Truman Brewery
91-95 Brick Lane
London E1 6QN
United Kingdom
Tel +44 (207) 247 7022
Fax +44 (207) 247 5290
Email fewer@fewer.org
http://www.fewer.org

Initiative on Conflict Resolution and Ethnicity (INCORE)
Aberfoyle House, Northland Road
Londonderry BT48 7JA
Northern Ireland
Tel +44 (0)2871 375 500
Fax +44 (0)2871 375 510
Email INCORE@incore.ulst.ac.uk
http://www.incore.ulst.ac.uk

International Alert
1 Glyn Street
London SE11 5HT
United Kingdom
Tel +44 (207) 793 8383
Fax +44 (207) 793 7975
Email general@international-alert.org
http://www.international-alert.org

International IDEA
Strömsborg
S-103 34 Stockholm
Sweden
Tel +46 (8) 6983 700
Fax +46 (8) 2024 22
Email info@idea.int
http://www.idea.int

Institute for Multi Track Diplomacy (IMTD)
1819 H Street, NW, Suite 1200
Washington DC 20006
USA
Tel +1 (202) 466 46 05
Fax +1 (202) 66 46 07
Email imtd@igc.apc.org
http://www.imtd.org

Jehangir Khan
Political Affairs Officer
Policy Planning Unit
United Nations - DPA
New York, N.Y. 10017
USA
Email khanj@un.org

Jonathan Goodhand
School of African & Oriental Studies
Thornhaugh Street
Russell Square
London WC1H 0XG
United Kingdom
Tel +44 (207) 637 2388
Fax +44 (207) 436 3844
Email JonathanGoodhand@aol.com

Justitia et Pax Netherlands
P.O. Box 16334
2500 BH The Hague
The Netherlands
Tel +31 (70) 313 6800
Fax +31 (70) 313 6801
Email jupax@antenna.nl

Manuela Leonhardt
Development & Conflict Consultant
Berliner Strasse 12
65760 Eschborn
Germany
Tel +49 (61) 9677 7497
Email manuela leonhardt@hotmail.com

Michael Lund
Management Systems International Inc.
600, Water Street, S.W.
Washington D.C. 20024
USA
Tel +1 (202) 484 7170
Fax +1 (202) 488 0754
Email mslund41@aol.com

Dutch Ministry of Foreign Affairs
P.O.Box 20061
2500 EB The Hague
The Netherlands
Tel +31 (70) 348 6486
Fax +31 (70) 348 4848
E-mail dvl-voorlichting@minbuza.nl
http://www.minbuza.nl

Nairobi Peace Initiative-Africa
5th Floor New Waumini House
Chiromo Road, Westlands Nairobi
P.O. Box 14894
Nairobi-Kenia
Tel +254 (2) 441 444 / 440 098
Fax +254 (2) 440 097
Email npi@africaonline.co.ke

National Council of Churches of Kenya
Church House
MOI Avenue
P.O. Box 45009
Nairobi
Kenya
Tel +254 (2) 338 211
Fax +254 (2) 215 169

Netherlands Institute of International Relations 'Clingendael'
P.O. Box 93080
2509 AB The Hague
The Netherlands
Tel +31 (70) 324 5384
Fax +31 (70) 328 2002
http://www.clingendael.nl

Norwegian Church Aid
Sandakerveien 74
P.O. Box 4544 Torshov
NO-0404 Oslo - Norway
Tel +47 (22) 09 27 00
Fax +47 (22) 09 27 20
Email nca.oslo@sn.no
http://www.nca.no.org

Oxford Research Group
51 Plantation Road
Oxford OX2 6JE
United Kingdom
Tel +44 (1865) 242 819
Fax +44 (1865) 794 652
Email org@oxfordresearchgroup.org.uk
http://www.oxfordresearchgroup.org.uk

Pax Christi The Netherlands
P.O. Box 19318
3501 DH Utrecht
The Netherlands
Tel +31 (30) 233 3346
Fax +31 (30) 236 8199
Email paxchristi@antenna.nl
http://www.paxchristi.net

PRONI: Kontakt der Kontinenten
Amersfoortsestraat 20
3769 AS Soesterberg
The Netherlands
Tel +31 (346) 351 755
Fax +31 (346) 354 735
Email peacebulding@kdk-nl.org
http://www.kdk-nl.org

Responding to Conflict
1046 Bristol Road
Selly Oak
Birmingham B29 6LJ
United Kingdom
Tel +44 (121) 415 5641
Fax +44 (121) 415 4119
Email enquiries@respond.org
http://www.respond.org

Saferworld
46 Grosvenor Gardens
London SW1W 0EB
United Kingdom
Tel +44 (207) 881 9290
Fax +44 (207) 7881 9291
Email general@saferworld.co.uk
http://www.saferworld.co.uk

Search for Common Ground
1601 Connecticut Ave. NW
Suite 200
Washington, DC 20009
USA
Tel +1 (202) 265 4300
Fax +1 (202) 232 6718
Email search@sfcg.org
http://www.sfcg.org

Stockholm International Peace Research Institute (SIPRI)
Signalistgatan 9 SE-169 70 Solna
Sweden
Tel +46 (8) 655 9700
Fax +46 (8) 655 9733
E-mail sipri@sipri.org
http://www.sipri.se

Swedish International Development Cooperation Agency (Sida)
105 25 Stockholm
Sweden
Tel +46 (8) 698 5000
Fax +46 (8) 20 8864
Email info@sida.se
http://www.sida.se

Swiss Peace Foundation
P.O. Box 517
CH - 3000 Bern 8
Gerechtigkeitsgasse 12
Switzerland
Tel +41 (31) 310 2727
Fax +41 (31) 310 2728
Email spfinfo@swisspeace.unibe.ch
http://www.swisspeace.ch/

Trocaire
169 Booterstown Avenue
Blackrock
Co. Dublin
Ireland
Tel +351 (1) 288 5385
Fax +351 (1) 288 3577
Email info@trocaire.ie

Robert Ricigliano
University of Wisconsin
Peace Studies Programme
Department of Communication
P.O. Box. 413
Milwaukee, WI 53201-0413
USA
Email robr@uwm.edu
http://www.uwm.edu

Voluntary Organisations in Cooperation in Emergencies (VOICE)
10, Square Ambriorix 10
B-1000
Brussels
Belgium
Tel +32 (2) 743 8775
Fax +32 (2) 732 1934
Email voice@clong.be
http://www.oneworld.org/voice/

World Vision
599 Avebury Boulevard
Milton Keynes
MK9 3PG
United Kingdom
Tel +44 (1908) 841000
Fax +44 (1908) 841001
Email info@worldvision.org.uk
http://www.worldvision.org.uk

Annex 9

The European Platform for Conflict Prevention and Transformation/
The European Centre for Conflict Prevention

The *European Platform for Conflict Prevention and Transformation* is a network of more than 150 key European organisations working in the field of the prevention and/or resolution of violent conflicts in the international arena. Its mission is to facilitate the exchange of information and experience among participating organisations, as well as to stimulate co-operation and synergy.

The *European Centre for Conflict Prevention* is an independent non-governmental organisation based in the Netherlands. Its mission is to contribute to prevention and/or resolution of violent conflicts in the world, like in Kosovo and Rwanda. The Centre acts as the secretariat of the European Platform for Conflict Prevention & Transformation and initiates, co-ordinates and implements the activities of the Platform.

The main objectives and activities are:

Networking and information exchange
- **European Platform meetings** are organised annually. The last meeting took place in Sweden, May 2001, and was organised in co-operation with the Swedish Peace Team. The conference, called 'Gripsholm- II' addressed issues such as: priorities for the European Union to enhance the EU's conflict prevention capacities; lessons learned from conflict interventions; national infrastructures for conflict prevention; and establishing Civilian Peace Services.

- The European Platform aims to include participant organisations from all European countries. Optimally, these should be **national platforms or networks,** such have already been established in e.g. Finland, Germany, Switzerland and the UK. In countries where no such focal point exists, the Platform aims to support the creation of one.

- The **Conflict Prevention Newsletter** is one of the few general newsletters on conflict prevention and resolution in the world. It has a circulation of 2,500 world-wide. Regular contributions to the Newsletter from prominent organisations such as International Alert, Saferworld and the African Centre for the Constructive Resolution of Disputes (ACCORD) greatly enhance its international focus as well as its quality of information. In 2001 thematic specials focussing on the Swdish Presidency of the EU and on Lessons Learned were included. For 2002 specials will pay attention to Central Asia, Media & Peacebuilding, and Women and Peacebuilding.

Clearinghouse
- The **Platform's web-site** *www.conflict-prevention.net* is the successor of the successful website *www.euconflict.org*, which recorded an average of 100.000 hits per month. The new website is one of the most comprehensive sources of information in the field of conflict prevention, and Background information is presented on conflicts and peacebuilding activities, combined with other service information like contact persons, addresses of organisations, web sites and databases, all kind of networks in the field, new literature, conferences and other events in the world.

- Since the publication of the **International Directory** in 1998, which provided an overview of 475 organisations active in the field of conflict prevention and resolution, the overview has grown to about **1300 organisations worldwide.**

- The **Information Centre** maintains a large collection of material produced by organisations around the world involved in conflict prevention. Its focus is upon unpublished and unpublicised 'grey literature' produced by NGOs.

- The objective of the project on **Lessons Learned in Peace Building** is to collect experiences of people working in the field of conflict prevention and peacebuilding. Through seminars and conferences these lessons, both positive and negative, and evaluation practices, undertaken by field staff as well as academics, are collected and shared. The aim is to formulate future challenges and possibilities to improve the work. This process will lead to a more coherent and integrative body of knowledge in this field.

Searching for Peace programme
Searching for Peace is a regional programme aimed at recording, describing and analysing prevention and peacebuilding efforts in the main violent conflicts in the world. Surveys of conflicts are produced that combines background information, detailed descriptions of ongoing activities to transform the conflicts, and assessments of future prospects for conflict prevention and peacebuilding. Furthermore directories are produced of local and international organisations working in this field. The results are published in a series of books as well as on the European Platform's web site. The Searching for Peace series is the result of a process involving research and regional seminars as well as collaboration with local partners, practitioners and prominent international scholars. In 1999 *Searching for Peace in Africa - An Overview of Conflict Prevention and Management Activities (October 1999)* was published and in March 2002 Searching for Peace Europe & Eurasia will

be published in collaboration with Lynne Rienner Publishers. The programme is ongoing and in 2002 *Searching for Peace in Asia* will be available.

Lobby and advocacy

- The Platform is one of the initiators of the **European Peacebuilding Liaison Office**. This Liaison Office is based in Brussels and aims to enhance information exchange between its members and the EU institutions dealing with conflict prevention.

- **Lobby documents**: aiming at the Swedish and Belgian EU presidencies in 2001, the European Platform, International Alert and Saferworld produced the lobby document *Preventing Violent Conflict - Opportunities for the Swedish and Belgian Presidency of the EU in 2001*

- **People Building Peace** is a project aimed at collecting and publishing inspiring stories of peacebuilding, with special attention to examples of successful peacebuilding by different actors, such as women groups, churches, media, the corporate sector, etc. The first publication was issued in May 1999: *People Building Peace; 35 Inspiring Stories from Around the World*. The project is on-going.

- In the Netherlands the European Centre established a **Special Chair of Conflict Prevention and Management** at Utrecht University. The first courses started in September 2000.

- **Media & Peacebuilding** is a project aimed at developing an operational framework for peacebuilding activities of media. It will be implemented by the Platform in close collaboration with IMPACS (Canadian NGO) and the European Centre for Common Ground (Brussels based NGO).